About the Authors

Simon Raven and Chris Raven were born in the United Kingdom. A career in overland adventure travel was launched when they drove across Siberia from the UK to Vladivostok at the dawn of a new millennium. The brothers have since traversed the Trans-oceanic highway from the Pacific to the Atlantic coast of South America and in 2007 travelled the road to Damascus. In addition to co-writing four travel books, they have documented and photographed multiple off the beaten track destinations across the globe including China's deep south, tribal India and the Balkan peninsula.

Also by Chris Raven & Simon Raven

Leaving London

Driving the Trans-Siberian

Carnival Express

SIMON RAVEN   CHRIS RAVEN

BLACK SEA CIRCUIT

AN ADVENTURE THROUGH THE CAUCASUS

Published by Samosir Books 2015

Copyright © Chris Raven, Simon Raven, 2015

Simon Raven and Chris Raven have asserted their rights under the Copyright, Designs and Patterns Act 1988 to be identified as the authors of this work

This book is sold subject to the condition that it shall not, by way of trade or otherwise, be lent, resold, hired out, or otherwise circulated without the publisher's prior consent in any form or binding or cover other than that in which it is published and without a similar condition including this condition being imposed on the subsequent purchaser

First published in Great Britain in 2015 by Samosir Books

A CIP catalogue record for this book is available from the British Library

ISBN 9780954884284

To all the people living around the Black Sea
who gave us their time, their hospitality
and their friendship

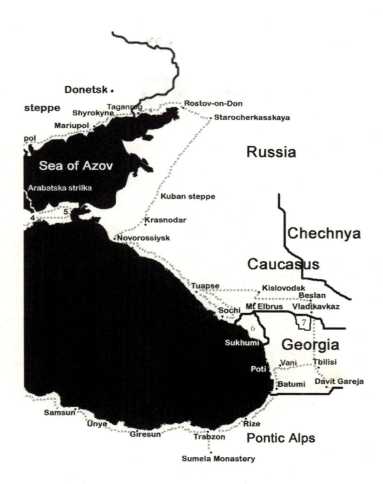

"Of all men's miseries the bitterest is this:
to know so much and to have control over nothing."
Herodotus (484-425 BC)

Contents

Introduction	11
Part 1 Ukraine to Russia (via Crimea)	15
Part 2 Russia & the Caucasus	68
Part 3 Georgia & the Kingdom of Colchis	127
Part 4 Turkey's Black Sea Coast	179
Part 5 Istanbul to the Danube Delta	221
Chronology	262
Bibliography	264

Introduction

In the shadow of rising tension in Ukraine, my brother and I agreed one sunny afternoon to drive full circle around the Black Sea.

For many years we had yearned to travel this region of the world, where Europe meets Asia, and to explore the six fascinating countries that share these colourful shores. With Russia hosting the Sochi Winter Olympics our eyes were drawn to the Caucasus. Naturally, we were a little dubious at first about venturing deep into what is considered to be southern Russia's "Wild West". This region bordering Chechnya conjured up images of war, violence and kidnapping. The thought of actually driving through the Caucasus made my spine tingle.

Following weeks of research, I joined Si for a barbecue in the spring of 2013 to discuss the risks of embarking on such a challenging journey.

Si flipped a burger on the griddle and told me to relax. 'Think lush green rolling hills, spa towns and traditional rural folk tending to their crops in vast open fields. There is relative peace in the region now and, besides, the Caucasus is our only way into Georgia.'

Si was right. Receiving conflicting reports from the Georgian and Russian consulates in London, there appeared to be a fifty percent chance that the 'Verkhny

Lars - Darial Gorge' border crossing between Russia and Georgia was now open to foreigners. Fellow adventurers had written on travel forums stating that this route was now indeed open, while others claimed it was only accessible to citizens of countries in the ex-Soviet grouping called the CIS (Commonwealth of Independent States). The thought of not knowing if we could make it through sounded fantastically exciting.

Epic overland adventure is nothing new to me and Si. In 2003, the year before Ewan McGregor and Charley Boorman set off on their motorcycle road trip across Russia with a film crew, we drove a Ford Sierra from the UK across Siberia to Vladivostok. Deep in the Siberian wilderness, the Zilov Gap section of the Amur highway between Chita and Khabarovsk was still being bulldozed at the time and it wasn't fully completed until Vladimir Putin officially opened the road in 2010. We wrote a book about the journey 'Driving the Trans-Siberian' and Lonely Planet kindly mentioned us in their Russia travel guide. In 2007, we somehow managed to coax a rusty Ford Escort from the UK to Damascus in Syria. The elections were taking place in this turbulent country at the heart of the Middle East, and president Bashar al-Assad was soon re-elected for the second term. I will never forget that eerie moment when the border guard looked at us both just before we crossed into Syria and said, "This is not Iraq". I often think of the many people we met along the way; the kind people who treated us like friends without asking for anything in return.

With limited means our road trips are not for the faint hearted and to save money we often sleep in the car. For many people the thought of grabbing a few hours shut eye with a steering wheel wedged between your thighs might be considered unacceptable. I struggle to disagree, but it's the pedals that get caught under the sleeping bag that I find the most annoying.

On that sunny afternoon in the garden, with my head buried deep in a world atlas, I looked down at the Black Sea. My eyes were drawn to the Crimean peninsula that hangs from the neck of the southern Ukraine like a sparkling diamond. Bounded by Russia, Georgia, Turkey, Bulgaria and Romania, this journey at the gateway of Eurasia had all the right ingredients for an expedition of a lifetime. Many thousands of years ago tribes of nomadic settlers born out of the Altai Mountains, Mongolia and the Central Asian steppes migrated to the Black Sea and fought great battles. Powerful civilisations have risen along these shores leaving behind ancient kurgan burial mounds brimming with gold and ruins of once great cities, opulent palaces, temples and forts. Thracians, Hittites, Scythians, Sarmatians, Greeks, Persians, Romans, Goths, Huns, Khazars, Venetians, Mongols, Genoese, Tatars, Turks and Russians, have all left their mark on the Black Sea. Enduring myths and legends inspire us to this present day, from Jason and the Argonauts to the tribe of fierce female warriors known as the Amazons. Since its transformation from a lake into a sea approximately 7,000 years ago, the Black Sea has witnessed the gravest of human misfortunes, played host to the most terrifying atrocities and suffered multiple apocalypses from the arrival of the Black Death to the near extinction of all life inside its waters.

'So, what d'you think?' Si grinned, offering me a cold beer. 'Fancy another adventure?'

What did we have to lose? Six countries, a sea and a twenty year old Volvo 440 – the plan was set. I jumped out of my foldaway chair and slammed the map shut. Our quest to drive around the Black Sea was about to begin.

14

PART 1
Ukraine to Russia (via Crimea)

One

A charcoal grey Ferrari roars through the sun-drenched streets of the Ukrainian port city of Odessa. With the International Film Festival in full swing, sleek movers and shakers hide behind shades and sip champagne in buzzing pavement cafes. There is a glamorous Monte Carlo vibe in the air that's heavily scented by the sweet smell of perfume. Model slim women wearing designer outfits wrapped tightly around their sculpted bodies, pout their glossy red lips and catwalk with care in sparkling high heels. Admiring the rococo style Opera and Ballet Theatre and the grand building that houses the Sea Fleet Museum, Chris slams on the brakes outside a busy seafood restaurant.

'Back me in, Si,' he smiles, grinding the gearbox into reverse.

I leap out of our silver chariot, which looks as rustic and weather beaten as a Cold War tank, and self-consciously wave Chris into the narrow gap between two sports cars. A gentleman wearing a leaden-blue jacket leans back in his chair and appears to enjoy watching our shunting fiasco. After numerous nail-biting attempts to squeeze the long boxy vehicle into the snug parking space Chris cuts the engine. Half expecting the entire restaurant to erupt in applause, thankfully the clientele return to their conversations and seafood cuisine.

Shaded by chestnut trees, the pleasant Primorsky Boulevard is a hive of activity. Youths on skateboards perform ankle-breaking flip tricks, loving couples sit entwined on park benches and two stony-faced police cops lurk in the shadows, waiting to pounce. We crank our necks and look up at the statue of the 5th Duke de Richelieu. Armand-Emmanuel was a royalist during the French Revolution and Napoleonic Wars, who narrowly escaped the guillotine. He was later appointed the first governor of Odessa in 1803 by his friend Tsar Alexander I. Surprised by a cool gust of wind from the powerful wings of a golden eagle, a guy asks if I would like my photograph taken with this magnificent bird of prey. I shake my head mutely and glance over at a group of women wearing black headscarves. They resemble extras from the cinematic masterpiece 'Battleship Potemkin'. A famous scene in the film had taken place on these steps, which depicted a massacre in a dramatised version of the mutiny that occurred in Odessa in 1905.

Joining Chris on the balustrade terrace, I look south towards the horizon in the direction of Turkey and take a moment to appreciate this grand entrance to the city from the sea. Connected to the Mediterranean by the Bosphorus strait, the Sea of Marmara and the Dardanelles, the Black Sea is the main focus of our adventure. After travelling 3,000km from the UK, across Germany and Poland to Kiev and then south to Odessa, we have reached the starting point of our quest to drive our trusty Volvo around this ancient body of water. To the east lie Crimea, Russia and Georgia, to the west Bulgaria and Romania. Observing dozens of large container ships and tankers in the bay, the thought of the journey ahead suddenly seems quite daunting. Over the coming weeks we will pass through six countries, cross the towering frozen peaks of the Caucasus Mountains, traverse the Turkish coastal highway at the foot of the Pontic Alps to Istanbul and end our expedition in Romania at the outfall of the mighty River Danube.

Returning to the campground ten kilometres east of Odessa, I see Annalise marching towards me clutching a bottle of wine.

'For you, Simon, and your brother,' she smiles. 'Come! Come!'

Curious, I follow the preternaturally friendly proprietor behind one of a dozen pastel blue wooden cabins that stand evenly spaced out along the top of the cliffs. She begins to point out apricots, plums, blackcurrants and walnuts, which she calls "Greek nuts", growing in the garden.

She hands me a plastic bag bursting with fruit that has fallen to the ground.

'Please, you eat,' she nods excitedly.

Wearing a lemon floral print nightgown and cream sandals, Annalise takes my arm and leads me across the orchard to a small rustic kitchen. She pushes open the door and I'm immediately struck by the overpowering smell of plums frothing on the stove in an enormous cooking pot. A bright pink tablecloth covers the small table in the corner, and a ticking clock above the sink tells the wrong time. Between the frilly net curtains hanging at the window, I see a thin old man with a bristly grey moustache pushing a wheelbarrow brimming with freshly chopped firewood. Stripped to the waist and wearing baggy black suit trousers, he has the complexion of tan boot leather. I watch with intrigue as he draws to a halt outside a small shed with hanging baskets either side of a faded blue door. He stretches his back and wipes his brow before stepping inside. Annalise grabs a large wooden spoon and begins to frantically stir the saucepan with her huge motherly arms. Leaning in close she inhales the sweet aroma, her face lights up and she mumbles away in her own little world.

Chris appears suddenly at the window. He pokes his head around the kitchen door.

'Good afternoon!' he sings, flicking his sunglasses on top of his head.

Annalise waves him inside and lifts the lid off the cooking pot. Through a cloud of steam Chris peers down at the bubbling concoction.

'What is it?' he frowns.

'It's plum jam, fresh from the tree,' I reply.

Annalise dries her hands on a tea towel and looks up at us both with wide eyes. 'Later, my family, you eat. Yes! Yes!'

She squeezes both our cheeks like we are seven years old.

Leaving Annalise to finish preparing the jam, we head down to the beach and follow a sandy path through the coarse yellow grass that clings to the crumbling sandstone cliffs. Terns and swallows dart overhead in the cloudless blue sky. Climbing steeply down to a small cove, we pass a woman with a sulky pout reading a book on the sand and set up base close to the jagged rocks at the farthest end of the beach. Crouching down, I scoop up seawater with my flip-flop and inspect a small crustacean that looks like a miniature transparent shrimp. The water is crystal clear and I can see small fish darting about in the shallows. Entering the sea from the beach, Chris dives beneath the surface of the water and swims a few metres before floating on his back and gazing up at the blue sky. Struggling over the rocks, I disturb a shoal of fish that disperse explosively. Noticing the water doesn't taste all that salty, we are reminded that five major rivers, carrying billions of tons of organic matter, empty into the Black Sea and the smaller adjoining Sea of Azov. Over thousands of years this has created one of the largest reservoirs of hydrogen sulphide in the world, where no life can exist below the depths of 150-200 metres.

Hungry as wolves, we return to the campground and see Annalise waving urgently from the top of the cliffs. My initial thought is that something terrible has happened; maybe the old man with the wheelbarrow has had a heart attack or Annalise's plum jam has exploded in a fireball and burnt down the kitchen. Out of breath, she escorts us hurriedly over to a group of people sat around a long wooden table at the bottom of the orchard. Seated in front of a large platter of barbecued meat, we are introduced to Annalise's son, Vlad, his wife, Yana, her sister, Kristina, and their mother and father. The father is a hulk of a man with a shaved head and hairy shoulders. He pours all of the men a shot of vodka before proposing a toast. I mop my brow with a paper napkin and Vlad, a muscular guy with detailed tattoos on his arms, suggests I remove my t-shirt. Reluctantly pulling it over my head, Chris follows suit and we both sit there looking rather pale and thin in the harsh sunlight. The friendly mother with cherry red cheeks offers us three types of bread; Ukrainian, Georgian and Armenian and our plates are heavily loaded with delicious fresh salad, green peppers and chunks of succulent pork and lamb. Kristina, an attractive woman in her early thirties with watery black eyes, olive skin and silky dark brown hair, speaks perfect English. She reveals that she works for Maersk Line, a

Danish shipping company based not far away in the port of Odessa. Intrigued, I ask her what kind of cargo arrives in Odessa by ship, and she replies that the majority of imports are cars and electrical goods from Asia and much of the exports are raw materials such as wheat and sunflower oil.

Over lunch we talk about the deluge hypothesis, a theory that the Black Sea may have formed thousands of years ago by a flood through the Bosphorus strait caused by rising seas after the last Ice Age. Kristina explains how some people believe this may have inspired the flood narrative about Noah's Ark in the Book of Genesis. Personally, she is sceptical about the literal events of religious texts, and explains how one shipping company tried to transport Persian horses from Iran across the Black Sea, but they would frequently die during transportation. She proposes that maybe Noah's Ark was not possible. Yana joins the conversation and we talk about Odessa's turbulent history, and she shares her fears that the city will someday collapse into the 1,000km of catacombs and tunnels that lie beneath its streets. Kristina quickly changes the subject and asks us what we are doing in Odessa. Chris reveals our quest to drive around the Black Sea, and our desire to draw inspiration from the people, history and many mythological stories that originated in this fascinating region of the world. Vlad tears off a large chunk of meat from the bone and nods, he appears to be impressed by our journey, but warns us to stay alert when travelling through the North Caucasus close to Chechnya. I ask Vlad if he has any idea if the 'Verkhny Lars - Darial Gorge' border crossing between Russia and Georgia is now open to foreigners. He shakes his head and shrugs his powerful shoulders. His friend had travelled from Russia to Georgia in 2011, but he was a Russian national. We had received conflicting reports from the Russian and Georgian consulates before leaving England, and fear this route around the Black Sea may still be impassable.

The father proposes a second toast before collapsing onto a makeshift bed beside the table. While he snores in the shade, the mother encourages Kristina to tell the story about her ostrich ride on their recent trip to Vietnam. Fighting fits of giggles, Kristina describes how scared her mother had been sitting on top of the huge bird. Her father wasn't allowed to participate due to his weight. They all turn to him and burst out laughing.

'They thought he looked like Buddha,' Kristina laughs, tears streaming down her cheeks.

The family's sense of humour, hospitality and warmth is humbling, and I'm intrigued to discover that Yana, Kristina and their mother and father are originally from Armenia. The family had moved to Ukraine in the 1990s during the 'Dark and cold years' of the energetic crisis in Armenia caused by the Nagorno-Karabakh War with neighbouring Azerbaijan and the Spitak Earthquake, which left 25,000 dead and half a million homeless. Even more surprisingly, Annalise reveals that she is Georgian, and tells the emotional story of how she had been forced to flee the country with her late husband and Vlad, during the Abkhazia conflict in 1989. She had witnessed much violence, with Abkhaz separatist carrying out a full scale ethnic cleansing campaign that resulted in the expulsion of up to 250,000 ethnic Georgians. More than 15,000 were killed. I glance at the three different types of bread nestled together in the basket on the table and find myself struck by its symbology. The Black Sea, it appears, is a complex cultural melting pot steeped in modern and ancient history. This road trip promised to be a journey through time.

Two

Si's hair dances in the wind as we drive east to Crimea. Vast fields of sunflowers reach to the horizon, resembling thousands of little faces at a concert all facing the stage. A seaport slides into view with cargo ships moored up near to a Soviet era power station. Brand new combine harvesters glow in the early morning light and work tirelessly to gather wheat that has grown on the fertile Pontic steppe since ancient times.

Around 800 BC, a tribe of nomadic horse bowmen called the Scythians emerged from Central Asia and settled right here on the vast plains of the Pontic steppe. Coming into close contact with Greek merchant colonies, the Scythians gradually adapted to settled agriculture and inhabited the entire northern shore of the Black Sea, from the border with Romania all the way to the Volga region in modern-day central Russia. Over the centuries, they played an important role in growing the grain and shipped wheat that fed the Greek Empire. The Scythians also became hugely wealthy from the slave trade, and left burial mounds "kurgans" brimming with treasure troves of gold. According to the Greek historian Herodotus, higher-ranking Scythian warriors were often covered in detailed tattoos and indulged in smoking marijuana. The

Greeks described the Scythians as "barbaric" warriors. Herodotus thought otherwise and saw them not as the barbarians of the Black Sea, but skilled hardworking communities who lived a nomadic way of life. In 512 BC, when King Darius the Great of Persia attacked the Scythians, he allegedly cut into their land after crossing the Danube. Herodotus related that the nomadic Scythians succeeded in frustrating the Persian army by letting them march through the entire country without one single swipe of a sword. After the collapse of the Roman Empire mass migration took place, partly stimulated by the arrival of the Huns in the 4th century AD. Emerging from east of the Volga River, the Huns were one of the first major ruthless nomadic groups to enter the Black Sea, hundreds of years after the Scythians were pushed west by a group of nomadic pastoralists called the Sarmatians.

Munching on sunflower seeds, we cross a bridge over the Southern Bug River and drive through the city of Mykolaiv, an important ship building centre. Si reveals that it was here at the mouth of this mighty river, where it empties into the Dnieper estuary, that the ancient city of Olbia once thrived. Meaning "happy" in ancient Greek, Olbia was founded by adventures from Miletus in the 6th century BC and was used as a major port. The city imported wine and olive oil from Greece and traded these products for grain, fish and slaves with the steppe tribes. Home to as many as thirty to forty thousand people at its peak in the 4th century BC, Olbia was a heavily fortified and guarded city that withstood a major siege by one of Alexander the Great's armies in 331 BC.

Looping around Kherson, we cross the Dnieper River and see signs pointing to Cossack Churches and the Black Sea Biosphere Reserve. The engine of our Volvo, which rolled off the production line in 1994 (the same year Boris

Yeltsin ordered troops into Chechnya), purrs effortlessly in the heat of the day. We turn into a bustling rest stop, and browse the makeshift stalls that sell fresh fruit and vegetables and salted mackerel and anchovy that are hung up on string. Si purchases a honey melon from the trunk of a Lada, the weight on the suspension tilting the vehicle comically to one side. A beat up old minibus screeches to a halt nearby and a group of unshaven men pile out. They immediately spark up cigarettes and readjust their crotches.

Powering the Volvo south through the last wild grasslands of the Pontic steppe, we cross a bridge that transports us to the east coast of the Crimean peninsula. At brief intervals we catch glimpses of white salt flats, with multiple shades of pink and orange minerals fading to a rusty red colour around the shoreline. This region of marshy inlets and coves form Lake Syvash "Rotten Sea", a body of water that stretches south along the coast of northeast Crimea. Joining an arrow straight highway that cuts through the lush green hills, we are carried swiftly to the Crimean Tatar capital of Bakhchysarai. The Tatars are thought to have evolved their cultural identity in the 16th century, through the merging of the Greeks, Armenians, Italians, Goths and Ottoman Turks who once inhabited this region. During the invasions of the Golden Horde in the 1230s Mongol influence was added along with Turkic-speaking Kipchaks and Cumans of the steppe. Tragically, under Stalin's orders, many Crimean Tatars lost their lives during mass deportation to Central Asia in 1944. A quarter of a million Crimean Tatars were bundled aboard freight trains and physically removed from the peninsula to remote regions of Uzbekistan, Kazakhstan and Siberia. Nearly half died during the journey and the following year after. In the late 1980s, they slowly began to return to their motherland where they exist as an approximately 12% minority today, numbering around 250,000 people.

We arrive in the small dusty town of Bakhchysarai in the stifling midday heat. Si is ushered into a parking space by an unshaven guy wearing an orange high-visibility vest. Walking along the main street to the palace, we are offered jeep tours of the surrounding countryside and a peppermint tea by a young lad touting for business outside a restaurant serving Central Asian cuisine. Crossing a bridge over a moat, we eagerly enter the grounds of the strikingly beautiful Khan's Palace. The Hansaray was built in the 16th century by Ukrainian and Russian slaves under the instruction of Ottoman, Persian and Italian architects. Following Russia's annexation of the Crimean Khanate in 1783, Catherine the Great found the palace to be "romantic and sweet" and spared it from destruction. Suffering from neglect the palace had fallen into disrepair over the centuries, but has since been restored to its former glory since the return of the Tatars in the 1990s.

A Turkic-speaking Muslim state, the Crimean Khanate was one of the most powerful confederations in Eastern Europe. The rulers "khans" of the Crimean Tatars were the progeny of Haci I Girai a Jochid, descendant of Genghis Khan. Up until the beginning of the 18th century the Tatars were slave traders on a grand scale. They would make frequent raids into Ukraine and Russia, and became incredibly wealthy from the supply of women and workers to the Ottoman Empire and the Middle East. Adopting Islam in the 14th century, by 1783 there were approximately 1,600 religious schools and mosques in Crimea.

Leaving the sunny courtyard, we explore the Khan's main residence. I admire the impressive chandeliers in the opulent dining hall and we pop our heads into the tranquil Summer Pavilion, with colourful stained glass windows. Si leads the way into the Small Khan Mosque, where we view a mihrab that is beautifully decorated with seven bands, symbolising the seven levels of heaven. An ornate window above the mihrab displays a hexagram star, which is the official seal of Suleiman. Tagging along with a Viking Cruise tour, we stand in front of the Fountain of Tears and learn it was built for the last Crimean Khan, Qirim Girai, who fell in love with a beautiful Polish girl from his Harem. A red rose for "love" and a yellow rose for "chagrin" lie on the small white marble fountain; a tradition that was introduced by the Russian writer Alexander Pushkin. He first visited the Hansaray in the early 19th century and loved the fountain so much, he wrote a poem about it in 1823 'The Bakhchysaray Fountain'.

Wandering through the internal courtyard, we seek out a display of Scythian gold. Many of the items in the collection were unearthed inside ancient kurgan burial mounds found close to Bakhchysarai. Along with gold, archaeologists also discovered Chinese lacquered boxes revealing evidence of ancient trade between east and west many centuries before the birth of Christianity. Peering into a glass cabinet, we admire the fine detail and beautiful craftsmanship of a Scythian grave circlet, a golden deer, an ornamental breastplate, a cone-shaped headdress and a gold wolf's head.

* * *

At the foot of the Shatir Dagh mountain range, we ditch the Volvo at the entrance gate to the cave fortress of Mangup Kale. Hiking through the dark forest we reach an ancient Jewish cemetery, with moss covered tombstones that are engraved in Hebrew. Squatting down, Chris explains the earliest graves here date back six hundred years and belong to a people known as the Crimean Karaites. A Jewish sect that began in Mesopotamia in the 8th century AD, the Karaites branched away from rabbinical Judaism two hundred years later and were pushed out of Palestine and Egypt by the First Crusade. The Karaites reached Crimea in the 12th century and settled here in the Crimean Mountains. They eventually took over Mangup Kale after it was destroyed by the Turks. In the eerie forest I examine various tombstones nestled amid the leaves and notice the majority appear to have been carved in the 16th and 17th centuries. Pushed on by the raucous cawing of a hooded crow in a nearby tree, we scramble over rocks and continue our hike to the top of the mountain plateau. We turn a sharp corner, and are brought to an abrupt halt by the surprising sight of two women bathing completely naked in a natural spring. Fearing I may be experiencing some kind of bizarre hallucination induced by fatigue, I blink in disbelief at seeing their slim naked bodies and soft white skin that is enhanced by the dark green setting of the forest. Rinsing their hair with water from a porcelain jug, the women spot us through the trees. They both giggle and modestly cover their breasts. Chris tugs my arm and, breaking out of my trance, we push on up the trail.

Emerging out of the forest, we cross a beautiful wild meadow and climb the last few metres to the crumbling ruins of Mangup Kale. The entrance gate and a towering wall are all that remains of this huge block fortress, which was formerly the ancient city of Feodor. Fortified by Justinian I in the 6th century AD, Mangup Kale was inhabited by the Crimean Greeks, who were actually descendants of Greeks, Goths and Sarmatians. The view into the valley from the top of the flat upper plateau is truly breathtaking, with vertical cliffs dropping steeply away on three sides. Clambering around the ruins, I follow Chris down a flight of smooth steps carved into the rock that lead to a burial chamber with tiny cells. The setting sun floods the cave in golden light; our elongated shadows casting temporary graffiti across the stone walls. Russian and Ukrainian hippies used to live at Mangup Kale in the 1980s, and they would wander around the rocky plateau barefoot soaking up the ghostly energies. Providing sanctuary over the centuries to pagans, Christians, Tatars and the Karaite, we look down into the lush green valley and begin to understand why these mountains are known as the spirit of Crimea.

Conscious of the setting sun, we slip and slide back down the mountain. Reaching the Karaite cemetery, we bump into two cyclists setting up camp. Aleksander and Sasha invite us to join them, and we sit on a blanket outside their tent and eat delicious cured pork with thick white fat. Aleksander is tall and thin and wears round spectacles, whilst Sasha is short and stocky with a receding hairline. Sasha proudly informs us that the meat we are eating is produced by feeding the pigs six litres of cream everyday.

'In England we feed our pigs chocolate candy,' Chris smiles.

Alexander looks surprised. 'You make joke?'

I nod my head. 'I'm afraid it's true.'

Sasha laughs hysterically. 'I have this image of a pig with chocolate around its mouth.'

Continuing to feast on the meat, Sasha breaks the silence. 'So, tell me English brothers. What is it like living in England?'

'It's great,' Chris replies, 'if you don't mind cloudy skies, congested roads and CCTV cameras spying on your every move.'

'Yes, we know about the cameras. You are the most watched country in the world.'

Aleksander furrows his brow.'Things are not so great here also. We are not one country, we are two.'

'How do you mean?' I ask.

Aleksander looks serious and prepares to answer the question. 'Our problems in Ukraine are nothing new. Since Roman times we have been a border country. The disunion between Catholic and Orthodox Christianity in 1054 split our country down the middle.'

'I had no idea. I thought Ukraine was unified?'

'I'm afraid the opposite is true, Simon,' Aleksander replies, pushing his glasses up the bridge of his nose. 'It does not help when we have interference from the outside.'

Sasha disappears inside the tent and reappears with a bottle of vodka. 'I hear you British guys like to drink.'

'Absolutely,' Chris sings, rubbing his hands together.

Glancing over my shoulder, I can see the faint outline of the moss-covered gravestones dotted across the forest floor.

'Great place to get drunk,' I smile.

Sasha laughs. 'You know about this place, right? The Karaites were bohemian people. They lived in this forest for hundreds of years.'

Chris looks up into the trees. 'It's kind of creepy.'

Aleksander fishes a candle out of his rucksack and puts it inside a plastic water bottle that acts like a lampshade, while Sasha pours everyone a shot of vodka.

'What were you saying Aleksander, about interference from outside of Ukraine?'

Aleksander looks surprised. 'You do not know this? For many years the Russians and the US have been fighting a new Cold War in Ukraine, and also in Georgia. They have been competing for control of Eurasia.'

'Where did you hear that?'

'It is common knowledge. I study history and politics at university. Did you know that the Russians own more than seventy percent of businesses and industry in Ukraine, and supply approximately thirty percent of gas and oil imports to Europe? The US and the EU does not like to be dependent on Russia for energy, and over the past decade they have been supporting pro-Western politicians, NGOs and oligarchs in our country. The Russians are of course doing the same. It is a dangerous game to play here, as we are an unstable country. People are becoming vocal. They are provoking civil war!'

'But with what purpose?'

'To profit from the control of fossil fuels, of course. All these wars in Afghanistan, Iraq and Gaza are about the control of energy and the ultimate goal of controlling economics. When Poland became a member of the EU, it was the beginning of changing times for us here. We became the frontline between East and West.'

'I must apologise for my friend,' Sasha laughs. 'He is not good in a party.'

Aleksander shrugs his shoulders before knocking back his shot of vodka. 'What I say is true.'

Chris leans forward. 'Who do you think Ukraine should side with?'

'We're really quite screwed,' Aleksander sighs. 'My parents are pro-Russian Crimean's. They grew up under communism and had a very good quality of life during the Sixties and Seventies.'

'Surely there must a peaceful solution.'

'What I want is a united Ukraine - united in a popular revolt against corruption. I dream of a Federal Republic of Ukraine, with a high level of autonomy for the two parts, East Ukraine and West Ukraine. This would be the intelligent thing to do, but the media is so plagued with propaganda that no one can see clearly anymore. No one knows what to believe. If only people could see the bigger picture, instead of thinking only about themselves and dreaming about being able to work in Germany or the UK, or of Crimea returning to Russia "the Motherland". If that were to happen, then maybe we could have unity and diversity in our country. Did you know Ukraine is a founding member of the United Nations? It is a country, yet the different identities of the east and west have for many years been fully respected. If we were clever, we could be both an associate member of the EU and the Russian federation. We could have the best of both worlds.'

'Have you ever thought about going into politics?' Chris asks with a smile.

Sasha bursts out laughing. 'Chris, please don't tell him that. He already thinks he is Mahatma Gandhi.'

Aleksander playfully punches him in the arm. 'And you like only to fuck and smoke.'

Finishing our drinks, we thank Sasha and Aleksander for their incredible hospitality. They insist we take the candle and water bottle lampshade, and in the dead of night we walk the last few kilometres back to the Volvo through the eerie forest.

Three

We arrive in the maritime city of Sevastopol in time for breakfast. Home to the second largest port in Ukraine after Odessa, Sevastopol was a "closed city" until 1996, with access to large areas around it prohibited to foreigners. With virtually no road signs we quickly become lost. Si pulls over at the roadside and I ask a charismatic chap for directions. Bearing an uncanny resemblence to the British entrepreneur Richard Branson, he has white shoulder length hair, a neatly trimmed goatee beard and a tanned complexion. We are fascinated to discover he is a cargo ship captain on vacation with his family. Using nautical terminology "starboard" for right and "port" for left, he uses his finger to draw a map in the dirt on the roof of the Volvo. Thanking the captain for his help, we drive for a couple of kilometres before Si is forced to pull over once again and flick on the hazard lights so I can check the map on the roof of the car. In the distance, I can see the towering masts belonging to a number of enormous naval warships and to my right I look curiously at a large wrought iron gate with the Tryzub symbol emblazoned across it. The "trident" was adopted as the coat of arms of the Ukrainian People's Republic in February 1918. With a history dating back two thousand years, this symbol of a three-pronged fork on an azure background, is believed to have derived from the classic mythological symbol of Neptune's trident spear. The oldest examples of the trident were discovered by archaeologists on Ukrainian territory dating back to the 1st century AD.

Walking through the shaded back streets, we race up a flight of steps that lead to the elegant Russian headquarters of the Black Sea Fleet. For centuries Sevastopol has been an important hub to project Russian naval power in the Black Sea, the Mediterranean and beyond. Si voices his concerns that if Ukraine were to join the European Union and become a member of NATO, it seems incredibly unlikely that Russia would sit back and potentially lose its major militarily strategic naval base on the Black Sea. Prince Grigory Potemkin founded Russia's Black Sea Fleet in 1783, and it defeated the Turks in 1790 and fought the Ottomans during World War I, the Romanians during World War II and Georgia during the 2008 South Ossetia war.

High above the city, we pass guards wearing navy uniforms standing outside grand official buildings, and we admire an imposing statue of Vladimir Lenin on vulitsya Voronyna. He points south across the Black Sea, with the gold dome of Vladimirsky Cathedral in the background. Descending a sweeping flight of steps leading down to the bay, Si uses his razor sharp instincts to seek out a coffee machine by the bustling ferry terminal. Modern glass hotels tower over the harbour, and boats of varying shapes and sizes cut frothy white channels in the surface of the turquoise Artilleriyskaya Bay. Making our way along the promenade, a group of soldiers scrub the deck of a boat while their supervisory officer sits in the shade and plays with his mobile phone. Close by, locals and holidaymakers swim off the rocks in the shadow of the Eagle Column. This monument commemorates the many Russian ships that were deliberately sunk in the bay to protect the harbour from invasion by the Allies in 1854. With the Ottoman Empire in ruins, Russia saw an opportunity to gain control over parts of Moldavia and Wallachia (modern-day Romania), and secure access to routes from the Black Sea to the Mediterranean. A surprise attack on the Turkish town of Sinop in 1853 signalled the beginning of the Crimean War, which led the British and French to join forces with the Turks to prevent the threat of the Russians taking over routes to their India and North African colonies. The first target to be bombarded was right here in Sevastopol, with the Allies attacking the city for 349 days. History repeated itself in 1942 during the Second World War, when Sevastopol fell to the Germans after a brutal 250-day siege.

Si seizes the helm and we drop by the pretty seaside town of Balaklava on the Yalta-Sevastopol highway. On a hill a few miles north of the town, the infamous Battle of Balaklava had been fought on 25th October 1854 during the Crimean War. This bloody battle had witnessed the tragic slaughter of many British soldiers during an event that became known as the 'Charge of the Light Brigade'. As part of the Anglo-French-Turkish campaign to capture the port and fortress of Sevastopol, the Earl of Cardigan was ordered to prevent the Russians from snatching their weapons supplies. Loyalty and a complete misunderstanding of orders and position of the enemy were the reasons the brigade charged down the wrong side of the valley into a frontal assault on Russian artillery. The British nurse, Florence Nightingale, "The Lady with the Lamp", saved many soldiers' lives at her field hospital on the plateau above Balaklava.

We make a loop around the suburban neighbourhood,

where almost the entire population of the town at one time worked at the formerly classified nuclear submarine base. Operational until 1993, the base was apparently designed to survive a direct atomic impact. Avoiding the parking hustlers close to the marina, where the Russian elite moor their yachts alongside fishing boats, we climb into the forested Baydarskiy hills on the road to Yalta. We spend the night outside the gates of a German war cemetery near to the village of Gontscharnoje. During the small hours we come under attack by a group of feral cats. They climb onto the roof of the car and scream, wail and fight.

Dawn finally arrives and, after a sleepless night, we traverse the mountainous southern coastline of the Crimean peninsula. Cruising along the strikingly beautiful Baydarski Vorota Pass, we catch a glimpse of Mt Mshat-Kaya that towers above the village of Foros; where Mikhail Gorbachev was held under house arrest in 1991. With the smooth highway clinging to the side of the steep mountains that plunge into the sparkling Black Sea below, ravens soar high above the alpine forests as we make our aerial descent into Yalta.

Once a fashionable resort for the Russian aristocracy and gentry, Yalta has grown into a popular holiday destination for predominantly Russian and Ukrainian working people on their summer vacation. We pass dozens of tour boats and giant inflatable bouncy castles along the waterfront promenade. The smell of candyfloss and fried food fills the air. On the crowded beach a group of pale, bare-chested guys drink beer hidden inside brown paper bags and ogle a couple of girls wearing microscopic bikinis. A painfully skinny old man in a string vest devours a burger next to his plump wife, while families and couples enjoy the warm waters of the Black Sea. The energetic and slightly tacky nal Lenina waterfront promenade, with a funfair and a McDonalds at its centre, is chock-a-block with screaming kids zipping around in electric toy cars. Si stops dead in his tracks, and we watch an attractive girl dressed as a rock chick straddling a big shiny motorcycle. Wearing a wig, black leather hot pants and thigh length boots, she poses in front of the camera for her grinning boyfriend. Palm trees, nightclubs, commercial shops and fast food joints dominate the upper pedestrian street. Stumbling across a stolovy canteen, we devour a delicious bowl of borscht; a traditional Ukrainian beetroot soup with large chunks of beef, onion and a dollop of cream.

Further along the coast we discover a section of the beach has been sponsored by National Geographic. It occurs to me that this popular magazine and TV channel may have identified Russia as a lucrative new marketplace. Si photographs an advertisement for the Russian Winter Olympics, which is due to be held in Sochi in six months time. Admiring the snow-capped mountains on the poster, I begin to feel excited about the prospect of driving to the furthest point of southern Russia, where the Caucasus Mountains meet the Black Sea.

* * *

In serious need of an injection of culture, Chris weaves through the steep narrow backstreets of Yalta. We screech to a halt outside a house where the much loved Russian playwright, Anton Chekhov, once lived. I had started reading a collection of Chekhov's work before leaving England and, inspired by a man who had a great talent for projecting empathy, I'm sad to learn about his long-term illness and premature death aged only 44. Anton spent the last four years of his life here in Yalta from 1898 to 1902. Having sold the rights to his complete works to a publisher, he built this beautiful house that he called the White Dacha.

An eccentric woman in her early seventies shows us around the house. She is wonderfully animated and reveals that she used to perform on the stage. Chris asks her if she can dance, and with an air of confidence she expertly rises onto the balls of her feet and performs a pirouette. The wooden floorboards creak as we explore the sparsely furnished rooms that appear frozen in time. Glancing inside Anton's office, where he wrote one of his most famous short stories 'The Lady with the Dog', I imagine him sat at the wooden desk still deep in thought over the paragraph he is writing. Anton shared this house with his mother and sister and later his wife Olga Knipper, an actress of the stage who performed in a number of his plays. He regularly hosted dinner parties for friends including Leo Tolstoy, the great writer, philosopher and political thinker who wrote 'War and Peace'; Maxim Gorky, a political activist and founder of the Socialist realism literary method and Isaac Levitan, his close friend and landscape artist. I imagine I can hear laughter and the sound of the piano drifting through the house.

We return to the main administrative building where Chris greets a woman with a bird's nest perm and penetrating green eyes. She personally walks us through a chronology of Anton Chekhov's life in black and white photographs, and points out his actress wife, Olga, performing in the play he wrote 'The Seagull'. Anton married Olga in 1901, and they lived unconventionally with Olga residing mainly in Moscow and Chekhov in Yalta. He had once written to the book publisher and friend, Aleksey Suvorin, "give me a wife who, like the moon, won't appear in my sky every day." In 1890, Anton undertook an arduous journey by train, horse-drawn carriage and river steamer across Siberia to the Far East of Russia and the katorga, or penal colony on Sakhalin Island north of Japan. During his stay he spent three months interviewing thousands of convicts and settlers for a census. He then sailed on a long voyage back to Russia via Ceylon (Sri Lanka). Travelling full circle around the room, voyeuristically examining every aspect of this man's life, we reach the door where our journey first began.

A short drive outside Yalta, we drop by Livadia Palace that is located on the cliffs with breathtaking views of the Black Sea. This beautiful Italian Renaissance-style white mansion house was built in the 1860s as a summer retreat for Tsar Nicholas II. It later hosted the Yalta Conference in 1945. We enter the palace between tour groups and stand in front of a reproduction of the round table where the victors of World War II, Winston Churchill, Franklin Roosevelt and Joseph Stalin confirmed decisions on the carve-up of Europe. In two months time Bill Clinton and Tony Blair will gather in this luxurious palace to attend the 10th Yalta Annual Meeting in Ukraine. Joining them will be more than 250 influential politicians and world business leaders from companies including oil and gas giant Shell, Visa Inc and Ukrainian oligarch owned Smart-Holding Group. Under the title, "Changing Ukraine in a Changing World: Factors of Success", the YES (Yalta European Strategy) annual meetings are promoted as, "A platform to share ideas and views on paths to European, Ukrainian and global development." Peering into an elegant banqueting hall, I try to imagine Tony Blair addressing a room full of business people and politicians, and imagine the unimpressed frown of Sergey Glazyev, Advisor to President Vladimir Putin, who is due to attend the event. Divided down the middle, with predominantly Catholic Ukrainians in the west of the country and Orthodox Russian-speaking Ukrainians in Crimea and in the east, Aleksander's fears suddenly appear very real. With very little chance of Russia ever agreeing to join NATO, Ukraine is the final buffer zone between Russia and NATO allied Europe, as the European Union has slowly edged east of Berlin over the past two decades and absorbed the former eastern block countries. With a religiously and politically divided pro-European-west and pro-Russian-east, it seems terrifyingly clear that this region of Europe is at the centre of a power struggle, and has all of the right ingredients to erupt in bloody civil war.

Passing through the grand room where Roosevelt slept, we view the courtyard where the famous photograph was taken of the three chief Allied leaders sitting together. We discover the rest of the palace is dedicated to Nicholas II and his family. Photographs of the Tsar, with fellow bushy bearded men dressed in military uniform, are hung alongside portraits of his wife Alexandra and their five children. Chris points out a black and white photograph of a young Nicholas aged 22, standing outside a railway carriage. In 1890, before Nicholas became king, he was sent on a huge journey around the greater part of the Eurasian continent. This long trip, apparently for educational purposes, exceeded 51,000km, including 15,000km of railway and 22,000km of sea routes. During his time in Japan he was nearly assassinated. He later took part in the opening ceremony of the Trans-Siberian Railway in Vladivostok, which was completed in 1916. Entering the Tsar's office, Chris admires a large wooden desk with a throne-like chair, and we absorb the opulence of a family living in extreme luxury at a time when thousands of peasant serfs in Russia were dying of starvation. Nicholas II had become a puppet of his strong-willed eccentric wife, Alexandra, who was the granddaughter of the British monarch, Queen Victoria. Alexandra had herself fallen under the spell of a sinister Siberian peasant named Rasputin. In spite of his wife's bullying, Nicholas II apparently preferred to spend time with his family, rather than having to deal with the problems of running a nation. I narrow my eyes at the thought of the tragic and violent event that brought an end to Tsarist rule in Russia, when the family were executed by the Bolsheviks in Yekaterinburg in 1918.

Four

Sweeping across the top of Yalta we drive a stunning stretch of road through the mountains, with beautiful switchback corners and nail-biting hairpin bends. Returning to the coast, Si points out the impressive towers of an enormous 14th century Genoese fortress that is located high on the cliffs above the historic town of Sudak. Once a major stopover on the Silk Road from China, Sudak was an important trading centre heavily guarded by this impressive fort. In 1380, the whole Crimean Black Sea coast was effectively controlled by the Genoese, from Caffa (now known as Feodosiya) in the east, to Chembalo in the west. The Genoese and the Venetians competed for a lucrative trade in slaves and spices; transporting slaves from Eastern Europe via Crimea to Egypt and trading them for spices, silk, linen and aromatic woods brought by traders from India and Ceylon. For over one hundred years, Sudak remained in Genoese hands until they were driven out in 1475 by the arrival of the Ottoman Turks.

Driving through a particularly wild and picturesque region of Crimea, we admire the Kara-Dag volcano "Black Mountain" that rises from the earth in a fortress of jagged rock. We make a pit stop in the buzzing seaside town of Koktebel. It's been raining this side of the mountain and muddy puddles force pedestrians to walk in the road. For fear of his scrawny neck being wrung like a chicken, Si avoids splashing a sunburnt colossus of a man who is pushing a baby in a pram. Located halfway between Sudak and Feodosia, Koktebel was once a deserted hamlet populated mostly by Bulgarian refugees. It became an oasis for artists and writers during the Soviet years, and in recent decades it has grown into a popular Black Sea tourist spot. Taking the opportunity to stretch our legs and mingle with predominantly Russian holidaymakers, we walk along the promenade and jostle through the half-naked crowds. Artisans sell jewellery, clothes and souvenirs and posters advertise the forthcoming jazz festival, hang gliding, horse riding tours and night jeep safaris of the surrounding hills.

We pass a large concrete building near to a water amusement park, and Si hears the distinct sound of a dolphin clicking and whistling. Standing on tiptoe, we peer through a salt stained window and see one of these water dwelling mammals splashing around in a swimming pool. The Black Sea is home to the bottlenose dolphin, seals and approximately 180 fish species including sturgeon, anchovy, grey herring, mullet, mackerel and tuna. Utilising dolphin's intelligence and strong swimming capabilities, bottlenose dolphins (such as the American combat dolphin "K-Dog") have been trained by the US and Russian military over the years to perform tasks under the sea; such as detecting enemy divers and locating mines. According to a British newspaper, US trained dolphins from San Diego are scheduled to participate in eight joint NATO-Ukrainian military exercises in the coming months. Their mission is to test a new anti-radar system that is designed to disorientate enemy sonars. New armour for dolphins, developed at a specialised research centre at the University of Hawaii, will also be tested in the Black Sea. This will be the first time in history dolphins have participated in a NATO drill. The exercise may also become the first time that US military dolphins meet their Russian counterparts in the open seas, as San Diego and Sevastopol host the world's only military dolphin training facilities.

Feeling revitalised after a refreshing swim, we head for the cone-shaped hills that rise above the town. Si keeps his eyes peeled for sharp rocks and potholes, as we follow a jeep trail to a peak covered in yellow grass with views over the bay. From our vantage point on top of the hill, the gold sea shimmers as it fans out to the horizon. A lone woman silhouetted in the shallow water below appears to be paralysed, seduced by the beauty of the setting sun.

Squatting down to light the gas stove, I suddenly notice a guy approaching us on a bicycle. He is wearing professional cycling gear and has a long beard and a red face that has been heavily scorched by the sun.

'Hallo, you are from Great Britain?' the guy asks, pointing at our licence plate.

Si glances over his shoulder. 'Hey, you speak English.'

'Ya, of course. You will stay here the night?'

'Yes,' I nod. 'Fancy a brew?'

The guy's face lights up. 'That would be most kind. Please give me moment to pitch my tent.'

In the time it takes to boil a kettle of water, the guy reappears out of the murky darkness. He immediately hands us both a business card, and we all shake hands and introduce ourselves. We learn Jan is from Friesland in the Netherlands and is an amateur cyclist and photographer. He spends most summers peddling around Europe, and in his life he has cycled more than 250,000km. That is nearly six times around the planet and two thirds of the way to the moon. He left Friesland one month ago and plans to cycle 20,000km by the time he returns home at the end of September.

Si fixes Jan a mug of tea, and he declines a seat preferring to stand after spending nearly the whole day on his bike. I ask him where he is heading, and he explains that he rode into Crimea along the Arabatska strilka, a thin strip of sand in the east that joins mainland Ukraine to Crimea. He reveals that the unpaved track was hard, wavy sand like a dried sea bed and possible to drive across. His only problem was not being prepared for the many mosquitoes that inhabit this marshy region.

'Without wind to blow them away I was eaten alive,' he sighs, slapping a mosquito dead on his forearm.

Si returns from the Volvo with a mosquito coil and a large bottle of Ukrainian beer. He offers Jan a glass, but he declines at first, fearing that alcohol can cause him muscle pain in the morning. Watching Si pour the lively beverage into two mugs, he suddenly changes his mind and within a matter of seconds we are merrily sipping the frothy beer beneath a bright starry sky and laughing together like old friends. We discover Jan is fifty years old. I ask him if cycling such great distances becomes more difficult with age. Like a wise guru, he warns us that although his fitness levels have not declined, sadly peoples' perceptions do. Due to only speaking a few words of Russian he has found this particular journey quite challenging. He admits to have been feeling down the past couple of days and suffering from lack of human interaction. But when he is in his tent, a Long Wave radio brings him great comfort on those lonely nights in the wilderness.

'The benefit of cycling is that you always have the open road and the kilometres to achieve,' he informs us with a smile. 'I find I'm busy most of the time.'

Si suggests that maybe it is almost meditative. He nods his head and agrees that there could be some truth in this. Jan loves to cycle in Norway, with the stunning fjords mirroring the mountains, very few mosquitoes and quiet open roads. Over the past few years he has started to explore new places, and also loves Albania and Moldova where the local people had made him feel so welcome.

He laughs. 'Here in Crimea they are shocked if you do not speak the mother tongue, it is like Russia.'

'Yes,' I smile. 'I read the Russians only handed it over to the Ukrainians in nineteen fifty-three, and over seventy percent of the population here are ethnically Russian.'

'Ya, this is true. When the Russians defeated the Ottoman Empire in the eighteenth century they annexed Crimea from the Tatars. Many Russians settled here, as well as Germans and Jews.'

The alcohol takes effect and Jan becomes animated as we share stories in the warm night. He asks us about our journey, and appears worried when we explain to him that we plan to try and cross the Caucasus border from Russia into Georgia.

'I do not wish to sound negative,' he frowns, 'but I believe it is impossible at this time.'

Disappointed to hear Jan confirm our worst fears, we agree that we will stay true to our plan and drive to Sochi and the Caucasus Mountains, even if it means driving all the way back to Odessa for thousands of kilometres to catch a car ferry to Georgia. The mention of the Sochi Winter Olympics has Jan excited, and he tells us that he had met a Russian guy who was critical of the Olympics. He had told Jan that it seemed ridiculous that they planned to host the event in the only part of Russia that doesn't get snow. Sochi is considered to be the Florida of

Russia, a tropical holiday destination where palm trees and bananas grow. Fascinated by what Jan has told us, any doubts that we have about driving such a long way without knowing if we can make it through immediately disappear. We had to see this region of the world with our own eyes.

* * *

Checking out of the Hotel Volvo before breakfast, we wave goodbye to Jan who cycles west like a Scythian nomad on a personal quest to explore new horizons. Inspired by his enthusiasm, Chris strikes the engine and we head east in the direction of Russia. We arrive in the ancient port city of Feodosiya around mid-morning, and walk through a colourful crowded market. A train looms over the stalls and sounds its horn, as this giant metal monster crawls towards Feodosiya's seafront station. The smiling faces of excited tourists from cities as far away as Moscow, St Petersburg, Minsk and Kiev peer out of the windows of the clattering carriages. Passing a row of grand seafront mansion houses, we observe a statue of the 19th century seascape artist, Ivan Aivazovsky, before popping our heads inside the Feodosiya Museum of Antiquities.

Wandering through a labyrinth of rooms we study ancient Greek vases, terracotta amphora and necklaces made from beads and shells. I stand in front of an old wooden door dating back to 1587, which has an intricate carving of an angel, a sun and a cross that is surrounded by grapevines. Next to the door is a painting in pastel colours on stone of a mosque from 1623. Chris waves me over and we look at medieval chainmail, a heavily deteriorated sword, stirrups and a necklace and ring belonging to a Kipchak warrior from the 11th-12th century. A tribal confederation, the Kipchaks conquered large parts of the Eurasian steppe during the Turkic expansion, and were in turn conquered by the Mongol invasions in the early 13th century.

The adjoining room is brimming with Greek statues, vases, togas, stone tablet carvings and a magnificent three-metre statue of a Griffin from the 4th-3rd century BC. This winged creature with an eagle head and the body of a lion was a common feature of "animal style" Scythian gold, and was believed in mythical Scythian folklore to inhabit the steppes that reached from modern-day Ukraine to Central Asia. According to the legend, when strangers collected gold and precious stones on the steppes, the griffin would leap on them and tear them to pieces. The Scythians had cleverly used giant petrified bones as proof of these creatures existence, and I contemplate the idea that these legends may have inspired the mythical monsters and dragons in Greek chronicles and odysseys, such as Jason and the Argonauts. Adrienne Mayor, a classical folklorist, has suggested in her book 'The First Fossil Hunters: Paleontology in Greek and Roman Times', that these "griffin bones" were actually dinosaur fossils that are commonly found in this part of the world. I smile at the thought of this rather effective myth; possibly invented to deter ancient pioneering gold prospectors in this once gold rich region of the world.

On the second floor of the building, we browse a display of WWII weaponry including a six-metre torpedo and a large machinegun on wheels. Posters of war propaganda cover the walls, one depicting a chain and padlock with a swastika emblem on it that has been broken down the middle. A second poster shows a Nazi soldier pointing a pistol at a Crimean Tatar, and the second frame the Tatar slicing off the Nazi soldier's head with a sword.

Down by the seafront every inch of Kameshky beach is crowded with Russian and Ukrainian tourists enjoying the summer sun. We pass the towering administration offices belonging to the 'Port of Theodosia'. Chris points out the Tryzub (Neptune's three-pronged trident fork) on a blue shield on the side of the building, next to a red emblem of the Griffin; two ancient symbols echoing Ukraine's ancient past. We study a black bust of a naval officer in a small park, with the gold emblem of the hammer and sickle on his hat set inside a red communist star. In Medieval times, this park was the location of the largest slave market on the Black Sea coast. I try to picture the faces of the people from multiple ethnic backgrounds, who may have passed through here as traders or slaves from regions as diverse as North Africa, the Middle East, Asia and Europe. According to work by the 17th century Polish poet and essayist, Samuel Twardowski, the famous slave who became Ottoman queen, known as Roxelana, was possibly sold right here where we are standing. Not to be confused with the girl who captured the heart of the Khan Qirim Girai at the Khan's Palace in Bakhchysarai, Roxelana was born in the town of Rohatyn in a region that used to belong to the kingdom of Poland. In the 1520s, it is believed she was captured by Crimean Tatars during one of their frequent raids into the region and sold as a slave; possibly first to the slave market here in Feodosiya before being shipped to Constantinople, where she had been selected for Suleiman the Magnificent's harem. Becoming the legal wife of Suleiman, it is alleged she was the mother of a long dynasty of rulers during the Ottoman Empire.

On the edge of town, Chris eagerly seeks out the ruins of Feodosiya's mighty citadel. Built by the Genoese in the

14th century, we traverse a colossal eleven-metre high sandstone block wall that stretches between impressive towers for a hundred metres to the bay. Entering the citadel through a narrow doorway, we weave around overgrown gardens and stumble across a collapsed archway at the back of the fortification. Neal Ascherson wrote in his book 'Black Sea', "Six hundred years ago, columns of slaves in irons would enter this gate, and gangs of men carrying bales of Chinese silk shipped across the Sea of Azov from Tana. But one day in 1347…the Black Death came to Europe through this gate, the pandemic of pneumonic plague which within a few years had reduced the European population by one-third or more."

The Black Death was thought to have originated in the plains of Central Asia, or China, and was carried along the Silk Road with Mongol armies and traders. It reached Crimea's Caffa here in modern-day Feodosiya in 1346, and spread quickly to Western Europe via rat fleas that were often passengers aboard merchant ships. Not even the two-metre thick stone walls could keep the Black Death out, and Caffa's demise was brought about, not solely by war, but by the rapid spread of an aggressive plague. Weakened, the Genoese fled the city aboard ships bound for southern Europe, as the Mongols catapulted the infected corpses of their victims over the walls; a futile but effective manoeuvre that brought an abrupt end to a long and drawn out siege.

Five

A cowboy on horseback skilfully herds cattle across the vast open plains of the Kerch Peninsula. Absorbing this snapshot of life, as it might have looked thousands of years ago, Si dryly points out that a Scythian or Sarmatian horseman would probably not have worn a green bomber jacket and jeans. The sky turns black as coal, and rain thunders down for approximately ten minutes before the clouds disperse and the hot sun reappears and instantly dries the tarmac. With the Volvo showroom clean we soon arrive in sunny Kerch, which is considered to be one of the most ancient cities in Crimea.

In the main square we check out the memorial to the victims of war, with an eternal flame at its centre, and admire the beautiful red and white stone Byzantine Church of St John the Baptist; Ukraine's oldest church that was built in 717 AD. An attractive woman with auburn hair, catwalks past wearing a long flowing white summer dress. Two elderly ladies sitting on a bench shake their heads in disapproval, either envious of her sparkling youth or annoyed to see the hem of her pretty frock brushing against the ground. Down by the waterfront we visit the Kerch Museum of Antiquities, and study stone tablets from the 2nd and 3rd century BC and gravestones from the 1st century AD. One tombstone reads, "Bidding son of Coss, goodbye". Si makes a quick sketch of a 2nd century AD sculpture of the goddess Nike killing the bull, which was unearthed on top of nearby Mount Mithridat. In the adjoining room, we study two elongated skulls in a glass case that look like they may have belonged to creatures from an alien world. The fashion for cranial deformation was popular among a race of nomadic pastoralists called the Sarmatians, and was attained by bandaging the head of a child in infancy. The Sarmatians first appeared on the Pontic steppe and the Crimean peninsula around 300 BC, five hundred years after the Scythians had first settled in the region. Speaking an Iranian language, the Sarmatians evolved their cultural identity in Central Asia, and moved out of the steppes around the Caspian Sea and the outfall of the Volga River with herds of horses and covered wagons. For centuries the Sarmatians are thought to have lived in relative peaceful co-existence with the Scythians, but in the 3rd century BC they fought on the Pontic steppe to the north of the Black Sea and came to dominate these territories. The Sarmatians remained on the steppe for five hundred years, until the onslaught of the Goths and finally the Huns in the 4th century AD pushed them west into modern-day Romania and south into the Caucasus Mountains.

Si asks the woman on reception if she can direct us to the rare statue of Mixoparthenos. Disappointed to learn it is on loan to the Museum of Bonn, she slides a postcard of the sculpture across the desk. Female above waist and snake below, divided into two coiled serpents, Mixoparthenos is the mythological Scythian godmother. The Greek historian Herodotus had retold the story of how she was rumoured to have lived close to the once great city of Olbia in a forest on the left bank of the lower

Dnieper. According to Greco-Scythian myth, Mixoparthenos had lured Heracles into a cave and fallen pregnant to Scythes, the first king of the Scythians. Wealthy Scythian nomads had jewellery made of this mythical snake goddess and engravings on swords; examples of which have been unearthed in kurgan burial mounds across the steppe. Fascinatingly, this lasting symbol of one of the first ancient multi-ethnic cultures living around the Black Sea can still be found today, most notably on a Starbucks coffee cup.

Wandering back to the main square, we begin to climb the steps leading to the top of Mount Mithridat. A young Russian guy swoops up his surprised girlfriend in his arms and proceeds to carry her up the hill.

'Love inspires you to commit to the most exhausting tasks,' Si smiles, impressed by the guy's display of commitment.

Approximately halfway to the top, I photograph the stone griffin statues either side of a balustrade terrace. The young guy carrying his girlfriend hides his pain well, as he staggers up the steps with a bright red face. Reaching the summit, we are rewarded with magnificent views of the Kerch Strait. An obelisk stands proud on top of the hill, which was built in 1944 to commemorate the soldiers that defended Kerch during World War II. Seventy years ago, fierce battles between the Soviet Union and the Nazi troops left the city of Kerch in total ruins and, despite the resistance of the Soviet army, Kerch fell to the German onslaught in May 1942. The Red Army lost over 170,000 men, who were killed in battle, executed or sent to concentration camps. For Hitler seizing Crimea was a prized goal. He wanted to annex the peninsula directly to Germany and name it Gotenland, securing a launch pad for further offensive in his bid to seize control of Eurasia and, ultimately, the world.

* * *

Exploring the ruins of the once great city of Panticapaeum, Chris examines Greek columns and ancient steps carved into the rock. Much of the wealth of artefacts we had seen on display in the museum were found right here, at the site of a powerful city located at the intersection of trade routes between the steppe and Europe. First founded in the 6th century BC by Greek colonists from Miletus, Panticapaeum became the capital of the Bosporan Kingdom by 480 BC. A large percentage of the city's population was Scythian and later Sarmatian. They minted coins and made wine, but Panticapaeum's main exports were grain and salted fish that fed the Greek Empire and Hellenistic period. In 438 BC, a man called Spartocos became the sole ruler of Panticapaeum. Neal Ascherson, author of 'Black Sea', believes he may have been a Thracian mercenary officer. As the Bosporan State began to grow, an army of Greek and Thracian soldiers were recruited along with Sarmatian and Scythian horsemen. They took control of this entire region within a matter of decades, around the Sea of Azov all the way to Tanais at the mouth of the Don River. The descendants of Spartocos ruled for more than three hundred years after declaring themselves kings. "The kingdom grew into an empire, an early Byzantium of the north," wrote Ascherson, "whose merchants, shipping magnates and urban governors were Greek, but whose rulers and soldiers were Thracian, Scythian and, increasingly, Sarmatian." Tribal chiefs in the countryside became incredibly wealthy from growing wheat and would buy gold and silver work produced by skilled artisans in the city.

Chris stands between two Greek columns and we look out across the vast plains. Along with nearby Theodosia, the Bosporan Kingdom eventually became a Roman client kingdom, despite fierce resistance from the heavy armoured Sarmatian soldiers who forced the Romans to completely rethink their entire method of warfare. Panticapaeum became a Roman province under Emperor Nero from 63 to 68 AD. It continued to thrive for many more centuries, until the arrival of the Huns destroyed it and the entire Bosporan Kingdom forever.

The Huns were first recorded as occupying land in a region of Scythia to the east of the Volga River around the 1st century AD. Emerging onto the steppe, they are thought to have sparked the migration west and south of a group of Sarmatian tribes called the Alans. Living near the Caspian Sea in 91 AD, by about 150 AD it is said they migrated southwest into the Caucasus. Unlike the Scythians or the Sarmatians, the Huns were a plundering force who appeared to have little interest in trade or putting down roots. By 370 AD, the Huns had established a vast Hunnic Empire in Europe which over the following three-quarters of a century stretched under Attila the Hun (434-453 AD), from the Ural River to the Rhine River and from the River Danube to the Baltic Sea.

Chris interrogates the road atlas as we go in search of the 4th century BC Tsarskiy Kurgan, a 15-metre tall burial mound covering one of the royal tombs of Spartocids. A local mechanic points us in the right direction and, turning down a residential street on the outskirts of the city, I'm forced to slam on the brakes when a woman collapses in front of the Volvo. A guy stripped to the waist swaggers out of a nearby house and marches up the road with clenched fists. The woman screams after him with blood pouring from her nostrils. Her greasy hair hangs in front of her face, and her ankles are covered in cuts and bruises. Seeming completely unaware of our existence, she struggles to her feet and limps barefoot after him. Curtains twitch at the neighbour's window, and a woman speaking into a mobile phone appears at the door. Chris gestures over to her, but she waves us away. The police will be here soon, so we agree to leave the local community to deal with this violent domestic dispute.

Driving to the end of the street, we cross a vast waste ground and in the distance I see a grass burial mound that looks like a strange eco-pyramid. We look in awe into the entrance of this magnificent tomb that is over two thousand years old. Mesmerised by a V-shape cut in the side of the mound, that creates the illusion of passing through a gateway into another dimension, we walk along the narrow corridor into the eerie darkness. Chris examines the stone block walls with fascination, as we approach the main burial chamber with a vaulted dome roof. Historians believe Leukon I was buried here, ruler of the Kingdom of Bosporus during its peak of economic development in the 4th century BC. The Tsarskiy Kurgan was only discovered fairly recently in the 19th century, and when archaeologists opened up the tomb they found it to be empty. Thankfully, many gold treasures from the barrow were later discovered elsewhere and are now on display in the Hermitage Museum in St Petersburg.

Snacking on plums picked from a nearby tree, we stroll over to the impressive Monument to the Defenders of Adzhimushkay Quarry. Enormous twenty-metre tall stone figures, clutching shovels and pick axes, defiantly guard the entrance to the catacombs hidden beneath the earth. During the counter offensive by the Germans against the Red Army in 1942, approximately 10,000 soldiers and civilians were besieged below ground for six months; many dying of hunger and thirst. The Adzhimushkay campaign was largely covered up by Soviet propaganda until the end of Joseph Stalin's rule.

Driving ten kilometres north of Kerch along a potholed road, we reach a small one-horse town. We pass two farm workers wearing flat caps who are carrying shovels over their shoulders. One of the guys has his shirt unbuttoned, revealing a strong barrel chest and firm gut. Chris powers the Volvo along a narrow track to a viewpoint that overlooks the Kerch Strait. Scrambling to the top of a nearby hill, I check out a memorial to the Soviet soldiers who died here fighting against the Germans during WWII. From my 360-degree panoramic viewpoint, I glance over at the plump white lighthouse on the adjacent hillside that looks like a pepper pot. A warm wind blows across the strait, causing each blade of grass and the many pale lime and crimson wildflowers to quiver. I watch a large tanker pass through the narrow strait. It joins a group of ships and two smaller vessels that sit between the headland and the thin strip of sand that juts out from Russia's Taman peninsula like a crooked finger. As the sun slowly sinks in the sky, the hills and the lighthouse and the tiny village are illuminated in an orange glow. The colour of the water changes from deep grey to navy blue. I look past a small church with a yellow spire on the edge of the village, and see a train waiting to be loaded aboard a ship in the harbour. Two large tankers drift behind. Hearing a lone dog barking in the distance, I watch a swift pushing into the wind and then dart overhead.

Making my way back down the hill, I see Chris with his head under the hood of the car. It looks like a giant metal monster is devouring him. He slides the dipstick back in place and points towards the Tuzla Spit; a sandy island in the middle of the Kerch Strait between the Kerch Peninsula and the Taman Peninsula. A territorial dispute between Ukraine and Russia in October 2003, over the ownership of the island, brought a halt to Russia's plans for a proposed bridge linking the Russian mainland to Crimea. Multiple attempts have been made in the past to build a bridge over the Kerch Strait. Early in 1943, Adolf Hitler ordered the construction of a 4.8km rail and road bridge to assist a campaign aimed at pushing through the Caucasus to Iran. The project was brought to a halt in September of the same year, as a result of the demand for extra-strength girders of precious steel that were needed because of minor earthquakes that regularly occur in this region. A second attempt was made in 1944 by the Red Army, who built a provisional railway bridge across the strait using supplies captured from the Germans. Completed in November 1944, the bridge collapsed in February 1945 as a result of moving ice floes. Reconstruction was not attempted, and it seems the possibility of a new bridge being built today will depend on changing politics in the region. Putin's plans for a bridge to be constructed in time for the Winter Olympics in Sochi have been put on hold, due to reluctance by the Ukrainian government to sign a deal allowing the Russians to create a new entrance point into Crimea. Looking out towards the Russian mainland, only 3km away, it seems clear that it would take a regime change in Crimea before a bridge would ever be built.

Fireworks explode above Russia. The moon shows itself for a brief moment, as a large oil tanker covered with thousands of fairy lights cuts through the silver water below.

Six

With twenty-four hours to kill until our Russian visas are valid, Si proposes we drive the Arabatska strilka; a 112km strip of sand that our trusty friend Jan had told us about. It's a brilliant idea! We can then enter Russia from the Sea of Azov in the Donetsk Region of east Ukraine and explore Don Cossack country.

Hurtling across farmland in the early morning light, we top up with fuel and follow an unpaved road leading north to the Bay of Arabat. Reaching the forgotten ruins of a Genoese fortification, I pull up outside an abandoned two-storey building with a heap of rubbish piled outside. Peering up at the crumbling balcony, I look in surprise when I see a military soldier wearing an old fashioned helmet with a rifle hooked over his shoulder. Our eyes lock, and I quickly turn away. Suspecting this may be some kind of unofficial checkpoint, or a restricted route into Crimea, I nudge Si with my elbow and point over in the direction of the soldier. He flicks on his sunglasses and looks up at the balcony.

'What am I supposed to be looking at?' he sighs, wiping sweat from his forehead.

I glance back, but the soldier is nowhere to be seen. An unshaven guy wearing a trilby hat suddenly steps into view. Not wishing to appear suspicious, I point in the direction of the sandy spit.

'Ok?' I ask.

The guy mutters to someone lurking in the shadows, before responding.

'Da, da,' he nods firmly.

We choose to not hang around and launch ourselves onto the Arabatska strilka, known locally as the Arabat Arrow. This strange strip of sand was formed by sedimentation processes around 1100–1200 AD, with the Don and Kuban rivers depositing large quantities of sand, silt and shells into the Sea of Azov. Driving across a terrain, more suited to a 4x4 than a family saloon car from the 1990s, we grit our teeth as the Volvo's suspension is tested to its limits with each dip in the sand track. Si thrusts his head out of the window and howls at the swifts and swallows that chase alongside the car. I feel an enormous rush of adrenaline that flows through my mosquito marked body, as we slip and slide across the golden sand like competitors in the Dakar Rally. We begin to see a lush green marsh to the left of the track, where colonies of terns, herons, egrets and bitterns cluster around the shores of Lake Syvash; a salty system of lagoons we had seen from the opposite shore on our arrival in Crimea. After two hours of intense concentration, I whack on the brakes approximately halfway along the Arabatska strilka. We collapse out of the car and shake the dust out of our hair. So far not one single vehicle has driven by, and I begin to fear that if we breakdown out here we will be little more than food for the mosquitoes. Si takes over the driving, and in the rising heat of the day we continue our uncomfortable dusty adventure to the never-ending horizon.

We eventually reach the end of the Arabatska strilka,

and begin to see signs of civilisation in the form of a small house with a cow grazing outside. Crossing into Khersons'ka oblast, we grab a couple of well-earned beers from a local grocery store in Strilkove and join the hundreds of tourists wild camping along the coast. Diving into the warm shallow green water of the Sea of Azov brings instant relief to my mosquito bitten limbs. In ecstasy, I float on my back and try to imagine our location on a satellite map. Known in Classical Antiquity as Lake Maeotis, the Sea of Azov is the shallowest sea in the world, with the depth varying between 0.9 to 14 metres. Because of the huge intake of river water, the sea is pleasantly low in salinity with a positive outflow through the Kerch Strait into the Black Sea. Si wades out of the water like a swamp monster, and I'm reminded that the sea also has a high content of organic matter, such as algae, that affects its colour and covers everyone in green slime.

We pack up and hit the road. Si whacks the gearbox into reverse, but the front wheels struggle to gain traction and the car rapidly digs itself into the sand. Unable to open the car doors we are forced to climb out through the windows. Squatting down, I see the chassis is lying flat on the beach.

'We're screwed,' I sigh. 'The only way to get out of this sand pit is to dig a big hole.'

Secretly enjoying the survival element of our predicament, we set to work at scraping away the sand with our bare hands. Sweat pours from our faces and mosquitoes buzz around our ears. We lay towels, rope, an old rubber bicycle inner tube and a pair of Si's flip-flops behind the front wheels to help the tyres gain traction. A guy who is camping nearby walks over with his teenage son and kindly offers to help. Revving the engine a couple of times I engage the clutch, and with Si and the new recruits pushing from the front the Volvo reverses out of the sand with relative ease. The guy orders his son to help us fill in the enormous crater, and we pause momentarily to study a Praying Mantis that has landed on a nearby rock. The large green insect looks up at me with its bulging alien eyes. We learn Robert is a chemistry teacher from the industrial city of Donetsk in eastern Ukraine. He brings his son to this beach every summer for one week. His wife died last year, so it is a chance for them to spend time together. The young kid beams a smile and points at the Volvo. I get the distinct impression he likes the car. Whipping off his t-shirt he runs into the sea. Si asks Robert about his city. He drops his smile and explains that he fears if Ukraine forms closer ties with the European Union, pro-Russian nationalists will take up arms against the government. Shaking his head gravely, he looks over at his son swimming in the sea. 'Putin no allow another NATO country to Russia's borders. I no care about myself, but I am afraid for my son.'

* * *

Crossing a bridge over the Tonkyi River, we pass through the small town of Heniches'k in the southeast corner of mainland Ukraine. Spying a car wash, Chris skids into a bay and we greet two kids clutching power hoses. It's illegal to drive a dirty car in Russia, so we happily sign up for a full power wash and polish. They do an immaculate job and I stand back and admire our sparkling chariot. The eldest of the duo points at the "GB" sticker on the rear of the car and asks where we are from. He breaks into an enormous grin when he hears we are from England. Disappearing into the office at the side of the bay he returns with a newspaper. We study the photograph on the front page of Prince William and Kate Middleton, who is clutching a baby. The future king of England has been born. A police car suddenly screeches onto the forecourt. The kids immediately drop their smiles and leap into action. They grab their power hoses and set to work at washing the vehicle. The police cop smokes a cigarette outside while the duo blast away the dirt and corruption. Chris waits patiently for the owner to make his chess move before he hands him the money.

With the Azovo-Syvas'kyi national park hazy in the distance, we skirt around Melitopol in the Zaporizhia oblast, and drive east along the north shore of the Sea of Azov. At frequent intervals, suicidal Russian drivers overtake dangerously on the long straight highway that leads to the Russian border. Chris loses count of the many kurgans dotted across the flat landscape as we zip by a field occupied by hundreds of sheep. On the Azov coast we pass the town of Berdyansk, which is known in Ukraine for its mud baths and climatic treatments. Chris informs me that the beautiful Bond Girl, Olga Kurylenko, who starred in 'Quantum of Solace', was also born here.

Most people living in the east of Ukraine speak Russian and belong to the Orthodox Church, but echoes of the Black Sea's multicultural past still persists here with Greek, Roman Catholic, Protestant, Judaic and Islamic communities inhabiting the region. A steel plant and several coal mines were first established around Donetsk by a Welsh businessman called John Hughes in 1869. John was a Merthyr Tydfil steel worker, with a contract from the Tsarist government to provide steel plating for the navy. Ukraine honours the Merthyr Tydfil man, and in a few months time they will celebrate the 200th anniversary of his birth. After the Bolshevik revolution, the city was renamed Stalino (after Joseph Stalin) and was finally called Donetsk in 1961. The east of Ukraine boomed under the Soviet Union, with the main pillars of the economy being metallurgy, coke chemistry, steel and coal mining. As recently as 1979, the city was granted the Order of Lenin and recognised by UNESCO as the cleanest industrial town in the world. Following the collapse of the Soviet Union in the 1990s, this industrial region in the east of the country rapidly began to deteriorate. With a desperate need for investment into the oblast, particularly in the agricultural sector, political and bureaucratic issues urgently needed to be resolved to win the trust of investment from foreign companies.

The stagnation of this region is a prime example of Ukraine's current role as a boundary country caught in a tug of war between East and West. Russian investors own a large share of business and industry in the country and cling jealously to this relic of the USSR. The EU and IMF (International Monetary Fund) circle like vultures overhead, neither sides seeming to care much about the terrifying prospect of a new Cold War that the hunger to profit or control may cause. Ukraine has become so riddled with the disease of corruption that it can no longer function as a normal nation. The people desperately need to take a stand and unite, but deep divisions in the east and west, it seems, would make this highly improbable. Despairing at a world of greedy self-interested nations, and our species collective inability to empathise or try and mediate together to find a fair solution to an individual nation's crisis, I fantasise about the utopian ideal of a global intellectual stand.

Chris suddenly springs up in his seat. 'Tractor!' he shrieks.

The Volvo's anti-lock brake system kicks in, and I swerve around an ancient rusty tractor that has turned sharply into the road. Escaping near death, I adjust my speed and continue to drive on in silence.

The Sea of Azov appears at brief intervals, as we weave through pretty seaside towns and quiet villages with traditional wooden houses. I pull over and buy an enormous watermelon from a strong farm girl with gold teeth. Chris spots a truck from Kazakhstan as we journey east on a tide of curiosity. Hurtling past yet more enormous fields of sunflowers, in a country that is the world's largest producer of the crop, we pass unhindered through a police checkpoint. Entering the Donetsk oblast, we roll into the industrial port of Mariupol, a city founded by the Cossacks in the 16th century at the mouth of the Kalmius River. Located only 50km south of Donetsk, the city of Mariupol is predominantly Russian speaking and is home to the largest Greek population in Ukraine. Around the middle of the 15th century, much of this region north of the Black Sea and the Sea of Azov fell under the control of the Crimean Khanate and became a dependency of the Ottoman Empire. Close to the city lies the infamous Kalmius trail; one of the branches of the Muravsky trail, which was a historic Tatar transit route that stretched almost to Moscow. For hundreds of years, frequent raids and plundering by the Tatar tribes prevented permanent settlement in the region around Mariupol, with as many as 80,000 Tatar soldiers with 200,000 horses marching along this route during harvest time invading villages and capturing women and children.

We begin to see billboards advertising Levis Jeans and McDonalds in the suburbs of the city, where Soviet era apartment blocks tower above the main street. Edging our way through the congested rush hour traffic, Chris identifies classic pre-Revolutionary architecture belonging to century-old hotels and administrative buildings. The city centre is a hive of activity, with people going about their business and crowding outside restaurants and bars. A woman clutching a bunch of flowers totters along the street in impossible high heels, and an old chap with a cigarette protruding from his mouth talks animatedly to a burley security guard outside a bank. The road splits around City Square with a theatre at its centre. Chris works hard as my second pair of eyes and directs me around a yellow city bus that speeds along Lenin Avenue. Skirting past a tranquil park we exit the city centre and are struck by the monstrous sight of the rusty structure of the ex-Soviet Ilyich Steel & Iron Works, which looms above us. With chimneys coughing brown smoke into the atmosphere the factory dwarfs the cars and the surrounding apartment buildings. Enormous heaps of coal tower behind a barbwire fence. Chris points out the striking view to the left of the road of many more chimneys stretching to the horizon. The nearby Azovstal Iron and Steel Works is owned by the second richest oligarch in Ukraine, Rinat Akhmetov, who is estimated to have a net worth of around US$6.9 billion.

Crossing the Kalmius River we pass an old red and white tram, and weave around large potholes before returning to the countryside. Close to a cluster of wind turbines, we pause at the roadside to pick wild apricots. I peer over a hedge beneath a willow tree, and watch a deeply tanned farmer carrying a bail of hay in one hand across a field. As the sun begins its descent to the horizon, we grab a few supplies from the village of Shyrokyne and stumble across a track that leads to a scenic viewpoint overlooking the Tahanroz'ka gulf. A powerful guy in his mid-fifties with a bristly moustache sprints past with a chocolate Labrador at heel. Chris acknowledges him with a nod. The tough looking guy has the appearance of a military man, and it occurs to me that he could be a Cossack soldier.

Drinking a glass of beer, we watch the full moon rise blood red over Russia. I scribble madly in my notepad. "Sometimes we're distracted by the traffic police or weariness from our journey, and then it shows itself to us again; a turquoise strip of water peering above the horizon, over a field of golden wheat, a ploughed field of black earth, or above the heads of a thousand yellow sunflowers. Its constant presence makes it impossible for us to forget the purpose of our journey."

PART 2
Russia & the Caucasus

Seven

On the outskirts of Novoazovsk, a thickset guy with faded tattoos on his arms sits outside a rundown café and stares into a breakfast beer. I begin to feel anxious as we prepare to enter the complex multi-ethnic region of southern Russia. The Southern Federal District of Russia is one of nine krais (borders or frontiers) that together form the largest country in the world. Following years of tension in the Caucasus region, the district was split into two halves in 2010, with its former southern territories forming a new North Caucasus Federal District. Long considered to be Russia's "Wild West", this region has witnessed Greek, Scythian, Sarmatian and Russian expansion in the face of fierce resistance from Mountain peoples and Tatar tribes.

We are welcomed at the east Ukraine border crossing by a long line of trucks. We breeze through customs and join a second queue of vehicles at the Russian frontier. Si nervously shuffles the car documents on his lap. A green light appears and I approach a border guard with a stern face, who carefully interrogates our tourist visas. He gestures for me to step out of the Volvo. I'm about to open the trunk when a baby bird, purple and featherless, falls from a nest in the roof rafters and lands right beside the guard's shiny boots. He fails to see it, and I watch helplessly as he crushes this fragile creature beneath his heel. Opening the trunk, he quickly rummages through our possessions and takes a peek inside a canvas bag that is stuffed full of electrical tape, old rope and fishing line. He then instructs me to open the rear passenger door. Scanning the interior, he retrieves the bottle of red wine that Annalise had given to us as a gift in Odessa. He studies the label before throwing it onto the back seat. Satisfied, he waves us through to a second checkpoint. A military police officer with a shaved head orders us to fill out an immigration form. He then marches us both into a small office, where a guy wearing half-moon spectacles inputs our car details into a computer. Punching the keys with two fingers, he squints at the screen and prints out a customs certificate for our vehicle. Waiting to be presented with a huge bill, I'm surprised when he welcomes us to Russia with a kind smile. Driving to the final gate, we approach a military soldier wearing full combat gear with an assault rifle slung over his shoulder. Si hands him a small pink receipt and he raises the barrier.

Ecstatic to have arrived on Russian soil, we purchase car insurance with relative ease from a small roadside kiosk and, within less than an hour, we are drinking coffee with a Moldovan truck driver who speaks impeccable English. Marian worked in Southern Ireland for five years, and recently returned to the Republic of Moldova to be closer to his family. These days he regularly travels this route delivering apples by the container load from Moldova to Moscow. He warns us to keep an eye out for the traffic police, and advises us that if we stick to the rules our journey in Russia will be trouble free. We wish Marian luck, before heading east into the unknown realms of the Southern Federal District of Russia.

Cruising alongside enormous Soviet-size fields of corn,

we overtake a tractor with a white ceramic teapot wedged over the tow bar. A large steppe buzzard is perched on a fence post and watches our metal monster zoom by. We soon arrive in Taganrog; a port city founded by Peter the Great in 1698. The Azov Flotilla of Catherine the Great was hosted here in Russia's first navy base, which later grew into the Russian Black Sea Fleet. Weaving through the quiet suburbs of the city, we pass a row of traditional one-storey houses and park the Volvo near to the large central market. A pot-bellied chap standing at the back of a truck rammed full of watermelons, whistles into the street as we go in search of the house where Anton Chekhov spent his childhood years. I ask for directions inside a small electrical shop that smells strongly of cannabis and the mellow guy behind the counter kindly points us in the direction of the Chekhov house museum.

The buildings along Chekhov Street have an air of faded grandeur. An old chap wearing a sailor's cap and a blue and white striped t-shirt exits his house with a scruffy terrier, and an elderly woman wearing a brown dress sits on the steps outside her home and listens to classical music on a small radio. Admiring a statue of the writer in the suitably named Chekhov Square, we reach the gate of a small house set back in a well kept tranquil garden. An attractive woman in her mid-fifties called Nina greets us at the front door. She is ecstatic to hear we are from England. Her daughter studied law in London, but she now lives in Paris. Escorting us around the tiny house, Nina explains Chekhov's father, Pavel, was raised in extreme poverty in central Russia and lived as a serf; the lowest social class. He later moved to Taganrog and made a living as a merchant, renting this outbuilding for his wife and two children in 1859. A year later in 1860, baby Anton was born. Nina points out Pavel on a family portrait hung on

71

the wall. He is a tall man with a long beard and staring eyes. Pavel ruled his household with an iron fist, and would regularly beat Anton and his brothers and sisters. He worked for a wealthy merchant, but so desperately wanted to be free. It tormented him that he had to rely on other people for his survival.

Pavel experienced financial ruin in the 1870s, which caused him and his wife to leave Taganrog in a hurry to escape debtors' prison. They stayed with their sons, Nikolay and Alexander, who were attending university in Moscow. Aged only sixteen, Anton was left behind to finish school and sell the family possessions. He lived during this period with a family friend called Selivanov, who Anton is thought to have later drawn inspiration from for the character Lopakhin in 'The Cherry Orchard'. In the story, Lopakhin had assisted the family financially in return for their house. Anton had to support himself during these difficult years and finance his education. He would catch and sell goldfinches and found work tutoring other students. He also began to write humorous short sketches for newspapers and magazines. Any spare money he had left he would send to Moscow, and he used his talent for writing to cheer up his family with comical letters from Taganrog. Anton discovered a love of books during these years living alone, and eventually wrote one of his own - a dramatic comedy titled 'Fatherless'. His brother Alexander had allegedly dismissed the story as "an inexcusable though innocent fabrication." Arching her neatly groomed eyebrows, Nina reveals that Anton also enjoyed a series of love affairs, one with the wife of a teacher.

Thanking Nina for such a brilliant insight into Anton Chekhov's early life. She confesses that she had not expected English people to be so friendly.

'People from your country are always portrayed in Russian films and on the news as cruel and cold,' she smiles. 'Yet you both seem so nice.'

Si explains to her that the same is true with how Russians and people from the former Soviet countries are portrayed in Britain; yet everyone we have met so far, from border officials to shopkeepers, have been helpful and kind. We debate the possibility that this negative portrayal of the two countries is an example of the propaganda that plagues both our societies, and a reflection of the tension that still exists between our governments; not the majority of peaceful individuals who live within invisible borders.

Keen to be a good ambassador to her much loved town, Nina recommends we visit the harbour where Anton used to watch the merchant ships arrive and set sail.

'Anton loved to travel like you,' Nina smiles. 'He would have travelled more if it had not been for his poor health.'

In addition to his career as a writer, Anton was a trained physician and treated patients for free during the cholera epidemic that struck the country during the Russian famine of 1891-1892. The disease had emerged along the Volga River, and spread rapidly as far as the Ural Mountains and the Black Sea. A chain of unfortunate natural events had led to the famine that caused the outbreak, with unfavourable weather conditions leading to an enormous percentage of the yearly seedlings being destroyed. This resulted in a catastrophic harvest. By the end of 1892 approximately half a million people were dead; mostly as a result of the cholera epidemics that had been sparked by the famine. Russian writer, Leo Tolstoy, blamed the Tsarist government and the Orthodox Church for the famine, and the church responded in a typically unreasonable manner by excommunicating him and banning peasants from accepting his charity. Si reveals that the Tsarist government's poor response to the disaster is believed to have caused the reawakening of Russian Marxism and populism in Russia.

We follow Nina's advice and drop by a small urban park that looks down over the port from the top of the cliffs. Below we can see factories and train carriages piled high with coal. A large ship in the harbour looks ready to set sail. Weaving down a steep coastal road, we stumble across a small beach. Two old men wade through the shallow green water of the Taganrog Bay in their underpants and enjoy an evening swim. Close to the shore, I see a fish thrashing around in the reeds. Scooping it up, I plop it into a pan full of water. A fisherman is perched like a gnome on the edge of a small wooden rowing boat. He stares down at the float, and appears to be hypnotised by its bobbing motion.

The Black Sea and the Sea of Azov were once one of the most plentiful seas in the world, with fish stocks easily supporting the many great civilisations that lived around these shores. In recent decades this has radically changed, and their capacity to support life is being greatly threatened. According to the Biological Sciences department at the University of California in Irvine, the five major rivers that drain into the Black Sea and the Sea of Azov are polluting the waters with synthetic organic compounds, heavy metals, untreated sewage and radionuclides from Chernobyl. Dams have severely decreased the quantity of freshwater flowing into the sea, altering the salinity and threatening the delicate balance of the Black Sea's ecosystem. The introduction of excessive nutrients into the water is damaging to most living organisms, as it decreases the concentration of dissolved oxygen that they depend on for life. In total, the exploitation of the fisheries has led to the commercial extinction of 21 out of 26 species of fish including perch, bonito, bluefish and pike. The Dnieper, Dniester, Don, Kuban and Danube rivers are the source of huge quantities of nitrates and phosphorus, which are the cause of increased algal and plankton blooms which are now so large they can be seen from outer space. The ports around the Black Sea are a large source of oil contamination and are responsible for the importation of alien species, such as the warty comb jelly, which has been transported in the hull of ships from foreign waters. In recent decades this organism has become established in the basin, exploding from a few individuals to an estimated biomass of one billion metric tons. The catastrophic environmental damage to the Black Sea that has been caused by humans over the past century is in grave danger of becoming irreversible.

Si prods the fish. 'Shall we eat it?'

With slight hesitation and a feeling of remorse, I quickly bash the fish over the head with a rock and begin to gut it. Si admires my speedy preparation, and within seconds the carp is sizzling away in the frying pan with garlic, black pepper and fresh lemon. The mouth-watering smell is carried on the breeze and the fisherman, who is still hunched over his rod, sniffs the air and glances over in our direction. Suspecting it may have been "the one that got away" I slide the frying pan out of sight with my foot. We sit back in our foldaway chairs and watch the sun swap shift with the moon and the stars.

* * *

Powered by protein, Chris seizes the wheel at dawn and drives in the direction of Rostov-on-Don. Seeing signs for the UNESCO world heritage site of Tanais, we turn sharply off the highway and follow an asphalt road that leads to the entrance gate of this once important Greek colony on the upper bank of the Don River Delta. A group of student archaeologists work on an excavation close to the ticket office, and scrape away the red earth under the watchful eye of a security guard. We cross a wooden walkway over a moat and look down into the deep footings of this once great fortified city, located at the farthest north-eastern extension of the Greek cultural sphere. Presented with a view over the tranquil marshes at the mouth of the Don River, Chris tries to imagine the brave pioneering Greeks, who first arrived here thousands of years ago in search of new fishing grounds and trade opportunities. A permanent settlement in this district had existed since the 7th century BC, long before merchants from Miletus founded an emporium here late in the 3rd century BC. A nearby necropolis contains over 300 burial kurgans, providing evidence of Scythian occupation from the Bronze Age. I smile at the thought of having arrived at this ancient crossroads, where pioneering Greeks may have first traded olive oil and wine for fur and slaves with the nomadic steppe tribes. Over the centuries Tanais grew from a small emporium into a large centre of commerce and handcraft production. The Sea of Azov was known to the Greeks as Lake Maeotis, and Tanais became a meeting place for trade between two very different cultures; the settled and the nomadic. Easy to reach by river or land, the influence here of the surrounding steppe peoples had been much stronger than in other Greek colonies around the Black Sea and consequently a new original culture evolved.

Tanais later became a colony of the Bosporan Kingdom. But it was successful at maintaining a certain degree of independence, partly with the aid of the Sarmatians who came to dominate the Pontic steppe around 300 BC. Instead of firing bows and arrows, the Sarmatians used heavy cavalry, wore chainmail and iron helmets and carried long lances. In contrast to the Scythians, the Sarmatians are thought to have been tribal warriors who conquered and then assimilated with the civilisations they encountered. In the Greek colonies, in particular Panticapaeum (on the hill above Kerch) and here in Tanais on the Don delta, the Sarmatians married Greeks and took an active role in society. They remained on the Pontic steppe for 500 years until the volatile arrival of the Huns from the east in the 4th century AD drove the Sarmatians west (into modern-day Romania) and south into the Caucasus Mountains. In the west, the Sarmatians settled in the agrarian societies on the fringes of the Roman Empire, and are thought to have introduced to Europe the concept of the knight in shining armour. "They ride in disguise as the class of mailed horsemen who hold land and whose manner of living is called 'chivalrous'," wrote Neal Ascherson. "To the extent that we have not yet completely escaped from that notion of aristocracy, the Sarmatians are among us."

We arrive in Rostov-on-Don in the uncomfortable midday heat. Chris asks a young guy of African descent if he knows where we can find a budget hotel. He nods and points to the open doorway of a grand mansion building. Surprised by our lucky find, we enter the dimly lit hallway. We scale four flights of stairs and meet a tall blonde guy painting over graffiti in the corridor. Welcoming us inside, we step into a large room with ornate wooden floors and high ceilings. A large desk and a throne-size chair are positioned under a colourful abstract painting. We introduce ourselves and discover Vladimir is the joint owner of the hostel. It is only the second week they have been open, and already they have accommodated guests from Japan, China, Benin, Germany and Finland. Vladimir looks like a Tsar behind the desk as he strokes his soft blonde stubble.

'This is the first hostel in Rostov-on-Don,' he reveals proudly. 'We are extremely excited about this project.'

Kindly offering to register our Russian tourist visas for a small fee, Chris asks Vladimir what inspired him to open a hostel. Pressing his fingertips together in the shape of a pyramid, he reveals that after finishing his education he had travelled around Germany with a backpack and stayed in many budget hostels. It seemed like a fun job, so he had decided to go into partnership with his friend. Discovering Vladimir is a Cossack from the southern Ukraine, he explains that his father was in the Russian military. He had spent the first few years of his life in the German Democratic Republic (GDR) during the Soviet years.

Vladimir leaps out of his chair and unrolls a map of the world on the desk. He tells the story of how a German guy had turned up at the hostel last week and bought him this map as a gift.

'He suggested I ask visitors to mark where they are from,' Vladimir smiles.

Handing Chris a red marker pen, he draws an arrow pointing to central England and scribbles, "Raven brothers".

The telephone on the desk begins to ring. Vladimir excuses himself and takes the call. I scan the front page of a local newspaper. The cover story displays a photograph of a guy called, Ali Taziev, who is currently on trial in Rostov-on-Don for various acts of terrorism. Taziev was originally born in Grozny in Chechnya and became one of the top leaders of the Caucasus Emirate. The Russian government listed him as one of the terrorists killed during the tragic 2004 Beslan School hostage crisis in the southern Russian Republic of North Ossetia. After discovering these reports were incorrect, security forces captured him in 2010 and his trial in Rostov-on-Don is ongoing. Pointing the story out to Chris, he looks concerned. Even though large numbers of militants from the North Caucasus are now fighting in Syria, terrorism attacks in this region still remain a fearsome reality, with the Islamic leader, Doku Umarov, only last month calling for terrorists to target the Sochi Winter Olympics.

Vladimir finishes his call and places down the receiver.

'Ok, so, I can register your visas today. They will be ready at three o'clock.'

'Great,' I smile.

Vladimir glances down at his watch, and then suddenly springs out of his chair. 'A tour party from Moscow is arriving in twenty minutes. I must prepare for their arrival.'

We thank Vladimir for his help, and shake him firmly by the hand.

Returning back down the stairs, we stroll through the wide avenues to Gorodskoy Park and browse stalls selling handcrafted jewellery and souvenirs. A group of colourfully dressed Peruvian musicians perform electro-Andean music with a keyboard and panpipes. These talented South American guys stand out in stark contrast next to the old men playing chess on nearby picnic tables. We sit on a wall and soak up the atmosphere of a city enjoying the peak summer temperatures. The genes of the people in this region of the Black Sea are a mishmash of the many immigrants who migrated here over the centuries including Greeks, Italians, Germans, Armenians and Turks. Considering we are now less than 800km away from neighbouring Kazakhstan, I'm surprised there does not appear to be more people of Central Asian descent especially in a region of the world that has witnessed countless invasions, migrations, colonisations and assimilations. Chris reminds me that during Stalin's regime in the 1930s and 1940s, millions of immigrants were deported from the Black Sea despite having lived here for many hundreds (and in the case of the Greeks) for thousands of years. This region today is considered to be the home of the Don Cossack; an independent or an autonomous democratic republic in present-day southern Russia and the Donbas region of Ukraine, which existed around the end of the 16th century until the early 20th century. The Cossacks are mainly considered to be of East Slavic ethnicity, who originated from Ukraine as warrior peasants. Following the annexation of the Crimean Tatars by the Russian Empire these democratic semi-military communities were utilised by the Tsarist government and fought many wars in southern Russia and the Caucasus. Controversially, the Cossacks were recently recognised as an ethnic group in 2010, and there are now Cossack organisations in Kazakhstan, Ukraine, Poland and the United States.

Hugo Boss, Cartier and a five-star hotel dominate the street that leads down to the market in the shadow of the Virgin's Nativity Cathedral. Stalls sell mountains of fresh seafood, vegetables and fruit, and we look through the window of an antique shop and study a faded portrait of Vladimir Putin, a Russian ushanka fur hat with ear flaps and a beautiful set of hand painted Russian dolls. Enjoying a refreshing glass of kvass, a fermented beverage made from rye bread, we stroll down to the Don River and watch cargo boats and a steam boat cutting through the water. The Don is one of Russia's major river arteries, flowing for a distance of 1,950km (1,220 miles) from Novomoskovsk, southeast of Moscow, to the Sea of Azov. Ocean-going ships can now sail across Russia from the Arctic to the Mediterranean, and we fantasise about a future journey travelling across Russia and Siberia by river and sea.

After collecting our newly registered visas, we leave Rostov-on-Don and drive 30km east to the old Don Cossack capital of Starocherkasskaya. For nearly two centuries Starocherkasskaya was the centre of Don Cossack culture and politics, until regular spring flooding forced it to be moved to Novocherkassk in 1805. Wandering around this small rural community, we pass cute wooden houses painted pastel blue and green, with ornately carved window shutters. Stalls selling souvenirs line the street and beautiful multi-coloured woollen shawls hang from a washing line. An elderly woman dressed in black sits in the entrance to a church, and chats to a man with a bicycle that looks like it pre-dates World War One. Chris photographs the enormous official seal of the Cossack Army that has been painted on the side of a red brick house. The Cossack seal was first introduced by Peter the Great to the Cherkassk Cossacks, and displays a naked Cossack soldier with a gun sitting on a wine-barrel. According to the myth, this image relates to a true event when the Tsar tried unsuccessfully to persuade a group of Cossack soldiers, who had sold their clothes to buy alcohol, to top up their supplies in exchange for their weapons. The Cossacks refusal to give up their rifles, despite their state of undress, had allegedly pleased the Tsar immensely at what he felt to be a proper sense of priorities. The Tsar routinely recruited the Don Cossacks during the early 18th century, and they fought many successful wars that ultimately resulted in vastly expanding the Russian Empire.

At sunset, we step inside the large 18th century Resurrection cathedral with a magnificent gold alter, and witness a ceremony conducted by a group of eight Orthodox priests wearing long black robes. Chris hides his smile when the priest elder with a long white beard, scolds one of the younger priests for not removing his hat. To the delightful sound of the eight men's baritone voices echoing throughout the cathedral a smartly dressed Cossack soldier, with an arrow straight posture and neatly trimmed beard, strides around the holy men and lights candles. He is wearing traditional military uniform, with a red stripe down the seam of his navy blue trousers and black leather riding boots. In a moment of drama, a young messenger boy runs up to the head priest during prayer and whispers in his ear. The priest mumbles behind his Rasputin-size beard, causing the boy to spring into flight out of the cathedral door. Fascinated to watch this display of ritual tradition, depicting a time before modern communication and dress, it occurs to me that religion frequently appears to be caught in an inescapable time warp.

* * *

Driving at dusk along a narrow unpaved dirt track that runs alongside the Don River, Si finds a place to park up for the night in the shelter of a cluster of trees. We snack on peanuts, potato chips and wild plums. I'm about to crack open a beer when I see a flickering headlight approaching us across the meadow. A motorbike skids to a halt beside the Volvo, and two youths collapse off the scrambler in fits of laughter. They appear to be completely intoxicated. A second motorcycle covered in blue neon lights arrives on the scene carrying two younger kids. The gang crowd around and excitedly fire questions at us. We try to guess what they are asking and reply with "London" and "England". Vadim, the eldest of the group, is big and clumsy and reminds me of an American High School jock. His friend, Georgiy, who is of a similar age, talks about Chevrolet, BMW and Chinese motorcycles, James Bond and Justin Bieber. One of the two younger kids, with olive skin and narrow eyes, looks distinctly Mongolian. The boisterous youths smoke cigarettes and take turns swigging beer from a large two-litre plastic bottle. Georgiy sits on the hood of the Volvo. He slides down and playfully rolls across the long grass like a circus clown. His friends burst out laughing. Vadim runs towards the car and rolls across the hood. I glance over at Si and see his concerned face in the flicking torchlight. Vadim stumbles to his feet and drunkenly pushes into me. Deeply irritated, I snap and push him away. Dropping his smile, he narrows his eyes and casts me a menacing stare. What happens next renders me speechless and, with utter surprise, I watch as this idiot kid suddenly whips a gun out of his bag. He points it at me and I look wide-eyed into the barrel. My mind races. Vadim bursts out laughing and begins to shoot at the ground beside Georgiy's feet. The skinny youth leaps high into the air and sprints off across the long grass. Much to our relief the gun appears to be gas propelled.

Thankfully, our night of teenage revelry is brought to an abrupt end when a mobile phone begins to play

Michael Jackson 'Thriller'. The gun-wielding Cossack kid hesitantly answers it, and we can hear the angry voice of a woman on the other end of the line. With a worried expression plastered across his dumb face, Vadim quickly slips the phone back into his pocket and the gun into his bag. He says something to his friends and they all quickly shake our hands and throw us a high-five. Leaping onto their bikes, they sound their horns and disappear into the night.

We eat 300km of tarmac for breakfast as we hurtle south to Krasnodar. Si quietly reads a book of poetry by Mikhail Lermontov, while I look out across the wide-open plains of the intensively cultivated Kuban steppe. The majority of the Kuban Cossacks, who inhabit this region, are descendants of two distinct groups that migrated to the western Northern Caucasus during the Caucasus War in the late 18th century. In 1792, 25,000 Black Sea Cossacks, originally the Zaporozhian Cossacks of Ukraine, settled in the western part of the Taman Peninsula and the adjoining region to the northeast. The eastern and south-eastern part of the region were previously administered by the Khopyour and Kuban regiments of the Caucasus Line Cossacks, who were re-settled from the Don from 1777. Both these groups played an important role in the Russo-Turkish War (1787–1792). Rewarding them for their service the Russian Empress Catherine the Great gave them unlimited use of the Kuban, which was inhabited at that time by what remained of the Nogai people. The Nogai Horde were a confederation of about eighteen Turkic and Mongol tribes that occupied the Pontic-Caspian steppe from around 1500 AD, until they were pushed west by the Kalmyks and south by the Russians in the 17th century.

On the outskirts of Krasnodar, we crawl past the wreckage of a flatbed truck that has smashed into the back of an articulated lorry. The cab has been completely destroyed in the impact and blood covers the twisted driver's side door. Si suggests we avoid the city traffic and instead head for the Kuban Sea; a 40km manmade reservoir created in 1973. We cross over the Kuban River that winds 750km from its source at Mt Elbrus in the Caucasus Mountains to the Sea of Azov. I begin to see a twenty-metre high grass bank and rows of stalls selling multi-coloured inflatable rubber rings, beach balls and boats. We turn off the main highway and drive down a narrow track that passes through a number of remote Cossack villages. Pulling up outside a small wooden house, I leap out clutching the road atlas and ask an elderly gentleman wearing a flat cap and moth eaten suit jacket for directions. He shrugs his shoulders and points back to the main road. A woman tending to a vegetable patch looks over and a girl with Down syndrome peers curiously from the doorway. Thanking the old chap, we spin the Volvo around and wave goodbye to a party of blank faces.

We stumble across a trail leading into a dark forest. I park up between two trees and we speedily prepare lunch before it rains. I'm about to pour tea into my cup when I see two large dogs scurrying towards us. The rouge hounds hesitate and sniff the air before disappearing into the undergrowth. A stocky guy wearing black tracksuit trousers and a white t-shirt suddenly appears at the entrance to the wood. He looks annoyed, and my immediate thought is that we are not supposed to be here. Si rises out of his foldaway chair and points across the clearing in the direction of where we had seen the dogs. I notice the guy is wearing a thick gold chain around his neck and has dark hair and penetrating black eyes. With the confident posture and demeanour of a warrior, I'm reminded that this region of southern Russia was once ruled by the Sarmatians. I find myself imagining this powerful man wearing a suit of heavy armour in the atmospheric setting of a forest. Respectfully shaking our hands, the guy appears to say something like, "enjoy your food", before walking off in search of his dogs.

A flash of lightning forks dramatically across the dark sky, it's closely followed by a deep boom of thunder. Keen to get back on firm tarmac, I direct Si out of the woods in a torrential downpour. With the heater on full blast, we loop around the city of Krasnodar and drive west towards the Black Sea coast and the port city of Novorossiysk.

We pause at the roadside and buy fresh fruit and vegetables. I hand over a 200-ruble note to the tall gentleman standing in front of an ancient wooden farm trailer. I suspect he may be of Assyrian descent and, feeling brave, I ask him. He looks at me at first with suspicion and then cracks a smile.

'Da, Assyrian,' he nods, flashing a mouthful of gold teeth.

The Assyrian people had migrated to this region of the Caucasus over the past century, following the mass slaughter of the Assyrian population of the Ottoman Empire during the 1890s and the First World War. Originating from ancient Mesopotamia, the Assyrians trace their ancestry back to the Sumero-Akkadian civilisation that emerged an astounding 6,000 years ago (circa 4000–3500 BC) in a region of the Middle East that is today the north of Iraq, part of southeast Turkey and northeast Syria. Adopting Christianity in the 1st to 3rd century AD, those who still practise religion today follow various Eastern Rite Churches. Since the Assyrian Genocide by the Ottoman Empire, emigration has also been caused by the Simele massacre in Iraq (1933), the Islamic revolution in Iran in 1979, Arab Nationalist Baathist policies in Iraq and Syria and the Al-Anfal Campaign of Saddam Hussein. Nearly 40% of the approximately one million Iraqis reported by the UN to have fled the country since the 2003 Iraq war are Assyrian, which is a considerable number when you take into account they only comprised around 3% of the pre-war Iraqi population. Many Assyrian refugees have also migrated to North America, Australia and Europe. Most recently, the war in Syria has displaced the regional Assyrian community and its people have faced new ethnic and religious persecution at the hands of Islamic extremists.

With our cargo of fresh fruit and vegetables, we cut across huge fields of sunflowers and begin to see nodding donkeys working tirelessly to extract oil from the earth. We reach the town of Krymsk, home to a community of approximately 2,000 Assyrians. Si informs me that flash flooding here the previous summer had claimed the lives of 140 inhabitants and destroyed thousands more homes across the region. According to reports, massive rainfall five times the monthly average had caused a river to burst its banks. The water had swept down the steep-sided valley and washed away homes and vehicles in its path.

Si continues to drive west and we make our way across the forested hills to the eastern shores of the Black Sea. As we inch closer, we begin to see locals selling jars of sprats, strips of sturgeon and salted Azov herrings. We are now only a short distance from Kerch, having driven clockwise around the Sea of Azov.

* * *

Looking out over Tsemes bay, we watch three tug boats help manoeuvre an enormous container ship from China into Novorossiysk's port. A row of yellow hydraulic cranes work flat out to load and unload containers in Russia's largest Black Sea port. From the harbour wall Chris photographs a guy wading through the shallow water to check his fishing nets. A machine grey artillery-cruiser towers behind him. This relic of Russia's military past was once the former flagship of Russia's Black Sea Fleet, and is now a memorial and museum. The Mikhail Kutuzov had a crew of 1,200 navy personnel. It was named in honour of Mikhail Kutuzov, a military commander and diplomat who was widely known for repelling Napoleon's invasion of Russia in 1812. A planned expansion will include a second large-scale multi-cargo deep port enabling more export of coal, iron ore and grain. A new Black Sea Fleet navy base is also currently under construction in Novorossiysk, which will expand the existing facility to accommodate 61 ships by 2020 and include a new submarine base.

Walking along the harbour wall, I admire the hills that shelter Tsemes bay. Known as Bata by the ancient Greeks, grain grown on the Kuban was once shipped from here to Athens. The bay was later utilised by the Genoese who maintained a trade outpost here until the Middle Ages. Further along the promenade a sailor in uniform leans against the harbour wall beneath the colossal Mikhail Kutuzov. I study a bronze statue of a woman clutching a child. She is wearing 1940s clothing and is waving a hanky in memory of the many ships that have set sail from the port. In the 1950s, our uncle, Trevor Raven, was the radio officer aboard a Greek merchant ship that was based in

Novorossiysk for five weeks. He had spoken about how well they had been treated by the Russians, and shared stories of the crew trading cigarettes and alcohol with the Russian sailors. The previous decade, the German Army had occupied the majority of the city. In 1942, a small unit of Soviet sailors heroically defended the Malaya Zemlya area for 225 days; allowing the Soviets to retain possession of the bay and preventing the Germans from using the port for supply shipments.

Chris sparks up a conversation with a guy in his early sixties at a coffee machine. He is wearing round metal-framed glasses and a crisp white shirt and flip-flops.

'You are not afraid of Russian bear?' the guy smiles.

Chris laughs, amused by his reference to a symbol of Russia that has appeared in cartoons, articles and dramatic plays since as early as the 16th century.

The guy seems pleased we are enjoying our time here in Russia. We introduce ourselves and I ask Yuriy if he lives in Novorossiysk. He explains that his family originates from Ulan-Ude in Siberia, near to Lake Baikal, but for many years he lived in Moscow. He has since retired to the warmer climate of Novorossiysk, to be closer to his son who works for an import export company in the port. Probing Yuriy further about his Siberian heritage, we're fascinated to discover that he is Buryat, the largest indigenous ethnic group in Siberia with a population of approximately 500,000 people. Descending from various Siberian and Mongolic peoples that inhabited the Lake Baikal Region, the various Buryat tribes were controlled by the Mongol Empire under Jochi, the eldest son of Genghis Khan in 1207.

Yuriy proudly reveals that the award-winning US actor, Yul Brynner, was Buryat and born in Russia.

'And Steven Seagal,' Chris adds, feeding coins into the

coffee machine.

Yuriy smiles. 'Yes. His grandfather is Buryat or Kalmyk.'

'Are his films popular in Russia?' I ask.

'Yes, yes. He is a good friend of our President. The people like him in Russia. He has made much work to stop terrorism.' Yuriy takes a sip of coffee. 'The Russian monk Agvan Dorzhiev was also Buryat. You know about Great Game?'

'Wasn't the Great Game played out in Afghanistan?' Chris replies.

'Yes, this was big competition with British Empire and Russia in Central Asia. It was like the game chess.'

'I once read 'Kim' by Rudyard Kipling,' I smile. 'Wasn't Britain worried Russia would invade India?'

Yuriy mutely nods his head before answering. 'In this time the Tsar was growing Russian land. After he took control of Central Asia, he had interest in China, Mongolia and Tibet,' Yuri grins. 'The British Lion did not like a Russian monk to be friends with the Dalai Lama...'

Moving the conversation away from politics, Yuriy asks us what we are doing in Russia. He seems genuinely intrigued that we are travelling south to Sochi. With a wry smile, he tells us that there has been much controversy in the Russian media over the astronomical sums of money invested in hosting the Winter Olympics. Chris confirms this and reveals he read in an article that it is predicted the games could cost as much as US$50 billion; making it the most expensive Winter Olympics in history. This breathtaking sum of money exceeds even the budget of the 2008 Summer Olympics in Beijing, which was reported to have cost US$42.58 billion.

Finishing his coffee, Yuriy explains that he has plans to take his grandson to the beach. Thanking Yuriy for the fascinating conversation, he firmly shakes our hands.

'Be careful on your journey, British Lions,' he smiles. 'While the Russian Bear is less of a threat these days, his fleas are strong.'

Eight

Babushkas shake keys at the passing traffic as the winding road snakes through the hills to the Sochi State borderline. Arriving in the prestigious resort town of Dagomys, we see willow trees and signs for a "Sanatoria". Both Tsar Nicholas II and Joseph Stalin owned a dacha in this area and the towns of Dagomys and Sochi were popular with famous artists and performers including the legendary opera singer Fyodor Chaliapin, poet Vladimir Mayakovsky and writer Isaac Babel.

An eccentric pensioner with a handlebar moustache cycles by wearing khaki shorts, a bright red Hawaiian shirt and a straw hat. There is a hint of Florida in the air with bananas growing at the roadside. Si reveals this region of the Black Sea has a subtropical climate with an average summer temperature of 24°C. To think Russia is hosting the Winter Olympics in this humid zone in six months time seems quite incredulous. But Putin, it seems, already has this covered. At enormous cost to the Russian taxpayers, plans are underway to construct a super highway into the Caucasus Mountains. The Winter Olympics is Putin's chance to showcase Russia as a country capable of glamour and sport. During the Soviet era, Sochi earned a reputation as a playground for criminals, gambling and mafia protection rackets for tourist hotels, and the rhyming phrase familiar to many Russians, "V gorodye sochi, tyomnye nochi", roughly translates, "In the city of Sochi, the nights are dark."

Following diversion signs, Si weaves around diggers and a major new road bridge that is under construction. We hit mass congestion with monster traffic queues and road works. The city centre appears to be in absolute chaos. Dust fills the air and the frustration of our fellow road users reaches boiling point. With their backs turned to the traffic, a group of construction workers puff on cigarettes and peer down into a muddy hole. Diggers move tons of earth and the noise of a pneumatic drill reverberates through the streets. A guy wearing a suit blasts his horn and attempts to turn round, which only creates more chaos and frustration. He mounts the sidewalk and tries to squeeze around a digger, only for the workmen to force him back into line. The driver of a black BMW, with "ABH" on the licence plate, leaps out of his car and runs over to Si's window. He has southern European features with a bronze complexion and a distinctive thin face and large nose. He points up the road and talks to us with some urgency. I assume he is late and wants to know a quick way out of this nightmare. I begin to see more cars with "ABH" on the licence plate and realise they are from nearby Abkhazia; a neighbouring disputed territory of Georgia that is now recognised by Russia as an independent state.

In the 14th-19th centuries the current location of Sochi, known as Ubykhia, was part of historical Circassia. It was controlled by the native people of the local mountain clans of the north-west Caucasus, under the sovereignty of the Ottoman Empire, who were their main trading partner in the Muslim world. The coastline was only given up to

Russia in 1829, as a result of the Russo-Turkish War and Caucasian War that took place in the nearby mountains. Despite the area of the current city of Sochi being absorbed into the Russian Empire after the Russian-Turkish War of 1828-29, the local population, the Adyghe, a Sunni Muslim people in what was then the historical country of Circassia, fiercely resisted the Tsarist troops. It was only after 1864, in connection with the end of the Caucasian War, that the area of the city became part of the Russian Empire. The defeat of Sochi, the last capital of an independent Circassia, was the final battle in the hundred-year Russian-Caucasus War between 1763 and 1864.

As the traffic begins to move, we pass a row of 1950s style mansion blocks and the unusual grand railway station, with its striking clock tower that sports a black clock face with Zodiac signs. Turning down Kurortny prospect, we head towards the sea and turn right and then left before stumbling across a shaded residential street. Si skilfully squeezes the car into a space behind a dust-covered burgundy Chevrolet saloon from Uzbekistan.

Strolling past designer shops selling jewellery, shoes and handbags, we cut through a small park brimming with palm trees. We join a group of tourists, who are crowding around the official Omega Olympic Countdown Clock. I take a photo of Si grinning into the sunshine beneath the digital display, only "191 days, 2 hours, 42 minutes and 6 seconds" until the games begin. We head down to the waterfront around the impressive Maritime Passenger Terminal of the Naval Station building, with its distinctive 71m high steeple tower that was built in 1955. Much of the seafront appears to be screened off with hundreds of construction workers using power tools in the heat of the day. Looping around the marina that is rammed full of luxury yachts and sailboats, we catch a glimpse of the beach teeming with holidaymakers. We chat to a friendly woman in a tourist information kiosk and discover the Olympic Park is located 17km south of the city, near to the town of Adler. She offers us the option of joining a tour group in two days' time, but warns that we will not be permitted to access many areas due to the large scale construction work that is taking place. Undeterred by the news, Si suggests we go and check it out for ourselves.

Returning to the Volvo that is now covered in a thick layer of dust, we join a quiet two-lane coastal highway heading south to the Abkhazian frontier town of Adler. We begin to see signs pointing in the direction of the mountain ski town of Krasnaya Polyana. An arrow for the Olympic Park directs Si onto a road that leads into what is currently one of Europe's largest building sites. Luxury apartment buildings await their new tenants and the white roof of the enormous Bolshoy Ice Dome sparkles in the distance. Parking right outside the main gates to the Olympic complex, a dumper truck roars past and leaves us choking on a cloud of dust. As the air clears, Si notices the silver Honda Civic nearby has Syrian licence plates. It suddenly occurs to me that we are now closer geographically to Syria than we are to Warsaw. Peering through the bars of a tall mesh security fence, we look in awe at the Alder Arena up close and study the white skeletal frame of the Fisht Olympic Stadium that looks a long way from completion. Making our way across a dry waste ground that is flooded in golden evening light, we join hundreds of construction workers wearing yellow hard hats, high visibility vests and work boots as they wait to start their shift. A beat up old bus crammed full of workers roars through the heavily guarded entrance gate. The majority of the men appear to be of Turkish and

Middle Eastern or Central Asian origin. The enormous Bolshoy Ice Dome looms in the distance and I can see hundreds of workers, who look like tiny ants, hanging from ropes attached to the roof of the dome. We stand by the fence on the edge of the new Sochi Formula One racetrack and photograph the stadiums under construction. A military guy wearing blue combat trousers and a black vest top glares over at us. An official emerges from a police jeep. Not wishing to appear suspicious, we head back to the Volvo and leave the construction workers to get the job finished.

* * *

Chris accelerates at speed along the newly constructed Adler-Krasnaya Polyana mountain highway. A symbol of the huge cost of the Sochi Winter Olympics, it is rumoured the construction of this 48km stretch of highway has escalated into the billions. We catch sight of the brand new Adler Thermal Power Plant (Adler TPP), as we cruise along an empty highway into the mountains. Half-owned by the Russian government, the energy giant Gazprom was commissioned in September 2009 to construct two gas pipelines running beneath the Black Sea. The 53cm pipes will deliver energy that will heat and power these enormous stadiums. With huge natural gas reserves, Russia is a geographically advantageous region of the world that has the capability to export its natural resources to both Asia and Europe via a huge network of pipelines. The controversial proposed Gazprom "South Stream" project (if ever built) would see the construction of a pipeline that would travel east to west across the entire width of the Black Sea from Anapa in Russia (52km north of Novorossiysk), to Tarvisio in northern Italy. This

Sochi and we wind our way up through the forested hills. In the early hours we park up close to the town of Sputnik and grab a few hours rest.

At sunrise, we stumble into a nearby café. The well-dressed woman working behind the counter fixes us a strong Nescafe Alegria from a brand new coffee machine. Her hair is jet black and she has petite features and a pale and flawless complexion. Chris asks her if she speaks English, but she shakes her head and replies Armenian and a little Turkish. Approximately 20% of the population in the Greater Sochi area are Armenian, and she playfully teaches us how to say "thank you". Sweeping her hand elegantly from left to right, as if presenting herself, she utters the word "shnorhakalutyun". We both attempt to repeat the word and she covers her mouth and begins to laugh hysterically.

Chris furrows his brow and casts the woman a comic look of paranoia. 'What?' he smiles.

Wrestling fits of giggles, she shows us to a table on the terrace outside. Chris flicks open the road atlas and identifies a short cut that will take us to the foothills of the Caucasus Mountains around Mt Elbrus.

Turning inland close to the coastal town of Tyance, we leave behind the speeding holiday traffic and drive along a deserted country road into the forested hills. We stop on the edge of a tranquil village and wash in a stream and rinse out a few clothes. Feeling fresh, we pass through the rural settlements of Yaableck and Nabnhck, and cautiously negotiate railway crossings without barriers and swerve to avoid cows standing in the middle of the road.

On the outskirts of Maykop, the capital city of the Republic of Adygea, we arrive at a large military base belonging to the 131st Motor Rifle Brigade of the North Caucasus Military District. This regiment fought in the First Chechen War in 1994. The discovery of extensive underground oil reserves has made this region a major centre for oil extraction, and at regular 10km intervals we pass through heavily guarded military checkpoints. Forced to slow down to a near halt, Chris creeps over sandbags and drives through a yellow chemical under the watchful eye of a soldier. Between checkpoints we are intrigued to see a group of women at a bus stop wearing Muslim hijabs. Further along the road we pass a Russian UAZ army van parked under a tree. Three guys with shaved heads pray on their knees in the direction of Mecca. These are the Adyghe people, an ethnic Circassian group that inhabit the Republic of Adygea, who fiercely resisted the Tsarist troops in Sochi after the Russian-Turkish War in the 19th century. Accounting for only 16% of the population of Maykop today, the Tsarist government had exiled the Adaghe to lands of the Ottoman Empire after defeating them in the Circassian War of 1862.

Continuing on our journey through the rural countryside, Chris acknowledges a military solider with a nod as we pass through yet another checkpoint. For reasons unknown, we seem to be of little interest to the soldiers. In the small village of Mockobckon, tobacco dries on wooden racks and an old woman relaxes on the porch of her humble home. A thickset guy wearing combat trousers, who sports a thick black moustache, stands on the forecourt of a rusty petrol station and eyeballs us curiously. The military checkpoints appear to have come to an end, and we cruise on an arrow straight highway across a vast flat landscape. Reaching Mcegan, we can see the pale blue Caucasus mountain range on the horizon, a spectacular 1,000km ethnic barrier between Europe and Asia. Deep in the heart of the Russian "Wild West", we hide the Volvo behind a thick hedgerow out of sight of the road. We eat heavily salted Black Sea anchovies in silence and watch the sky turn purple as mosquitoes buzz hungrily at the windows. Two Russian cowboys silhouetted on horseback pass close by, followed by a foal. They turn down a dusty track towards a remote farm or cattle ranch and dissolve into the darkness.

Nine

With a chill in the air, Si flicks on the Volvo's heated seats and we enjoy the warmth that soothes our aching backs. A morning mist hugs the valley and the rising sun illuminates the mountains. Passing through small rural communities, we weave around horses that waft their tails and shake their manes in a futile bid to keep the flies and mosquitoes away. A noisy Jay flutters at speed across a meadow that is bursting with lilac wildflowers. Si slows the car to a halt as a Russian cowboy on horseback, wearing a tar brown leather jacket and a cowboy hat, drives a large herd of cattle across the road.

Arriving in the small Muslim Turko-Tatar town of Karachayevsk, we are presented with the striking sight of a newly built mosque that looms over this vibrant community. The vast majority of the population of Karachayevsk are Karachay, which is the biggest ethnic group in the Karachay-Cherkess Republic. Similar in size to the Republic of Adygea, this region was once part of the historical region of Circassia. The Cherkess, who form around 12% of the population of the Republic, are mostly Besleney Kabardians. A highland people indigenous to the region, they speak the Cherkess (Circassian) language and are mainly Sunni Muslim. They generally call themselves

Adyge, as do most Circassians.

The town is buzzing with activity. Local people mill around market stalls and a group of taxi drivers joke around outside the mosque. Scanning the street, a guy with a dark complexion marches past with a big bunch of keys in his hand and slides behind the wheel of a Toyota saloon. Two Muslim women dressed beautifully in colourful hijabs and long skirts chat to a group of babushkas wearing paisley patterned print dresses, cardigans and flat sandals with thick woollen socks. An elderly couple climb out of an ancient machine green UAZ pickup truck with red curtains and unload crates of vegetables onto the sidewalk. Si checks out the market, while I grab a few supplies from a nearby grocery store. My heart skips a beat when the woman behind the counter glances up at me with large black feline eyes. She isn't wearing a headscarf and her silky black hair is tied up, revealing her long slim neck, perfectly proportioned features and high cheekbones. Purchasing a kilo of long grain rice, I bump clumsily into a shelf stacked full of canned food and exit the store with a bright red face.

On the horizon, the view of the snow-capped Caucasus Mountain range is breathtaking as we cross the Kuban River and drive east towards the spa town of Kislovodsk. Si points out honey for sale at the roadside and beehives neatly stacked on the back of a flatbed trailer. A group of kids in a high pasture meadow play cowboys and Indians with bows and arrows. We hesitantly enter Stavropol Krai, a region bordering Chechnya that has been known to inhabit militant groups of the Caucasus Emirate.

After the dissolution of the Soviet Union in 1991, the Chechen-Ingush ASSR was split into two parts, the smaller Republic of Ingushetia in the west and the Chechen

Republic. The latter sought independence, proclaiming itself the Chechen Republic of Ichkeria, which ultimately led to The First Chechen War from 1994 to 1996. During the conflict, it is believed that approximately 3,000-15,000 Chechen soldiers and between 30,000-100,000 civilians had been killed and possibly over 200,000 injured. It had taken the tragic event of the Budyonnovsk Hospital Hostage Crisis in 1995, a city only 184km northeast of Kislovodsk, to force a temporary ceasefire. On June 14th a group of 80 to 200 Chechen separatists, led by Chechen militant Islamist, Shamil Basayev, travelled 110km north of the border into Stavropol Krai from the de facto independent Chechen Republic of Ichkeria. Hidden inside military trucks, they attacked the main police station and the city hall and raised Chechen flags over official buildings. Fighting for several hours, it was reported they retreated to the main hospital in the city where they held approximately 1,500 to 1,800 people hostage. In a brutal display of the seriousness of their demands that Russian troops leave Chechen land, Basayev immediately ordered five hostages to be shot. It had taken until the fourth day of the siege, before Boris Yeltsin ordered a Russian strike force to attack the hospital building. Caught in the crossfire many innocent people lost their lives in the raid that lasted several hours. A second and third attack on the hospital saw many more deaths, with an approximate total of 129 civilians being killed and 415 injured.

On the sixth day of the attack, the majority of the hostages were released and Basayev's group, with 120 volunteer hostages, including sixteen journalists and nine State Duma deputies, travelled to the village of Zandak inside Chechnya near to the border with Dagestan. The remaining hostages were then released and Basayev, accompanied by some of the journalists, went to the village of Dargo, where he was apparently welcomed as a hero. The incident resulted in a ceasefire between Russia and Chechen rebels and peace talks, which later failed. In the years following the attack, Basayev served as Vice Prime Minister of Chechnya in Maskhadov's government from 1997 to 1998. He was considered to be the radical wing of the Chechen insurgency, and responsible for numerous guerrilla attacks on security forces and the 2002 Moscow theatre hostage crisis.

If the First Chechen War had not been brutal enough, the violent conclusion of the 1995 hospital crisis led to years of terror. The Chechen separatist hold over the republic was weak, particularly outside the war torn capital of Grozny. With few economic opportunities, lawlessness spread and abductions and raids steadily increased into other parts of the Northern Caucasus by extremist warlords. Heavily armed former separatist fighters made a business from kidnapping in Chechnya between 1996 and 1999, including a group of four engineers from the UK, who were held hostage for two months and then brutally murdered. With political violence and religious extremism becoming rife, the Russian Federation launched The Second Chechen War (1999-2009), following the Invasion of Dagestan by the Islamic International Brigade. The military campaign ended the de facto independence of the Chechen Republic of Ichkeria, and restored Russian federal control over the territory by February 2000. For many years after, resistance from Chechen extremists continued to dispute Russian government control over the republic resulting in heavy Russian casualties. It took until 2009 (only four years ago), before Russia was able to successfully bring the neighbouring Chechen separatist movement under control and large scale fighting came to an end.

* * *

With war and violence heavily on our minds, we arrive in the pleasant spa town of Kislovodsk "Sour Waters". Chris reveals that after the tragic Chernobyl nuclear disaster that occurred in Ukraine in 1986, during the Soviet era, victims were sent to Kislovodsk for the "Narzan treatment," which was believed to help wash out radionuclides. The medieval Arab traveller, Ibn-Battuta, first mentioned the healing waters in writing in the 14th century. In the late 17th century, Peter the Great ordered one of his leading naturalists German-born, Peter Simon Pallas, to explore the springs so they would one day rival those in Western Europe. Growing into a popular spa town in the late 1800s, Kislovodsk became a desirable retreat for painters, musicians and poets, and lays claim to being the setting of a number of scenes in the novel 'A Hero of Our Time' by Mikhail Lermontov.

Mikhail was a student with a passion for literature. His controversial early work 'Death of a Poet' written in 1837, in reaction to the death of the much loved Russian poet Alexander Pushkin, caused intrigue and thrust him into the limelight. Lermontov's poem accused the Russian aristocracy for Pushkin's death. He called them, "the hangmen who kill liberty, genius, and glory". Arrested for his work by the authorities, Lermontov was sent to the Caucasus as a low ranking officer in the Nizhegorodsky Dragoons regiment. Generations of Lermontov's family had served in the military, with his Scottish-born ancestor, Yuri Learmont, settling in Russia in the middle of the 17th century following a career as an officer in the Polish-Lithuanian army. Drawing inspiration from the Caucasus landscapes and fascinated by its people and mountain legends, Mikhail wrote in a letter, "Good people are here aplenty. In Tiflis (Tbilisi, Georgia) especially, people are very honest." Lermontov's first exile had been fairly short, and he travelled slowly back to St Petersburg. He quickly grew bored of the shallow pleasures offered by high society, and found himself in a duel with another officer over two women. Escaping with minor injury, he was sent back to exile in the Caucasus and fought in Chechnya in 1840, where he became hugely popular with his men. Returning to St Petersburg in 1841, he began to take his literary work more seriously following the success of his novel 'A Hero of Our Time'. Unable to escape the army and focus on his literary career, Lermontov was forced to return to his regiment in Stavropol. Faking illness, he travelled to the nearby spa town of Pyatigorsk. He drew much attention at parties and social events, and ruthlessly mocked his cadet friend, Nikolai Martynov, who dressed like a native Circassian and wore a long sword. On 25th July 1841, Nikolai challenged Lermontov, aged 26, to a duel and shot him in the heart.

Towering white Greek columns welcome us at the entrance to Kislovodskiy Park. Weaving around market stalls selling colourful prints and mass-produced paintings, Chris admires a beautiful watercolour of a mountain landscape. Scanning the faces of the local people and day-trippers, I struggle to identify the different ethnicities of the people who live in this region of the Caucasus. Approximately 80% of the population of Stavropol Krai are Russians, but with 33 ethnic groups, this federal district is considered to be one of the most multiethnic in Russia. I feel spots of rain on my skin as we traverse a river that cuts through the lush green park. The sky suddenly erupts in a torrential downpour. People wrestle with umbrellas and dash through the park in excited panic. We quickly seek shelter beneath a tree and wait patiently for the storm to pass. I notice everyone dotted around looks strangely frozen, and it feels like time itself has come to an abrupt standstill. A low rumble of thunder is closely followed by a lightning flash. Chris suggests we push on into the rain, so we tap dance through the puddles along the banks of the river and pass a row of large stone mansion houses and private sanatoriums. We weave through a cluster of market stalls at the rear entrance to the park, and see babushkas wrestling to cover their knitwear and souvenirs with plastic sheets in a futile bid to keep everything dry.

Ducking into a nearby supermarket we watch a scene of chaos unfold in the street outside, as hailstones the size of marbles power down from the sky. There is a feeling of panic and urgency in the air as people dive for cover to the eerie sound of car alarms. Within a matter of seconds the road is covered in a blanket of white ice. Water begins to creep under the door and we're pushed further inside the supermarket. In spite of the potentially life threatening natural disaster happening outside, I watch in bemusement as the supermarket employees on the checkout counters continue to scan products at ultra fast speed. Bunched together with a group of anxious locals, their panicked chatter is muffled by the terrifying roar of the hailstones crashing against the corrugated metal roof. An old lady glances up and smiles at me sweetly. Chris notices her sandals are submerged in the icy cold water, so he makes room for her on a ledge that runs along the length of the window.

Much to everyone's relief the storm eventually begins to subside. A guy hesitantly opens the supermarket door and we step outside one by one and inspect the damage.

Water gushes down the main street, vehicles are covered in tree branches and the gutters are overflowing with large ice marbles. We cut through the park and the once tranquil river is now a raging torrent of muddy brown water. A thick mist rises like steam from its surface and hangs eerily beneath its many footbridges. Glancing over the rooftops in the direction of Mt Elbrus, we both agree that it's time we paid the highest mountain in Europe a visit.

We chase a rainbow south to Baksan and Mt Elbrus. The road is congested with trucks from Moldova and Ukraine and cars from Azerbaijan, Armenia and the Republic of South Ossetia. We pass enormous apple plantations and see a road sign for Vladikavkaz; the capital of the Republic of North Ossetia-Alania. We enter the volatile Kabardino-Balkaria Republic, a region that was fought over by the Russian and Ottoman empires between the 17th and 19th centuries. Located in the North Caucasus, 50km west of Chechnya, this republic has extremely low living standards, unemployment is high, corruption is rife, and it has had more than its fair share of violence, kidnappings, organised crime and local rebels fighting the war in Syria. According to BBC News, since the 2004 Beslan school siege in neighbouring North Ossetia, Russia has repeatedly targeted what it says are Islamic militants operating in Kabardino-Balkaria. The late Chechen rebel leader, Abdul-Khalim Saydullayev, decreed the organisation of a Caucasus Front here against Russia in May 2005.

We begin to wrestle with paranoia as the light begins to fade. Reaching the outskirts of Baksan, we pass half a dozen security enforcement officers clutching assault rifles. They appear to be randomly searching vehicles and eyeball us as we turn right onto a smaller road that cuts across the Baksan Valley towards Mt Elbrus. Chris sticks to the speed limit through Tyrnyauz, a large mountain town that was devastated by a flood and mudslide in 2001. According to news reports, apartment buildings were buried up to the fourth floor. Two military police officers emerge from a police vehicle clutching Kalashnikovs, and sprint across the road into a small park. We are flagged down at a checkpoint on the way out of town. A soldier flicks through our passports before waving us on. Driving steeply into the mountains, we travel deep into the wilderness until we find ourselves at a safe distance from other humans. Chris turns off the road and parks up beside the fast flowing Baksan River; he kills the lights. Under the cover of darkness, we gaze up at the Milky Way and see dozens of shooting stars in the breathtaking clear night sky.

Rising early, Chris cooks a hearty breakfast of sausages and eggs while I type up my notes at a picnic bench. The Baksan River roars in the background, and one of the snow-capped peaks of Mt Elbrus makes a brief appearance before the dark clouds roll in. A number of cars begin to arrive around 8am. A group of guys in their early twenties claim a picnic bench nearby. We chat briefly to a kid with a pale complexion and shortly cropped ginger hair, who is wearing navy blue tracksuit trousers with black shoes. We discover he is from Nalchik, the capital of the Kabardino-Balkaria Republic and belongs to the Sunni Muslim Kabarda ethnic group. The Kabardin were originally the semi-nomadic eastern branch of the Adyghe tribal fellowship and speak Kabardian, a North West Caucasian language that represents the easternmost extension of the Circassian language group. The Kabardino-Balkaria Republic is also home to minorities of Turkic-speaking

Balkars (around 10% of the people) and Russians. Friction exists between the Kabardins and the Balkars and in 1992 the Balkars voted for secession. Our conversation with the kid is limited, and he seems curious to know where we are from. He interrogates our faces with penetrating black eyes before returning to his friends.

A short distance from the small ski village of Terskol, we stumble across a market where local Balkar people are selling souvenirs, food and refreshments to the tourists. I browse a stall selling jars of honey, sheep skin rugs and a surprised looking stuffed goat. A group of Muslim women laugh and take turns posing for photographs wearing a grey fur ushanka hat. I buy a coffee from a small wooden cabin and chat to the girl working behind the counter. She speaks good English, and we learn that her favourite TV show is the American vampire series 'Twilight'. Chris asks if her family are Balkar. She nods her head and explains that many of the people in this region are Balkar, but the young people just consider themselves to be Russian.

A Sunni Muslim Turkic ethnic group, the Balkar language is of the Ponto-Caspian subgroup of the North-western Kipchak group of Turkic languages. We came across the Kipchaks in Crimea, in the form of an 11th-12th century suit of armour in Feodosiya. Some scholars believe the Balkar people may have evolved from a cultural mix of the northern Caucasian tribes, with the Alans and Turkish-speaking tribes. The Balkars had slowly been integrated into the structure of the USSR after the Russian Civil War in the 1920s. In early 1944, the Balkars were accused by Joseph Stalin of allying with Nazi Germany. The penalty was deportation, and the Balkar people in this region were forcibly removed from their mountain home to Kazakhstan and various other regions of Central Asia. Fierce fighting between the Red Army and Nazi troops in the battle for the Caucasus took place on Mt Elbrus during the Second World War. Approximately 5,000 out of the 37,713 Balkars who were deported, died over the following three years from malnutrition and disease. The Balkars were allowed to return to their homeland in 1957-58. The girl's grandfather sits at a small table beside the gas cooker. He has the face of a hardy mountain people, and I try to imagine the world of poverty this proud man had no doubt endured as a child.

Ten

The rain thunders down as a veil of thick cloud swirls around the body of Mt Elbrus. Si turns on the squeaky windscreen wipers, and on the glass I draw a smiley face in the condensation. Rising 5,642 metres above sea level, Mt Elbrus is a double-coned volcano with a permanent icecap that feeds twenty-two glaciers. This majestic fortress of rock and ice is located on a moving tectonic area, and was formed more than 2.5 million years ago. The name Elbrus "Alborz" is believed to have roots in Middle Persian and derives from a mountain in Iranian mythology called "Hara Berezaiti", meaning "High Sentinel". Located at the crossroads of cultures at the axis of migrating civilisations, Elbrus has names in many other languages including "Mingi Taw" in Turkic, meaning "Eternal Mountain" and "Oshkhamakhua" in Circassian, meaning "Mountain of Happiness".

During the Hellenistic period the mountain was known as "Strobilus" (pine cone) in Latin; in reference to the volcanoes twisted peak. According to the curse of Zeus, everyday a giant eagle was to descend from the skies and devour Prometheus's liver. During the night, his wounds would heal and the torture would begin again. The Titan was eventually saved by Hercules who defeated the eagle.

In local Balkar mythology, they believe Mt Elbrus was trapped in ice by Allah as punishment for being too proud to bow in prayer to the Muslim holy site of Mount Arafat, east of Mecca.

Refusing to let the weather dampen our spirits, we drop by the 7Summit climbing shop and tour office in Terskol. Enjoying the novelty and warmth of being inside, we meet the assertive manager named Anna, who has shoulder length jet-black hair and rosy cheeks. We sip coffee and watch a group of climbers trying on hiking boots and choosing their ice axes and ski poles. There is an air of excitement in the room, an anxious anticipation. Si sparks up a conversation with a ruddy-faced chap from Moscow, who strides around the shop and tests out his new hiking boots. He tells us they hope to climb Elbrus in two days' time when the weather is forecast to improve. Two women from Norway inspect their poles, while a young couple debate about whether a blue or orange jacket looks better on the mountain.

I join Si outside and we meet a local guide who is chatting to his wife and young son on his laptop. I leap in front of the webcam and sing "dobryy vecher!" Pavel has a great sense of humour. When he hears about our expedition, he tells the story about the Russian adventurer, Alexander Abramov, who drove a Land Rover to the top of Elbrus in 1997. The vehicle had become stuck on the way down, and still remains on the mountain to this day. Mt Elbrus is considered to be Europe's highest summit, with regards to the seven highest mountains of each of the seven continents. F. Crauford Grove and a Swiss guide, Peter Knubel, made the first recorded ascent of Mt Elbrus in July 1874. Grove was one of the best British climbers of his time and wrote a book 'The Frosty Caucasus'.

Bidding Pavel goodnight, we retire to the shelter of the Hotel Volvo. I'm about to flick on the heater when Anna suddenly appears with her basset hound puppy. She looks shocked to see us sitting in the car.

'It is too cold to sleep in your car tonight. Please, sleep in the shop.'

Not wishing to be any trouble, she insists, so we quickly grab our sleeping bags and drag them inside. Anna leads the dog into the apartment at the back of the 7Summit office and pours us both a glass of Chilean Malbec, a present from a tourist. Overwhelmed by her kindness, we sip the delicious wine and learn about the many climbers who travel to this region of southern Russia from countries across the world. But Anna reveals tourism has been on the decrease in recent years, due to people in Russia being able to travel overseas more freely now. Si suggests that the publicity around the Sochi Winter Olympics might attract more international tourists here, but she seems doubtful. I ask Anna if climbing Mt Elbrus is dangerous.

She nods vehemently, flicking her hair away from her face. 'Of course, every year the mountain claims lives. But it is usually the result of poor organization and equipment. The weather can change very quickly here.'

Mt Elbrus is considered to be one of the most dangerous mountains on the Seven Summit circuit. In March 1963, even Tenzing Norgay, the first man to climb Mt Everest with Edmund Hillary, failed to reach the summit of Elbrus because of bad weather.

Anna asks what two English brothers are doing all the way out here in the remote Caucasus Mountains. 'Most tourists fly via Moscow, not drive from the UK in their car!'

'We are on a quest to drive around the Black Sea,' I

reply.

'Ah, so you are adventurers,' she smiles. 'I think if more people had the chance to travel, maybe they would realise we are not all so different.'

We chat late into the evening and I ask Anna if Mt Elbrus is in Europe or Asia.

'The mountains do not belong to anyone,' she laughs. 'They are bigger than we are. We must respect them.'

Finishing the wine, Anna locks the door and places the keys on the counter.

'I have an early start tomorrow, so I must sleep,' she smiles. 'If you want to go outside, no problem, but please remember to lock the door.'

Humbled by Anna's amazing hospitality and trust towards two complete strangers, we bid her goodnight and she disappears into her adjoining apartment. I curl up on the floor in my sleeping bag. An outside lamp floods the climbing shop in dim orange light that illuminates crampons, ice axes and climbing helmets that are hung on the walls. Expensive brand name hiking boots and winter jackets crowd the shelves. I hear a tapping noise at the window. I glance over and see a huge moth flapping madly around the outside light. It casts eerie shadows on the wall. Covering my head with my sleeping bag I drift into a deep sleep.

At first light, Si drives back down the mountain and we rejoin the busy M29. We pass through two checkpoints before arriving at the pleasant town of Nalchik (little horseshoe), the capital of the Kabarda-Balkar republic. An article in the Moscow Times in 2012 reported that, "these days, Nalchik tends to make the news only in connection with government-led crackdowns on Islamic militants". In October 2005, the city grabbed the world headlines when dozens of militants tried to seize local law enforcement offices in a raid that left 142 dead, including at least fourteen civilians. As many as 150-200 inexperienced fighters, took part in the assault on fifteen different Interior Ministry and state security buildings and police posts. According to reports, the rebels had ignored the advice of their mentor, renegade Chechen field commander, Shamil Basayev, who had warned them that they were not yet ready for combat. The operation was a complete disaster. The Guardian newspaper quoted a witness to the fighting, who recalled hearing one of the young attackers yelling to a comrade-in-arms, "How do you reload a grenade launcher?"

Taking the time to visit the 'Forever with Russia' monument in the main square, which is dedicated to Ivan the Terrible's wife, Maria, a native Kabardian, we push south and arrive at the border checkpoint for North Ossetia-Alania. Waiting patiently in a long queue of cars, we buy corn on the cob from a chubby kid standing in front of a military bunker. We creep forward and pull up alongside a control booth. Si hands our passports and car documents to an official. He asks where we are going.

'Vladikavkaz,' Si replies with a nervous grin.

He seems satisfied with his one word answer, and casually slides the documents over the counter. For many years, the Republic of North Ossetia-Alania has experienced terror and atrocities within its boundaries. The state had a predominantly Ossetian-Christian population, after Stalin deported thousands of ethnic Ingush Muslims from their homelands to Kazakhstan and Kyrgyzstan. The return of a second wave of Ingush Muslims in 1991, to the eastern part of North Ossetia's Prigorodny District, sparked violent clashes following the resettling of some 70,000 refugees from the Georgian province of South Ossetia. Prigorodny District was part of Ingushetia, which belonged to the Chechen-Ingush ASSR at the time. Dispute over lands and rising nationalism in North Ossetia-Alania led to the Ossetian-Ingush conflict, which according to Helsinki Human Rights Watch, was an Ossetian militia campaign of ethnic cleansing carried out during October and November 1992. It resulted in the deaths of more than 600 Ingush civilians and the expulsion of approximately 60,000 Ingush inhabitants from the Prigorodny district.

Si removes the magnetic "GB" sticker from the rear of the Volvo and we drive south to the small town of Beslan. We begin to see dramatic views of the white snow covered Caucasus Mountain Range. Looking towards the frozen peaks of Mt Elbrus, I imagine Pavel, the trusty mountain guide, leading his group of climbers to the summit of this towering fortress of rock. Multi-coloured bunting stretches across the road in a small village, and a babushka wearing a floral print dress sweeps her porch with a broom made of twigs. Si cautiously overtakes an old man driving a wooden cart that is powered by a donkey. His arms look strong as he confidently pulls on the reins.

We reach the suburbs of Beslan, home to a population of mainly Ossetian-Christians. With a community going about their daily lives, it is impossible to imagine the severity of the event that took place here in 2004. On 'The Day of Knowledge' (September 1st), when children all over Russia return to school, one of the bloodiest terrorist attacks in Russia's recent history took place in Beslan. The hostile takeover of School Number One by Chechen terrorists was to become the rebels answer to unleashing violence across the North Caucasus in order to strike at Russia's south.

After visiting the memorial cemetery, which is one of

the rare graveyards in North Ossetia where both Christians and Muslims are laid to rest, we drive around in circles trying to find School Number One. At a road junction, Si pulls over beside a fruit and vegetable stall. I leap out and approach a woman wearing a black crochet shawl. I ask her for directions to the school and she looks at me rather puzzled. Then she suddenly replies "Skooll, infants?" and draws a finger across her throat. I nod my head gravely. The woman points up ahead and then left. She seems curious to know why we want to go there, so I put a hand to my heart in an effort to communicate that we would like to pay our respects.

Following a railway track along a bumpy unpaved road we turn down a suburban street lined with two storey red brick houses. Near to a rusty abandoned sign warning of children crossing, a young woman lifts her baby out of a pram. It occurs to me that she could be one of the survivors of the siege, who now has a child of her own. We hang a sharp left into a side street with a row of garages, and I see a copper structure slide into view that covers a brick building in ruins. A new Christian church is under construction to the right of the memorial. We step inside the derelict sports hall, where twelve Chechen men and two Chechen women held over a thousand children, parents and teachers hostage. It is difficult for us to imagine the three days of suffering that occurred right here within these brick walls. Flowers and soft toys have been placed around the edges of the room, and colour photographs are on display of the children and teachers who tragically died here. A large wreath and a wooden crucifix have been positioned in the centre of the sports hall. Si points out the black and charred roof and the bullet and shrapnel holes scattered across the walls. The entire structure appears to have remained untouched since the day the school was brutally taken hostage. Homemade plastic explosives were attached to the basketball nets either side of the hall, and there are two holes in the wooden floor below caused by the blasts. TV news footage leaps into my mind, parents running with their dead and injured children in their arms, soldiers crouching behind walls and a scared little girl climbing back inside the school building to meet her fate. The news channel rt.com reported it was "the bloodiest terrorist attack in Russia's history" and claimed the lives of "186 children, 118 relatives or school guests, 17 teachers, 10 Special Forces officers, 2 Emergencies Ministry employees and one policeman." A further 810 people were injured. The Beslan terrorists requested the release of a group of gunmen who were being held, and demanded Russian armed forces leave Chechnya. In addition, they insisted specific individuals must be present at the negotiations including Putin's advisor, Aslambek Aslakhanov, and the presidents of North Ossetia and Ingushetia. An explosion occurred in the school ending the three-day siege. The government blamed the explosion on the terrorists, although, there had been some speculation that a terrorist bomb went off during a botched rescue operation by Russian security services. There can be no limit to the grief that the families of these innocent victims must feel.

* * *

Chris sits hunched over the steering wheel and skims along the border of Ingushetia. The small Republic of Ingushetia once formed part of the Chechen-Ingush ASSR before the dissolution of the Soviet Union in 1991. A republic plagued by corruption, the continuing military conflict in nearby Chechnya and Dagestan has on occasion spread into Ingushetia. In July 2006, less than 33km east of Beslan on the Ingushetia border with North Ossetia, Shamil Basayev, the man behind the Beslan School Hostage Crisis, was killed by an explosion. He was one of the most wanted men in the world. Controversy still surrounds who is responsible for his death, with the Russian authorities stating he was killed in an assassination.

The Caucasus Mountains create a stunning backdrop to an otherwise rather grey city as we reach the outskirts of Vladikavkaz. Chris pulls up to a set of traffic lights and I sneak a peek at my fellow road users. What am I expecting to see – a group of Islamic militants wearing balaclavas and clutching Kalashnikovs? No, of course not, instead it's a young family squeezed into a red Lada to my left and an overweight businessman in his fifties driving a smart Toyota saloon to my right. Ossetians are a proud people, who recognise themselves as descendants of the Alanic group of Sarmatian tribes. Most Ossetians are fluent in Russian, but they also speak an ancient Iranian language with multiple dialects called Ossetic that belongs to the eastern branch of the Indo-European family of languages. The Ossetians mostly live in the regions of North Ossetia-Alania in Russia and the neighbouring Georgian break-away state of South Ossetia; the latter of which has been de facto independent from Georgia since the 2008 South Ossetia War.

Byzantine missionaries first brought Christianity to the Alans in the 10th century, and a large percentage became Eastern Orthodox Christians in the 12th-13th centuries under the influence of Georgia. During the 13th century, Ossetia fell under the control of the Mongol Empire and the Alani were forced to flee into the mountains. The Kabarday (who we had met around Elbrus), introduced

Islam to the region in the 17th century and the Digor branch of the Ossetians in the west gradually adopted the Islamic religion and practises. The Encyclopaedia Britannica states that in North Ossetia-Alania, "Eastern Orthodox Christianity is the predominant religion, and Sunni Muslims make up a small but significant minority." Indigenous pre-Christian and pre-Islamic pagan practices also exist here alongside these and other faiths. With the establishment of a fortress in Vladikavkaz in 1784, Russian colonisation began in the northern Ossetian district. In addition to Ossetians - Russians, Ingush, Armenians, Georgians and Ukrainian Cossacks populate the Republic of North Ossetia-Alania.

Chris weaves around rattling trams that speed past Soviet-era concrete apartment blocks. For many years Vladikavkaz was the main Russian military base in the region. It grew quickly into an industrial centre following the completion of a railway line in 1875 that connected it to Rostov-on-Don and Baku in Azerbaijan. Failing to see any visible signs of the city's notorious reputation for violence, Chris reminds me that it was only a few years ago in 2010 when a suicide bomber detonated explosives that tore through the packed central market, killing nineteen people and injuring a further 240. Radio Free Europe-Radio Liberty reported that Emir Adam, commander of the Caucasus Emirate forces in Ingushetia, "formally identified the Riyadus Salikhiin suicide battalion as responsible for the suicide bombing in September 2010 in Vladikavkaz." Equally disturbing, the city is thought to have been a base for the Shahidka - Islamist Chechen female suicide bombers also known as the "Black Widows". Known for their involvement in the Moscow theatre hostage crisis in 2002, amongst multiple other attacks, a suspected Shahidka was thought to be responsible for an explosion at a taxi-van stop in Vladikavkaz in 2008, killing at least eleven people and injuring as many as forty others. The term Black Widow is thought to originate from the fact that many of these women are widows of men killed by the Russian forces in Chechnya.

We stroll down to the Mukhtarov Mosque (Sunni mosque) on the banks of the River Terek. Sitting on a bench in a pretty garden, we admire this historic building with its dome and twin minarets. The mosque was built in 1908 and was utilised by Ingush residents of Vladikavkaz before they were driven out of the city in the 1990s. From the river we wander back to the main square and observe the local people going about their daily lives. In the central market we pop into a local café. A plump woman behind the counter, with short bleached blonde hair, invites us to sit at a table in the sunshine. Ordering a coffee, she prepares the freshly ground beans on a stove and stirs each cup vigorously. Surprised to discover she speaks a few words in English, she asks "what country?" I reply "England", and she seems surprised why two citizens of the United Kingdom would travel all the way out here to the Caucasus. Chris shows her our route on the road atlas and points to Crimea, the Sea of Azov, Rostov-on-Don, Sochi, Mt Elbrus and Beslan.

I point out of the window. 'Vladikavkaz, good?'

She drops her smile, and shakes her head. 'No good, no good. Here no good. Mayor stupid alcoholic!' she snaps, her face bulging with anger.

She complains that the streets are dirty with chewing gum everywhere, and that people today have no respect for their elders. I'm intrigued that she appears to be more upset about the social decay of the city, rather than concerned about the political fighting, assassinations, kidnappings and continuing acts of terrorism and violence. She serves our coffee in white china tea cups with saucers and accompanies it with a slice of fruit cake. We discover Olga is Ossetian and has two daughters. One is married, but her youngest is 27 years old and she still doesn't have a ring on her finger. Olga is sad about this in the way a Greek or Jewish mother might behave. She uses the word "cho-cho" to ask if we would like "a little more" coffee. We gladly accept her offer. Chris tries to ask Olga if foreigners can pass through the 'Verkhny Lars - Darial Gorge' border crossing, but she shrugs her shoulders. Olga hasn't been to Georgia since she was a child and I get the impression she is not fond of the place. This is hardly surprising when you consider the Russo-Georgian War only took place six years ago. Approaching the counter to pay for the delicious coffee and cake, she shoos us away and refuses to accept any money. Disputing her kindness, Chris places money on the counter, but she looks so angry we feel it would be insulting to push her any further. I have heard of hospitality like this from travellers who have been to Iran and Armenia. Curious to witness this in North Ossetia, we embrace her in turn and leave the café with admiration for yet another proud people in this complex multi-ethnic region of the Caucasus.

Heading south of the city, we see the promising sight of a brand new road sign pointing to the Georgian capital of Tbilisi. Located only 195km away on the opposite side of the Caucasus Mountains, we are forced to repress our excitement as we speed into the mountains. This border at the frontier of the Georgian Military Highway is currently the only accessible route from Russia into Georgia, with Abkhazia now existing as a break-away state and South Ossetia de facto independent from Georgia since 2008. Before leaving England, Chris had read news reports that in 2010 Russia and Georgia had reached a deal under Swiss and Armenian mediation to reopen the checkpoint. But the crossing was only open to citizens of countries in the ex-Soviet grouping called the "CIS" (Commonwealth of Independent States). We had stumbled across various other conflicting reports on travel blogs and forums, with some people stating the border is now open to foreigners and others warning it is closed.

Traversing the Terek River through a rocky jagged mountain valley, we cautiously approach this remote frontier at the end of the line. Spotting a queue of cars in the distance, I inhale a deep breath. Smartly dressed Russian customs officials wearing green uniforms, with wide brimmed hats, shout orders at the drivers of the vehicles as they filter through the barrier. Reaching the front of the queue, we wait for the green light before drawing to a halt alongside a passport control booth. Experiencing a minor communication breakdown with the woman behind the counter, much to our relief we discover all she wants to see is our visa registration documents that we obtained at the hostel in Rostov-on-Don. Chris is instructed to open the trunk by a guy dressed in black. He asks if we are carrying any weapons or narcotics. Chris mutely shakes his head and he instructs him to close it.

We leave Russian soil and drive 8km through no man's land to the Darial Gorge border crossing. Workmen weld metal pipes alongside a newly constructed customs building. Serbond stickers have yet to be removed from the white plastic veneer panelling and unfinished wiring and cables hang loosely from ceilings and walls. An air of excitement buzzes around the place as this new border crossing, which is due to be officially opened by the Georgian president in six days time, is literally being unwrapped in front of our eyes. We approach a Georgian police officer with a shaved head and hairy forearms. He is wearing a tight black uniform and looks rather intimidating. We slide our passports across the counter. He flicks through the pages and without looking up he asks us for our visas.

I try to remain calm and Chris explains to the official that according to the Georgian Embassy in London, British citizens no longer require one.

He doesn't look impressed and shakes his head. 'This could be big problem, guys.'

The officer calls over his colleague and they have a quick chat. We both wait in nervous anticipation. The fate of our journey relies solely on this one man.

He glances up suddenly, and winks. 'Welcome to Georgia!'

PART 3
Georgia & the Kingdom of Colchis

Eleven

A dusty, unpaved stretch of the Georgian Military Highway winds through the Dariali Gorge the "Gate of the Alans". Pumped full of adrenalin, Si squeezes past a truck from Azerbaijan on a narrow shelf below a 1,800 metre vertical wall of granite. I try to remove the thought from my mind of rocks smashing through the windows, or a landslide forcing us into the steep valley below. This dramatic and ancient trade route is considered to be one of the most romantic places in the Caucasus, with both Lermontov and Pushkin drawing inspiration from the region. Concentrating on the road, Si reminds me to keep my eyes peeled for lammergeyers "bearded vultures" and griffon vultures nesting on the cliffs. In this remote region of Georgia there are plans to construct a new hydropower plant that would generate electricity to be used locally in winter and exported in the summer to Turkey, Syria and Iraq. If not built with care the threat of environmental disaster seems like a terrifying possibility.

After half an hour of negotiating switchback corners and hairpin bends, we cross the Tergi Bridge and arrive in the northeastern Georgian settlement of Kazbegi (1,797m). In the distance I can see the 14th century Holy Trinity Tsminda Sameba Church perched on the adjacent hilltop.

The setting sun kisses the jagged horizon and silhouettes a group of hikers making their way up the mountain. In the main square we are immediately surrounded by a group of hard-faced local men touting rooms. A guy appears suddenly at my window. He has flecks of grey in his wiry bushy hair and deep lines embedded in his face. Wearing a brown woollen tank top over a checked shirt, he has the manner of a mountain warrior and despite his age he looks as strong as an ox. I notice his teeth are yellow and decaying and his lips are dry and cracked. The smell of tobacco drifts inside the car.

'You want room?' he asks, the corner of his mouth curling upwards in a slight smirk.

I shake my head. 'No, we go to Tbilisi. Can we buy car insurance here?'

He drops his smile and raises his bushy, out of control eyebrows. 'What?' he growls, fixing his stare.

'We need to buy insurance, for the car,' Si adds, knocking his fists together to demonstrate a collision.

The tout mutters something under his breath to the sun-dried gentlemen standing around him.

'No room?'

'No,' I smile.

Exhaling a deep sigh, he turns sharply away and marches over to a young traveller struggling up the hill with his rucksack. Si swings the Volvo over to a nearby petrol station. I ask the guy working the pump about car insurance, but we are both suddenly distracted by the surreal sight of a camel walking along the road. A man with long white hair runs alongside the animal and barks orders at its backside. I turn back to the petrol pump attendant, who looks equally puzzled. He shrugs his shoulders and suggests we try in the capital city of Tbilisi.

We glide through the green mountains on a smooth

tarmac road with the menacing 5,047m Mt Kazbek looming above us. A turn off for Sno Valley zips by as we approach the small settlements of Sioni and Kobi in the Tergi Valley. Rocks stained red by the sweet mineral waters interrupts the alpine meadows. We head towards the 2,379m Jvari Ughelt "Cross Pass", the highest section of the GMH. Driving through deep water in an unlit tunnel, I grip the seat with my Gluteus maximus when two large trucks narrowly squeeze past. Sweeping from left to right, we observe crosses on sharp bends that suggest not all those who have driven this scenic highway have survived. In the winter months this section of the road is notorious for avalanches, and I try to imagine how beautiful it must look up here with the mountains covered in a thick blanket of snow. Devil's Valley glows in the evening light, and we make a pit stop at a scenic viewpoint balanced on a cliff edge. An unfriendly local guy wearing a big floppy hat sells honey and handcrafted souvenirs. Si photographs the enormous colourful abstract mural above the stone arches, depicting a medieval scene of a princess with a small redheaded boy at her feet and white royal battle horses. Since crossing the border we have been zapped to a region of eastern Georgia in the Southern Caucasus, known in Greco-Roman times as the kingdom of Iberia - home of the Caucasian Iberians. During Classical Antiquity and the Early Middle Ages, Iberia was a major state in the Caucasus. It later united with Colchis to its west, forming the nucleus of the medieval Kingdom of Georgia.

With nightfall rapidly approaching, we begin the familiar hunt for somewhere safe to park. Arriving at the mountain ski village of Gudauri, on the southern slopes of The Greater Caucasus Mountain Range, Si spots a sharp turn off below a luxury ski lodge. He sweeps the Volvo onto a grass verge and kills the lights.

Soft rays of morning sunlight creep slowly across the mountains revealing our dramatic location. Si coasts the Volvo down the hill to a small supermarket with a café, and I gaze dreamily at the poster in the window of a frothy cappuccino. With wild hair and pasta shell eyes I greet the friendly girl behind the counter. She has a very different appearance to the people we have seen living in the Caucasus region of southern Russia. Her nose is slightly crooked and she has thick wavy black hair and olive skin. Si returns from a trucker's wash with a skip in his step. We sip our cappuccinos and watch the supermarket employees arrive for work. The boss appears to be overly enthusiastic and orders a young lad to quickly mop the floors. He doesn't immediately jump into action and he shakes his head and trudges through a staff exit door. We listen to the employees chatter away and I'm intrigued to hear that the Georgian language sounds softer and more musical in contrast to their Russian neighbours. The guy operating the till eagerly teaches us how to say hello "gamarjoba" and thank you "gmadlobt".

High on caffeine, Si checks out the road atlas as I set to work at driving the remainder of the Georgian Military Highway. Traversing the Tetri Aragvi River, a warm westerly wind blows through my window and massages my freshly shaven skin. Losing myself in the drive, I power the Volvo through sweeping corners as we descend 500m to the deserted village of Kvesheti in the green Khada valley. We follow the Mtiuleti Aragvi River for 40km, from Pasanauri to the Ananuri fort that is located on a hill above the turquoise Zhinvali Reservoir. The fortress belonged to the Dukes of Aragvi, a feudal dynasty from the 13th century who ruled as far as the Tergi Valley.

The location of great battles, in 1739 the castle was set ablaze by Shanshe of Ksani and the Aragvi clan was massacred right here inside its walls.

Entering the larger Assumption Church that is covered in stone carvings, a woman wearing a headscarf scrapes candle wax out of an ornate freestanding candleholder. She has a striking face, round, pale and angelic. I observe a large cross on each wall and study the 17th and 18th century frescos; one of which depicts images of devils, snakes and agonising torture. A priest wearing black robes, with a long grey beard, appears from out of nowhere and scurries across the church with his head bent low. I watch with interest as he disappears mysteriously through a doorway hidden behind a fresco of The Last Judgement. I glance over at the woman scraping the candle wax and she looks up at me with her large watery eyes.

Joining Si on the battlements, we look out across the wild meadows and the lush green rolling hills of the Pankisi Gorge. Located in the foothills of the Caucasus Mountains, this region is home to an ethnic group known as the Kists, an ancient people that trace their origins back to the Chechens of the northern Caucasus. In an article on Pankisi, Romanian journalists Annina Lehmann and Rina Soloveitchik quoted the 19th century Georgian poet Vasha Pshavela, who described the Kists as "a vengeful yet honourable people, who were locked in blood feuds with their neighbours but would respect the laws of hospitality, even unto death." This remote poverty-stricken northeast valley in Georgia, south of the Chechen border in the municipality of Akhmeta, is associated with being a breeding ground for terrorists. Due to its reputation for radical Islam, drugs and arms smuggling, lawlessness and banditry, the region has for many years been viewed as a black hole beyond the reach of the authorities.

BBC News reported that during the two wars between the Russian government forces and separatist rebels in Chechnya in the 1990s and 2000s, the Chechen population grew in the Pankisi Gorge. Murad Batal al-Shishani wrote. "The valley became a refuge for those wanting to flee the fighting and, as the Russian state re-established control, rebel fighters seeking protection from attack". In the build up to the Iraq War in 2003, Georgia was pressured by Russia and the United States to repress the threat of al-Qaeda, with terrorist training camps believed to be located in this region. In 2005, France claimed al Qaeda operatives were manufacturing the biochemical ricin in the valley, and scrambled fighter jets to bomb the gorge. According to Sky News, the US also sent military advisers to train Georgian troops to fight the militants in a US$64 million dollar operation. Many Chechen fighters currently operating in Syria and Iraq for the Islamic State (IS) were recruited from the Pankisi Gorge, unemployed men who are believed to have been easy and willing jihadists. Daniel McLaughlin reporting for the Irish Times stated, "Beso Kushtanashvili (18) was at least the sixth young Muslim from Pankisi Gorge to die fighting in Syria. His parents told Georgian media they thought he was working in Turkey." One particular local fighter from Pankisi, with a distinctive red beard, was born in the nearby village of Birkiani and is today the commander of the newly formed al-Qaeda-affiliated Islamic State of Iraq and the Levant (ISIS). Growing up, Omar al-Shishani (real name Tarkhan Batirashvili) was a mountain shepherd boy, who decided to become a soldier. He served during the Russo-Georgia war in 2008, and was about to become an officer when he was diagnosed with tuberculosis. Katie Stallard, Moscow Correspondent for Sky News, reported that his life quickly spiralled out of control when he left the Georgian army on medical grounds. He was arrested in Birkiani not long after he left the army and was imprisoned for the possession of illegal weapons. A Sky News interview with his father, Teimuraz Batirashvili, revealed that Omar felt his country did not need him and he planned to start a holy war for god. His father, a Christian, still lives in a village close to Birkiani and has a small, simply furnished house. His son is now one of the most feared jihadists in the Middle East.

* * *

Leaving behind the wilderness of the Caucasus Mountains, Chris drives the last 70km to Mtskheta, a UNESCO World Heritage town north of Tbilisi. Parking outside the newly built Museum of Archaeology, we admire the beautiful Jvari church that sits atop a hill east of the town. Built in 585 AD, the church is located on the site where a sacred wooden cross was erected in the 4th century AD. Mtskheta was the capital of the early Georgian Kingdom of Iberia from the 3rd century BC to 5th century AD, and it was here that Christianity had first been proclaimed the state religion of Kartli in 337 AD. Still the headquarters of the Georgian Orthodox Church, we walk through the tourist town and make a circuit around a large defensive wall that surrounds the Svetitskhoveli Cathedral, or "the Living Pillar Cathedral". Built in the shape of an elongated cross, we crank our necks and look up at the stout cylindrical tower, with a steep cone roof and admire the carvings on the stone work.

In the arched entrance to the cathedral's main courtyard, a babushka dressed in black reaches out a hand with a twinkle in her eye. Chris drops a few coins into her palm and she thanks him with a toothless grin. We step inside this ancient monument, and feel immediately dwarfed by the enormous interior with towering stone columns. A group of women wearing headscarves sing and light candles at the gold altar, their soft voices echoing throughout the cathedral. Examining a giant pillar decorated with frescoes, I read a tourist leaflet in the light of my mobile phone, and discover that it is believed Christ's actual robe lies buried here. According to this ancient myth, retold by Roger Rosen in his book 'Georgia: A Sovereign Country of the Caucasus', a Jew called Elioz was in Jerusalem at the time of Jesus' crucifixion. He returned to Georgia with the robe that he had bought from a Roman soldier in Golgotha. On his arrival to Mtskheta, his sister Sidonia had apparently taken it from him and immediately died in a passion of faith. No one could prise the robe from her grasp, so it was allegedly buried with her.

On the spot where the robe was buried with Sidonia, a large cedar tree is believed to have sprouted from the ground. Three centuries later Saint Nino ordered the tree be cut down and used in the construction of a church. St Nino had travelled to Iberia from Cappadocia (Turkey) to carry out missionary work, and converted the Georgian queen, Nana, to Christianity. The pagan king of Iberia Mirian III eventually agreed to adopt Christianity as the state religion after St Nino helped cure him of an illness. From the cedar tree, the foundations of the church were built using seven wooden columns. Bizarrely, the seventh column is believed to have had magical properties, and rose into the air by itself. Thankfully it returned to earth after St Nino prayed through the night. A sacred liquid is rumoured to have flowed from the magical seventh column that cured people of all diseases. Chris examines the stone pillar for signs of this sacred liquid, and confirms that the construction of this new stone cathedral in the 11th century, must have plugged any leakages. The Svetitskhoveli Cathedral was named after this rather strange supernatural miracle; Sveti meaning "pillar" and tskhoveli meaning "life-giving" or "living".

Studying the tomb of Erekle II, who was the king of Kartli and Kakheti from 1762 to 1798, I observe a family of Georgian tourists who snap photographs inside the cathedral. I get the distinct impression they are not here to worship god, but rather to enjoy a day out visiting a historic monument in a pretty old Georgian town. We pass through an ancient stone archway that is tall and incredibly narrow. A woman lights a candle and crosses her chest. A western tourist wearing a Norwegian football shirt walks past with a sarong tied around his waist - an attempt by the church to prevent offending worshippers by hiding his skinny white legs. He sheepishly nods a hello and then gazes dreamily at the cathedral's ceiling.

Returning to the road, a police car tailgates us all the way out of town. It eventually overtakes, and a policewoman glances over her shoulder at our licence plate. Chris thunders south to Tbilisi and we enter into battle with the speeding traffic. The highway begins to feel more like a racetrack, with high performance vehicles cutting dangerously across lanes. Located in the south-east of Eurasia, Tbilisi grew up along an established East-West transit route, and has profited for many centuries from the trade of spices, silk and slaves and in more recent times from oil from Azerbaijan. A modern commercial city, the capital of Georgia has experienced rapid economic growth since the pro-Western Mikheil Saakashvili and his Georgian National Movement party came to power in 2003 following the Rose Revolution. In spite of this,

Saakashvili government suffered a political crisis in 2007, when opposition parties staged large street protests. They accused the new government of corruption and artificial price rises that had led to increasing poverty.

The impressive bow-shaped Bridge of Peace, which is covered in wafers of glass that are encased in a steel membrane, arches across the Mtkvari River. Chris identifies the grand Presidential Palace, with a beautiful glass dome on the roof and the Georgian national flag at full mast. Several times the size of the White House, the history of the presidential palace only dates back to 2004, after the Rose Revolution, when the newly elected Saakashvili decided to build this grand building. It officially opened in 2009, at a time when thousands of Georgians were still living in makeshift refugee camps after the war with Russia. Driving towards Freedom Square, steel and glass office buildings and international hotels rise like temples to the modern world. Chris screeches to a halt outside a bakery on Rustaveli Avenue. He returns with two slices of khachapuri, a delicious cheese pastry and two slices of kubdari, which is similar but with meat. The strong cheese tastes like ricotta and the meat pastry is bursting with minced beef and finely chopped onion. We pay a cheerful parking tout a few Georgian lari to keep an eye on the Volvo, while we tour around Tbilisi's fantastic world class museums and galleries and delve into Georgia's ancient past.

During Greek classical times in the 5th to 4th centuries BC, the two principal kingdoms in Georgia were Colchis in the west (home of the mythological Golden Fleece and the site of Greek colonies) and Kartli (also known as Iberia) in the east and south. By 66 BC the Roman Empire had conquered the Caucasus region, and for 400 years these Georgian kingdoms were partners and operated as

Roman client states. King Mirian III's adoption of Christianity as the state religion in 337 AD had the powerful effect of tying these kingdoms to the neighbouring Eastern Roman Empire, which grew into the Byzantine Empire and exerted a strong influence on Georgia for an additional thousand years.

Christianity was adopted in Georgia following the missionary work of Saint Nino of Cappadocia. According to the Orthodox Church of America, Nino belonged to a Greek-speaking Roman family from Kolastra (Cappadocia, Turkey). She was a relative of Saint George and came to Georgia from Constantinople in the 4th century AD. Conflicting sources state that she may have been from Jerusalem, Rome or Gaul in modern-day France. After her success at converting the Georgian king and queen to Christianity, Iberia became known as Kartli, with the Caucasian Iberian Georgians tracing their origins to the myth that Noah's great-great grandson, Kartlos, was their ancestor.

The Christian religion had begun as a Jewish sect in the middle of the 1st century AD. Originating in the Levant region of the Middle East, it was founded on the oral teachings of Jesus of Nazareth, as described in the New Testament. Similar to Judaism, Christianity (and Islam) recognised itself as an Abrahamic faith and spread rapidly to Syria, Mesopotamia, Asia Minor and Egypt. Growing in size and importance over a few hundred years, Christianity became the official state religion of the Roman Empire by the end of the 4th century AD and replaced other religions that the Romans had practised in the past. Despite there being no evidence to prove if Abraham ever existed, this mythological figure is believed by Christians, Jews and Muslims to be the son of Terah, the 10th in descent from Noah. He was thought to have been born in

Ur, in modern-day Iraq, near to the Euphrates River with approximate dates ranging between 2100-1800 BC, and is most famously thought of as the founder of monotheism (the belief that there is only one god).

In the centuries following the Roman Empire and Georgia's adoption of Christianity, a new alternative religion called "Islam" emerged in the Middle East. Born out of the teachings of Muhammad (570-632 AD) from Mecca, a city in modern-day Saudi Arabia, he became recognised as the last in a series of prophets, alongside Adam, Abraham, Moses and Jesus. In 622 AD, it is believed Muhammad moved to the neighbouring city of Medina, where he was successful at bringing surrounding desert tribes under his control. His following quickly grew, and by the time of his death in 632 AD (at the age of 62) he had successfully united the tribes of Arabia into a single religious polity following the conquest of Mecca. Islam spread with the distribution of the Quran along trade routes; a book believed to be of divine guidance revealed from god to Muhammad through the angel Gabriel over a period of 23 years.

The Islamic Seljuk Turk invasions of Christian Georgia in the 11th century AD, led to the Latin Roman Catholic Church launching The First Crusades against the expanding Seljuq dynasty. The Seljuqs had originated from the Qynyk branch of the Oghuz Turks, who lived in the 9th century on the edge of the Muslim world north of the Caspian and Aral Sea in Central Asia. During the 10th century, the Oghuz had come into close contact with Muslim cities and began a process of assimilation with Persian culture. Establishing the Seljuq Empire at the peak of its power, which stretched west from Persia into neighbouring Anatolia (Turkey), they became targets of the First Crusade. They were eventually driven out of

Georgia by the young Bagrationi king Davit Aghmashenebeli "David the Builder" in 1089-1125, who defeated them at Didgori in 1122 and recaptured nearby Tbilisi and made it his capital. Whether you view The Crusades as a defensive war against Islamic conquests or as an aggressive attempt by Christians from the West to expand their power, one fact remains; a new enduring form of human conflict had emerged in the region of the Black Sea and this time it was fuelled by religious militarism.

Exploring Tbilisi's Freedom Square, Chris points out the location of the Tiflis bank robbery. In 1907, Vladimir Lenin, Joseph Stalin and Maxim Litvinov held a secret meeting in Berlin to discuss staging a robbery to obtain funds to purchase arms. The group agreed that Stalin, then known as Koba and the Armenian Simon Ter-Petrossian, known as Kamo, would organise the robbery of the Tiflis branch of the State Bank of the Russian Empire. Stalin, aged 29, was living in Tiflis at the time with his wife Ekaterina and newborn son Yakov. Stalin was experienced at organising robberies, and his exploits had helped him gain a reputation as the regions leading financier. Stalin's childhood friend, Kamo, led a criminal gang called "the Outfit". He had been described by Stalin as "a master of disguise", and was referred to by Lenin as his "Caucasian bandit". On 26th June the twenty organisers, including Stalin, met near Freedom Square - previously called Erivan Square under Imperial Russia. The gang attacked the police and military using explosives and guns, and robbed a stagecoach that was transporting money through Freedom Square between the post office and the bank. Kamo's gang had smuggled explosives into Tiflis by hiding them inside a sofa. Forty people were tragically killed during the attack and fifty injured, with the revolutionaries successfully escaping with 341,000 rubles, the equivalent of approximately US$3 million.

Mesmerised by events in Tbilisi's turbulent past, I glance across Freedom Square towards the City Hall, and I try to imagine the thousands of demonstrators who had gathered here during the Rose Revolution in 2003. Widespread protests over the disputed parliamentary elections had ultimately led to a change of power in Georgia, and the election of a pro-Western government. This radical shift in political and economic direction in Georgia had not been without its opposition, and two years later Freedom Square had witnessed a violent act of protest at the new government's alliance with the west. BBC News reported, "In 2005, US President George W. Bush and Georgian President Mikheil Saakashvili addressed a crowd of around 100,000 people in celebration of the 60th anniversary marking the end of World War II." During the event, Georgian-Armenian Vladimir Arutyunian threw a live grenade at President Bush while he was speaking, in an unsuccessful attempt to assassinate him.

* * *

Standing in the centre of Freedom Square, Si shields his eyes from the sun and points out a beautiful gold sculpture atop a column depicting Saint George on horseback slaying the dragon. Under the Soviet Union, the square was renamed "Lenin Square" and accommodated a large statue to Vladimir Lenin, which was symbolically removed in August 1991. The Liberty Monument depicting St George slaying the dragon was installed on the same spot on 23rd November 2006. As a child, I had mistakenly considered the symbol of St George to be a legend that belonged exclusively to England, and I smile at the thought of how influenced our own country had been by stories that were spread to the farthest reaches of the Roman Empire. St George was in fact born in Lydda, Roman Palestine, and was a soldier in the Roman army before he was immortalised in the tale of St George and the Dragon. His father was a Greek Christian from Cappadocia in Turkey and his mother was a Christian from Roman Palestine. Despite the fact that this young soldier had never visited England in his lifetime, St George was admired by our ancestral countrymen as a man who, according to legend, fought on their side in The Crusades and the Hundred Years' War.

In 1348, King Edward III created the Order of the Garter under the patronage of St George. It was the recognition of the highest order of chivalry, and the most prestigious honour in England and the United Kingdom after the Victoria Cross and George Cross. Following the union of England and Scotland in 1707, the celebration of St George's Day became less popular. But in recent years, growing patriotism in England has seen people celebrating it on the 23rd of April (the day of his death in 303 AD) by flying or adorning the St George's cross flag. The story of St George and the Dragon is eastern in origin and according to the Golden Legend it took place somewhere in Libya. It belongs to the genre of chivalric romance that was popular in the aristocratic circles of High Medieval and Early Modern Europe, describing stories of fantastic adventures of heroic wandering knights.

I study the gold horse that rears up as St George bravely prepares to launch his lance at the dragon and save the king's daughter. Suddenly, I'm reminded of the nomadic horsemen, who once ruled the Pontic steppe around the north shores of the Black Sea, hundreds of years before the birth of Christianity. Instead of St George, I imagine a proud Sarmatian warrior wearing heavy armour standing in his place, or a Scythian horse bowman slaying a griffin. Debating this thought with Si, we come to the conclusion that national identity does not suddenly appear; it evolves slowly over time through the assimilation of cultures, borrowing from one another strengths and discarding weaknesses.

Heading east out of Tbilisi, Si pinpoints the World Heritage cave monasteries of Davit Gareja in the Kakheti region of Georgia. Reaching the small town of Sagarejo, 58km east of Tbilisi, we turn off the highway and traverse a narrow unpaved sand track towards the frontier with Azerbaijan. The further south we drive the drier and more barren the landscape becomes, and before long we find ourselves cutting across a semi-desert landscape void of any trees. It feels like we have arrived in the Middle East with a hot, dry wind scorching our tanned faces. The Volvo purrs effortlessly, seeming unconcerned by the dramatic rise in temperature as we scan the area for jackals and vultures that inhabit this region of Georgia. Passing through a chain of small rural settlements hidden deep in the Georgian countryside, we eventually join a deserted tarmac road that traverses a ridge across the vast open plains. Absorbing the striking otherworldly landscape at sunset, Si spots a derelict building atop a steep cone shaped hill that rises above the small rural settlement of Udabno. We agree to check it out, and turn sharply off the highway and climb at a forty-five degree angle to the summit. We look in awe over one of the most spectacular views we have ever seen. Small orange lights in the village below flicker in the windows of the houses, and in the far distance Tbilisi illuminates the horizon like a burning inferno. Talking in low whispers, we drink a beer beneath a dazzling night sky. Watching a shooting star zip above our heads, I quickly make a wish. I immediately regret what I wished for, so I sip my beer and wait patiently for the next shooting star to arrive before wishing for something a little more inspiring.

The enormous red fireball rises in the east and kick starts us into action. It's just after 6am and the desert landscape and low hills are flooded in a rich tangerine light. We edge the Volvo back down onto the road and pass through the small settlement of Udabno. We approach an exceptionally tall farmer with an eleven o'clock shadow, who drives a herd of cattle past a row of abandoned farmhouses. He taps a young calf's backside with his rubber boot, causing it to panic and run into the road. Si slams on the brakes and I hear the bottle of wine that Annalise had given to us as a gift in Odessa roll under my seat. A flock of blue-cheeked bee-eaters take flight, their bright green plumage glowing against the yellow landscape.

Continuing to push deeper into the Gareja Desert, we turn left off the tarmac road and drive down a steep, dusty unpaved track that leads to Dodo's Rka, literally meaning "the horn of Dodo". Dodo was one of the disciples of Davit Garejeli, one of The Thirteen Assyrian Fathers, who arrived from Mesopotamia in the 6th century AD to strengthen Christianity in the country. Scaling the last twenty metres on foot, we approach a cave that has newly fitted glazed windows. A black BMW is parked outside. While Si photographs a beautiful ornate cast iron bell, I look out across the colourful rock-hewn landscape towards the much larger Lavra monastery. The thick wooden door to Dodo's Rka creaks open and three women dressed in black scurry out. They avoid eye contact and make their way hurriedly down the dusty track. A large Orthodox priest, with a bushy beard and long hair tied back in a ponytail, fills the doorway and throws us an unwelcome stare. I ask him if it would be possible to take a look inside, but he shakes his head despairingly and says "No". Surprised by his unfriendly manner, in a country famous for its incredible hospitality, we both shift uncomfortably in the heat.

Si frowns. 'May I ask why?'

He folds his arms, and sighs. 'What country?'

'We have travelled here from England.'

I fight a smile at the realisation that it feels like we have suddenly been catapulted back to biblical times.

He points across the valley. 'You can visit the Lavra monastery, ten kilometres up the hill.'

Turning sharply away, the priest takes a moment to rub a dirt mark off the hood of his shiny BMW, before disappearing inside his cave and bolting the door.

* * *

Approaching the gates of the impressive fortified Lavra Monastery the luna landscape below looks dramatic, with the colours of the rocks fading from yellow to deep red and purple. Two soldiers walk past wearing military uniform with rifles slung over their shoulders. Chris informs me they could be Azeri guards, who last year took over the Udabno Monastery on top of the ridge. During Soviet occupation, the authorities had drawn borders in such a way that the complex had ended up partly in Georgian territory and partly in Azerbaijan territory. The border dispute seems a long way from ever being resolved, with the Azerbaijan government claiming the Udabno Monastery is an Albanian cultural monument.

Entering the heavily fortified stone structure through a gateway on the middle level, we study walls decorated with reliefs illustrating stories of the monks' harmony with the natural world. Ducking through a low doorway, we poke our heads into a network of caves that have been used to create cellars, bakeries, smithies and living quarters for the monks, which were intentionally uncomfortable since the monks believe they were meant for a life of asceticism. We descend to a courtyard where we find the caves of Davit (David) and his Kakhetian disciple Lukiane, and visit the Peristsvaleba "Transfiguration Church", which accommodates their tombs. The outer monastery walls and the watchtower were built in the 18th century, but the church and the caves were first established in the 6th century. Many important Christian manuscripts were copied and translated here and a celebrated school of fresco painting developed.

In the 12th century, Georgian king Demetre I, the author of the famous Georgian hymn 'Thou Art a Vineyard', chose Davit Gareja as his place of confinement after he abdicated the throne. In 1265, the Mongols destroyed the monastery complex and Giorgi V the Brilliant rebuilt it in the early 14th century. It was attacked soon after by the Turko-Mongol, Timur, who was one of the last great nomadic conquerors of the Eurasian steppe. Entering a period of relative peace, the monastery met its fate on Easter night in 1615, when Persian Shah Abbas soldiers killed 6,000 monks and destroyed most of their artistic treasures.

Wary of poisonous vipers that inhabit the southern Kakheti region, Chris scrambles up a steep path that leads to the Udabno monastery. Inside, 10th century frescoes show episodes from the life of St. David Garejeli, with one in particular depicting the story of the deer that had apparently given Davit and Lukiane milk when they were wandering hungry through this remote wilderness. We look down from the top of the ridge over the plains and low hills into Azerbaijan. Chris points to the southwest horizon and tells the story of how it was rumoured Davit once performed a pilgrimage to Jerusalem. According to the myth, when he left the holy city he picked up three stones and put them in his bag. That night he was visited by an angel, who told him that the three stones contained all of the spiritual treasure of the city and that he must return two of them. He was allowed to keep one for himself and, that stone, supposedly containing one third of the spiritual wealth of Jerusalem, was allegedly once kept inside the Lavra's main church.

I take a moment to appreciate the striking desert landscape. So much of our lives in the 21st century have been influenced by religion, philosophy, astronomy, mathematics and science that first originated in this region of the world. Humanity once lived a relatively nomadic self-sufficient existence. Tribes of hunter-gatherers would migrate with the seasons and their food source. But during a period of major climate change after the last ice age around 11000 BC, much of the Earth began to experience long dry seasons. This change in climatic conditions favoured annual plants that die off during this period, leaving behind a tuber or dormant seed. Putting more energy into making seeds than woody growth, these plants provided hunter-gatherers with large quantities of readily available pulses and wild grains, and enabled them to establish the first settled villages. This source of readily available food spawned the development of human technology, and a period in the evolution of humanity we call the Neolithic era.

The birth of Neolithic culture is considered to have first originated in the Levant in Jericho (modern-day West Bank), around 10200 to 8800 BC, but also separately and independently in northern and southern China. Developing directly from the Epipaleolithic Natufian culture, the peoples living in the Levant region were among the first humans to gather and consume these wild grains. Evolving a sedentary way of life, geological and archaeological evidence suggests that the onset of a second natural shift in climate associated with the "Big Freeze", may have forced these people to start planting and growing cereals. The Big Freeze (known as the Younger Dryas), was a period of cold climatic conditions and drought, which took place between approximately 10800 and 9500 BC and is thought to have been caused by the collapse of the North American ice sheets. The subsequent rise of farming communities in the Levant by 10200-8800 BC spread to Asia Minor, North Africa and North Mesopotamia and fuelled the development of modern civilisation.

Although the Levant and the Fertile Cresent lay claim to being the first known regions of the planet to be cultivated; farming evolved at least three times, with independent development of agriculture occurring in both northern and southern China. The earliest evidence found includes the Nanzhuangtou culture around (9500-9000 BC), that was unearthed under a peat bog on the Yellow River near Lake Baiyangdian in northern China. Along with evidence of the domestication of the dog, over forty-seven pieces of pottery were discovered at the site. It is also one of the earliest sites showing evidence of millet cultivation dating to around 8500 BC. The Peiligang culture (7000 to 5000 BC) was a Neolithic culture located around the Yi-Luo river basin in Hunan, southern China.

It existed during the same time as its neighbour, the Pengtoushan culture (7500–6100 BC), which was centred primarily on the central Yangtze River. The thought of these three very different civilisations in the Levant and northern and southern China, emerging during a period on Earth when humans had first been presented with the possibility of leading a settled existence strikes both myself and Chris with awe. Agriculture had enabled humans in these separate regions of the world to build strong communities and evolve common principles, shared beliefs and philosophy. Civilisation has only recently been given a start.

Twelve

In the blazing sun, Si slips on his shades and we drive west to Rustavi in the heart of the Kvemo Kartli province. Once a major industrial town that was established by Stalin during the Soviet era, it is home to a 45% population of Azeris; a Turkic-speaking predominantly Shia Muslim ethnic group who live mainly in the Republic of Azerbaijan and Iran. We cruise through the dusty streets, lined with decaying concrete tower blocks and Khrustchev apartments. Ironworks, steelworks and chemical plants once thrived here, some are still in operation, but after the collapse of the Soviet Union in 1991 the town hit rock bottom. Crime and unemployment today is high and the population has declined at an incredible rate.

Looping around Tbilisi, we continue to push west and enter the province of Shida Kartli. We arrive in Gori in the early afternoon; a city that is the birthplace of none-other than Joseph Stalin. We cut through the recently remodelled Stalin Square, where elderly folk, young families and courting couples relax on park benches and absorb the summer sun. Si locates the controversial statue of Soviet dictator, Joseph Stalin, and we look up at this effigy of a man who is synonymous with revolution, war and mass genocide. Beside the statue stands a small wood and mud brick house. It appears to have been physically removed from its original location and placed right here in the square. I read an information plaque, and discover it is the actual dwelling where Stalin lived for the first four years of his life.

Joseph Stalin was born in Gori in 1878 and was the son of a cobbler who suffered from alcoholism. He won a scholarship at the age of sixteen to attend the Tiflis Spiritual Seminary, but he was expelled in 1899 for failing to attend an exam. Around this time, Stalin discovered the writings of Vladimir Lenin and joined the Russian Social-Democratic Labour Party, a Marxist group. When Lenin formed the Bolsheviks, Stalin eagerly joined up and became involved with revolutionary activities in the Caucasus, by organising workers unions in Tbilisi and setting up an illegal workers press in Batumi. He later became involved politically with Lenin throughout the revolution of 1905 and 1917, and became close to Trotsky and Khrushchev, who helped to cement his political ideology. After the Civil War, Lenin wrote a political testament in 1922 stating that Stalin was too coarse and power hungry and advised Party members to remove Stalin from the post of General Secretary. By the time of Lenin's death in 1924, Stalin had grown too powerful for anyone to prevent him from carrying out the terrible purges in Tbilisi, the mass transportation of millions to the Gulag death camps and the starvation of an estimated five to six million people in Ukraine. Stalin's rule of the largest country in the world for three decades was a brutal journey, which resulted in the death of approximately 20 million people in his mission to rapidly turn a poor rural economy into a vast industrial nation.

On the outskirts of Gori we top up with fuel at a rusty petrol station. Si asks the guy operating the pump for directions to the town of Tskhinvali.

He looks concerned and shakes his head. 'No, no,' he mumbles, waggling his finger.

The guy hooks the nozzle back onto the pump and uses his hands to illustrate that the road is blocked. I show him the road map and he taps an oily finger on Tskhinvali.

He waggles his finger at us again, and shakes his head vehemently. 'No good.'

We suddenly realise the road passes through the disputed northern part of the Shida Kartli region, which has been controlled by the authorities of the self-proclaimed Republic of South Ossetia since 1992. During the Russo-Georgia War in 2008, the town of Tskhinvali was the centre of a three-day battle when Georgian forces launched a surprise attack to regain control of the region. In response, the Russian air force bombed an armament depot about 10km north of Gori, damaging several apartment buildings and killing sixty civilians. Tensions and the occasional outbreaks of violence in and around the borders of the separatist region of South Ossetia rose after Saakashvili's pro-Western government came to power in Tbilisi in 2003. By 2007, it seemed that if you did get through the many Russian, Georgian and Ossetian checkpoints around the border, there was a good chance you would either been turned around or hauled in for questioning. Reminded of the importance of researching the road ahead, we try to remove the thought from our minds of what might have happened if we had been using satellite navigation and had not needed to ask the petrol station attendant for directions.

Joining the E60 highway, our worst fears are confirmed when we see a speeding convoy of army trucks crammed full of soldiers heading in the direction of South Ossetia. During the three day war in South Ossetia in 2008, cyber warfare had coincided with military action for the first time, and diplomats in the United States and Europe blamed Russia for provoking the conflict and criticised the country for invading Georgia. Putin on the other hand, believed that the US had encouraged Georgia to attack the autonomous region, and accused the United States of orchestrating the conflict in Georgia to benefit one of its presidential election candidates. Although Georgia has no significant oil or gas reserves, its territory hosts part of the Baku-Tbilisi-Ceyhan pipeline supplying Europe and the US. According to Anne Grearan at the Associated Press, this was a key factor in the United States' support for Georgia allowing the West to reduce its reliance on Middle Eastern oil, bypassing Russia and Iran.

* * *

Chris takes the wheel and we head further along the highway to the bustling ancient town of Kutaisi. Georgia's second largest city, Kutaisi was once the capital of the ancient kingdom of Colchis, with archaeological evidence indicating that the city functioned as the capital as early as the second millennium BC. In the first half of the 3rd century BC the author, Apollonius Rhodius, wrote Argonautica; a Greek epic poem about Jason and the Argonauts and their journey to Colchis. Several historians believe that Apollonius considered Kutaisi on the Rioni River to be Jason's final destination, as well as the residence of King Aeëtes, while other academics believe it could have been nearby Vani. Today, the city of Kutaisi is the capital of the western region of Imereti. It is the gateway into the Caucasus from the west across the Black Sea, and witnessed the arrival of the Greeks and the Ottoman Turks. For long periods of time Georgia was divided into regions and ruled separately, but in the 11th and 12th centuries it was here that the great united Georgian kingdom got its start.

We pass dozens of roadside stalls selling handmade wooden deckchairs, large freestanding hammocks and beaded car seat covers. Chris spots a bustling market up ahead on the corner of a busy road junction, so we park up and go on the hunt for food. Absorbing the lively atmosphere, Chris weaves ravenously between stalls piled high with red onions and beef tomatoes, purple aubergines and enormous watermelons. I tap dance through the mud and the puddles as we make our way over to a white building at the far side of the market. Entering a cosy café, with starched white tablecloths and green paisley patterned wallpaper, we cheerfully greet the woman behind the counter with short black hair and piercing blue eyes. Chris rubs his hands together in anticipation of some tasty local grub. He points at the bowl of stew that an old man is slurping in the corner of the café. The friendly woman wearing a red apron brings two steaming bowls of kharcho to our table, which consists of rice, vegetables, herbs and large chunks of beef on the bone. Tucking into our spicy market traders' breakfast, the woman watches us with intrigue from behind the counter.

Chris puts up his thumb as he swallows a mouthful of food. 'Red chilli,' he grins.

I hold up a basil leaf. 'Fresh herbs, strong,' I add, flexing my biceps.

The woman laughs and quickly offers us more bread. Virtually licking our bowls clean, we sit back and nurse our swollen stomachs. She joins our table and we introduce ourselves. Mzia is originally from Abkhazia and it suddenly occurs to me that, like Annalise from the campground in Odessa, she too could be one of the 250,000 refugees who had been displaced from their homes as a result of the conflict. Mzia asks where we are from and gasps when she hears "London". She places a hand over her heart and says, "Big Ben." The door swings open and a crowd of hungry market traders march into the café. Not wishing to occupy the table longer than necessary, we pay for the food and bid Mzia good day before waddling back to the Volvo.

On the road to Baghdati, Chris battles against a car transporter from Turkey that tries to run us off the highway. We begin to see rural folk at the roadside selling flat loaves of bread, corn on the cob, a variety of mushrooms, handcrafted woven baskets and terracotta pots. Catching the disturbing sight of a guy snapping a stray dog's neck and throwing it into a ditch, we continue to head south to Vani through the green forested hills. Turning off the main highway, we wind our way through beautiful tranquil villages, with trees heavily weighed down with large red pomegranates. Palm trees grow in the garden of an old derelict house; a clear sign that we are returning once more to the warm semitropical climate of the Black Sea region of the Caucasus.

A brown sign pointing to a wine cellar grabs my attention. We walk down a narrow track to a large house with bunches of juicy green grapes spilling over the wall. I peer through the vines and call over to an old chap tending to his garden. He looks startled at first, but then breaks into an enormous smile and waves us over to the front of the house. Swinging open two towering metal gates, he greets us both like we are old friends. Chris asks the guy, with white shortly cropped hair, if he has any wine for sale. Completely unfazed by the request, Giorgi kindly invites us into his home. We enter a large farm kitchen with a stone floor and a cast iron stove. A rosy-cheeked grandmother wearing half-moon spectacles and a floral print apron, smiles at us warmly as she chops vegetables on a wooden kitchen table. Leading us through the house, we are shown into a grand dining hall with a beautiful handcrafted wooden staircase that leads to an L-shaped balcony. A large fireplace dominates the room with a height adjustable rack for barbecuing meat. Unveiling a banqueting table hidden beneath a dust sheet, Giorgi proudly shows us the unfurnished rooms leading off the balcony in this newly renovated part of the building. In November, after Giorgi has harvested his grapes and produced a fresh batch of homemade wine, he plans to open the house to guests. You can see from the excitement in his face that this renovation project has given him a new lease of life.

* * *

Exiting the house, we pass a small garage and I see a Russian army jeep parked on a ramp. Si grabs his camera and asks Giorgi to stand beside it. He throws back his shoulders with pride and strikes a pose. Herding us into a nearby outbuilding, Giorgi whips a hosepipe out of a barrel. He sucks firmly on the end of the pipe and siphons white wine directly into a glass. Expertly swirling the pale green liquid around to awaken the flavours, he offers us a taste. I take a sip and nod my head with delight at the cool crisp taste of the wine. Si follows suit and his eyes spring open. He enthusiastically congratulates Giorgi on its great depth of flavour and bouquet. Filling a large glass jug to the top, Giorgi invites us to sit at a table on the sunny patio. He explains that the grapes are crushed in a machine and the juice and skins are poured into an enormous ceramic clay jar called a "kvevri". He points down at a manhole cover and I presume there is a kvevri under the patio. Buried in the ground up to its neck, the kvevri can maintain a stable temperature for fermentation during the winter. This method of winemaking dates back 7,000 years, when the people living in this region of the southern Caucasus discovered that wild grape juice fermented into an alcohol when it was left buried in a shallow pit. The entire winemaking process takes place within the kvevri, from initial fermentation right through to maturation. I'm fascinated to learn that the skins are left on the grapes (and in hotter regions the stems as well), which produces wines of exceptional flavour and complexity and gives it the green hue typical to Georgian white wine.

During the Soviet period wines produced in Georgia were extremely popular, especially in comparison with other wines from Moldavia and Crimea that were also available on the Soviet market. According to statistics published by the Pacific Wine marketing group, in 1950 vineyards in Georgia occupied 143,000 acres of land and by 1985 it grew to 316,000 acres, with an annual production of 881,000 tons. The heyday of wine production in Georgia began to decline during Mikhail Gorbachev's 1985-87 anti-alcohol campaign, and it was virtually destroyed in 2006 when Georgian imports were banned by the Kremlin in reaction to Georgia's pro-Western stance and desire to join NATO. With news in February 2013 that Russia's import ban may soon be lifted Reuters reported, "Georgia's wine exports plunged from $81.4 million in 2005 to $29.2 million in 2007 and, have not fully recovered, reaching $64.9 million last year (2013)." Reuters also estimated that if the ban were to be lifted Georgia could potentially export 10 million bottles of wine to Russia every year.

Giorgi's wife calls from the kitchen and Giorgi returns moments later with plates of fresh home grown cucumber, pickled gherkin, beef tomatoes, red onion and a large metal platter filled with grilled shashlik lamb kebab meat, ham and strong soft white cheese. We sit in the sunshine and eat and drink until we are all red in the cheeks and feeling merry. Acting as toastmaster "tamada", Giorgi proposes numerous toasts throughout the meal and ensures the wine flows liberally. He explains in broken English that Georgians never toast with beer, only wine, beer being reserved for their enemies.

The grapevine is central to Georgian culture and tightly bound to their religious heritage, with most families growing their own grapes and producing their own wine. Other central pillars of Georgian culture are feasting and hospitality and we feel incredibly privileged to experience these ancient traditions in the authentic setting of Giorgi's garden.

After we have finished eating, Si shows Giorgi a few photographs on his camera from our trip. He seems intrigued by our journey, and reveals he has seen many changes in his country over the past fifty years. Life had been difficult during Soviet occupation as it had been after the collapse of communism, but Georgia was experiencing a new challenge – modernisation, at least for some, and tradition and family structure was breaking apart. Both his son and daughter have moved to Tbilisi, in the pursuit of careers that will allow them to own a brand new car and buy their own home. I get a sense Giorgi wonders how different his life might have been if he had been presented with the opportunity to travel, or the chance to enjoy more independence in his youth. I smile at the thought that life for Giorgi is changing too. The house and vineyard that had once provided wine for his family and community is now becoming a tourist business. The tradition of drinking wine shall continue inside these walls, only now it will be with strangers' friends and families instead of his own. Purchasing five litres of wine for 25 GEL (approximately €10), we firmly shake hands and thank Giorgi for his outstanding hospitality and fantastic tasting wine.

Stumbling back up the lane we grab an alcohol-induced siesta. Si immediately collapses onto the backseat and begins snoring like a wild beast. I recline my seat and throw a fleece over my head. I begin to dream we are sailing across the Black Sea in the Volvo. The rising motion of the water begins to build in intensity as we sail towards angry storm clouds. Carried steeply into the air by the growing swell, I grip tightly onto the steering wheel as the Volvo reaches tipping point and is launched down the steep side of a wave. Our cries are muffled by the tremendous boom of rain and sea water that smashes against the window screen. This action is repeated over and over again, carrying us steadily higher into the air and throwing us further and faster into the eye of the storm. Feeling the monstrous power of an enormous wave pick up the Volvo, we scream with all of our might as we are sent hurtling through the air and come violently crashing down into the foaming black water.

Approaching the once important city of Vani, at the spiritual heartland of the kingdom of Colchis, Si drives in circles around the deserted main square. Vani only received town status in 1981 and today has a small population of around 4,600 people. Asking a kid for directions to the archaeological site, he swings open the rear passenger door and leaps inside. Perched on top of our rucksacks, with his head pressed against the ceiling, he directs us up a steep hill and seems excited to meet a couple of old dudes from the country of Premiership football and Manchester United. Parking the Volvo below a derelict museum building, the kid leads us to the start of a footpath, before waving goodbye and sprinting hurriedly in the opposite direction. Unsure what it is we are here to see, we embrace the unknown and march along a trail into the open countryside.

This region of Georgia is shrouded in myth and legend, and it is thought to be the ultimate destination of Jason and the Argonauts in their quest to find the Golden Fleece. The mythological story of Jason first appeared in various literary works in the classical world of Greece and Rome. In the Greek epic poem Argonautica written by Apollonius Rhodius, Jason, a prince of Thessaly, was set a challenge by his uncle Pelias to sail to the land of Colchis on the eastern shores of the Black Sea. His quest was to find the Golden Fleece. According to the story Jason had a special ship built called the Argo, and this ship would carry him and 49 Greek rowers, known as the Argonauts, to the kingdom of Colchis. After surviving multiple hazards and life threatening challenges, the boat powered by the young men reached Poti and sailed up the Phasis (Rioni) River. It was here where King Aeetes received them in his capital, which experts think could be either the ancient city of Kutaisi or Vani. Rather sportingly, Aeetes agreed to give up the fleece if Jason sowed the teeth of a dragon with two fire-breathing bulls, which would produce a useful crop of armed men. Having travelled an awfully long way Jason accepted the challenge, but in a twist he secretly promised to marry Aeetes' daughter if she agreed to help him. This was advantageous to Jason as Medea was skilled with magic and potions, and she gave him a charm that enabled him to survive Aeetes' tests and to take the fleece from the dragon that guarded it.

* * *

A bronze BMW 4x4 draws up alongside us. Chris greets a friendly guy wearing a business suit who appears to be of Turkish origin. He is accompanied by an elderly gentleman dressed in a pale blue thobe and a white taqiyah (a short round prayer cap). They kindly offer us a ride to the top of the hill, where the archaeological site is apparently located. Dropping us off at the foot of a steep path, we thank them and walk the last hundred metres to a gate. I suddenly see a guy walking hurriedly towards us. Out of breath, he asks where we are going. He smiles when Chris explains that we had hoped to visit the ruins at Vani. Introducing ourselves, we discover Zurab is a professor of Archaeology at Tbilisi University. He kindly offers to show us around and escorts us to a newly excavated site. Still slightly out of breath, he pushes his glasses up the bridge of his nose and explains the ruins of a Roman wall with a moat has recently been discovered. So far they have unearthed a number of objects, including terracotta pots and amphora. Fascinated to have the opportunity to be one of only a handful of people to see a wall that has been hidden beneath the ground for more than a thousand years, we stand and absorb the sight of the mud covered stone blocks.

Zurab invites us to meet the director of the archaeological site, and we wander back down the hill to an awaiting taxi. Chris sits in the front with the driver and during the short journey I ask Zurab about his profession. With a smile he reveals that for a number of years he worked for the British petroleum company, BP Pipelines, as an archaeological and environmental advisor, but he now works as a lecturer at Tbilisi University. He informs us that the first excavations took place here at Vani in 1890, after locals reported gold ornaments being washed down the hill following heavy rain. They had since uncovered a city that is one of the main centres of ancient Colchis, which flourished from the 8th century BC (an astonishing 2,700 years ago). He believes that this could have been the city of King Aeetes, the ultimate destination where Jason would have sailed to in search of the Golden Fleece.

We arrive at an old wooden house with a porch and a beautifully carved fascia. Chris asks how old the property is and Zurab replies that it was built sometime at the beginning of the last century. The university had purchased the house and much of the land many years ago, in a bid to preserve the precious history that had been uncovered in this region. Leading us inside, we are introduced to the Director of Archaeology. He is a charismatic Georgian man in his early sixties, and is wearing a checked shirt and a camouflage green body warmer. Smoking a large cigar he reminds me of a military commander. Speaking German, the director kindly invites us to look inside the workshop where they are piecing together fragments of pottery using miniature bulldog clips and ceramic glue. It's truly fascinating to be given the opportunity to witness archaeology in progress.

Chris asks Zurab about gold panning with sheep's wool, and its connection with the story of Jason and the Argonauts going in search of a fleece made of gold. He smiles and confirms that this is almost certainly where the inspiration for the myth came from. When Zurab was a student at university he was involved in a field expedition in the Svaneti region in the north of the country. During his time there he had met an old man with a gold tooth.

When he asked the man where he came upon the gold, he revealed to Zurab that he had found a large gold nugget in the Inguri River. Geologists support the claim that villagers once used sheepskin to capture gold from mountain streams in the area. The fleece was used to line the bottom of the sandy streambeds, trapping any tiny grains of gold that built up there. This technique is a variation on panning used elsewhere in the world, and would have lead to sheepskins that were imprinted with flakes of gold and could have given rise to stories of a "Golden Fleece". Historic artefacts, including a bronze sculpture of a bird with a ram's head, were found in the villages of Svaneti and this provided support to the theory that the kingdom was once the source of the myth.

Leaving the archaeologists to continue with their work, we are driven further down the hill to an open-air museum. A woman wearing a white cotton shirt greets us at the entrance. Marine is the wife of the director, and first worked on the excavations at Vani in 1968 as a young student volunteer. She is hugely knowledgeable about the ruined city, and explains to us in perfect English that the site here at Vani was first established in 1947 and that the University of Tbilisi started excavations in 1950. Escorting us across the grounds, Marine reveals that Vani means "the place of rest". They had uncovered opulent burials from the 8th to the 1st centuries BC, and the archaeological research team believes Vani may have become a temple-city dedicated principally to the goddess Levcoteia. We stand around a strange stone altar from the 2nd to 1st century BC, and discover they had found many graves here and believe its existence may have been linked to the cult of death. Marine points out strong mud brick walls that were built towards the end of this period. The structure that existed here was destroyed in the 1st century BC, which they could conclude due to the fire damaged adobe bricks. According to historical records, Pompey the Great, the military and political leader of the late Roman Republic, had taken the city of Vani from Artoces - the king of Kartli. During this time, Pompieus was in pursuit of Mithridates the Great (the king of Pontus and Armenia Minor) who had fled to the kingdom of Colchis. Marine throws us both a sideways glance, and suggests that in pursuit of Artoces and Mithridates, Pompieus may have gone as far as the old capital of Mtskheta.

Continuing our walk around the site, Marine points out various walls and buildings and explains that a few years ago they had a fantastic new museum built. She had worked hard with her colleagues to make it the best museum imaginable. But in 2010 the local government had put into action dream-plans to construct a café inside the building, with a platform where tourists could drink coffee and look out across the beautiful countryside. They had been told to put all of the artefacts from the museum into storage and during the coming months they had set to work at completely destroying the museum building. Government funding was suddenly cut in the middle of the project, and the large museum has been left in a completely useless state ever since. Chris asks if many people come to visit the site.

She shakes her head. 'Nobody!' she cries. 'We've been completely shut down. The area is large with many interesting archaeological sites strung across the hilltops, but without the museum what is there for people to see?'

A security guard stands watch as we are invited to take a peek inside a temporary storage facility, where most of the artefacts are kept under lock and key. This is a great opportunity for us to examine ancient Greek columns up close, and ceramics typical to the region that date to around 500 BC. Marine excitedly points out various objects; ceramics glazed blue and green from the 3rd century BC, various items of pottery work and an adobe brick from the altar that had been preserved by fire. She explains that the battle that had taken place at Vani in the 1st century BC had actually been beneficial to their knowledge of the site, because the act of burning preserves certain materials, such as wood, better than if it had decomposed naturally. Marine stands close to a large temple carving of a cow's head. Sounding almost apologetic, she reveals that the truly valuable items are currently on display at the Museum of Archaeology in Tbilisi where her daughter works. On the upper floor of the museum they once had a fantastic bronze vessel depicting Greek gods, fine bronze casts and copies of gold adornments with animal designs. For a time they also had on display an original pair of pendants from an ornamental crown, with incredibly fine bird decorations. Chris asks Marine which items she had personally found, and she admits to having discóvered many great pieces. She is reluctant to lay claim to having found specific items as she feels that as an archaeologist you work as a team.

From the storage room we pass more ancient mud and brick walls and remains of monumental architecture. We follow Marine across a suspended metal walkway and view the museum that has been vandalised by the local government and temporarily abandoned. Scaffolding surrounds the walls of the structure and I notice a sunbleached billboard depicting the supposedly exciting plans for the new café that had never materialised. She explains that when they had first started work here at Vani in the 1960s and '70s, they had enjoyed a period of peace and a good standard of life in Georgia. The archaeological programs were well funded and education was valued. It was a golden age for archaeology in her country. She had worked on an archaeological dig with a female American student, who had visited Georgia many times since. This woman's generosity had saved them during the difficult years, following the collapse of the Soviet Union and Georgia's struggle for independence. By the 1980s, Mikhail Gorbachev had begun his policies of reform and the USSR disintegrated in just seven years. Chris mentions that we had seen the statue of Stalin in Gori, and Marine looks ashamed. Both her great aunt and uncle had been killed during the purges in Tbilisi after the Russian revolution, for no other reason than the fact that they were educated. Marine appears to be in a reflective mood. She shares with us how they had thought that after Georgia achieved independence from the USSR in 1991 their problems would be over. They had never imagined they would then suffer internal conflict, and that trouble would suddenly erupt in Abkhazia; people they had lived peacefully alongside for centuries. In the past, Georgians had married Abkhazians and vice versa. Russia's support of the Abkhazian separatists had caused a sudden and irreversible divide. Marine and her husband now live in Tbilisi during the winter and Vani in the summer months, but before independence they regularly made trips to the Abkhazian coast. With excitement in her voice she reveals that this beautiful region of the Caucasus is also home to the deepest known caves in the world, with the Krubera Cave stretching 2km beneath the Earth's surface. I ask her what would happen if she went to Abkhazia now, and she responds with surprise.

'We cannot go there. We would be put in jail. It is dangerous for us.'

Marine pauses sharply in front of a cluster of stone

ruins and her concerned face suddenly breaks into a smile. With great enthusiasm she explains that this was the main gateway into the city. Standing in the smooth stone doorway, she points out a ledge where a statue once stood. The inscription on the stone means goddess, and they believe the statue would have been female. Marine raises her eyebrows at the idea that this spiritual place has all of the hallmarks of the Dionysus cult. Dionysus was the god of the grape harvest, winemaking and wine and of ritual madness and ecstasy in Greek mythology. The polished stone step in the doorway is worn down in the middle by the many generations of Kartli who passed through these city gates. In front of this was a defence gate, which was made of wood and covered in iron. During the attack that had taken place here in the 1st century BC, the rope supports would have been cut and the defence gate slammed shut. She points out the vertical grooves in the pillars in which the gate would have slid down. Marine skilfully paints a mental picture of the events that may have occurred here in the seconds leading up to the end of this ancient city. In the moments of invasion, the people inside would have prayed for their lives at a shrine inside the gates. The grain found in these vessels was burnt, suggesting that eventually the gate had been destroyed by fire and the attackers had forced their way through.

Inspired by the absolute passion Marine feels for this magical site that looks out over the beautiful Georgian countryside, we thank her for taking the time to share it with us. Acknowledging our words of gratitude, we exchange contact details and make a promise to do all we can to share knowledge of the fascinating ongoing work here at Vani.

On our way out of town, we pause close to a road bridge that crosses the Sulori River, a tributary of the

Rioni. We stand at the railings and look downstream in the direction of the ancient Georgian port of Poti. I smile at the thought that during our journey there have been no fire-breathing bulls for us to yoke, dragons to slay, or gold and princesses for us to claim. But returning to the Volvo, our Argo, we drive into the fading light and continue on our path of knowledge, the most valuable prize.

Thirteen

A branch of the Tbilisi-Poti railway cuts northeast to Sukhumi on the coast of Abkhazia. Si finds our location on the map and we discover we are only 15km away from Zugdidi, a border town where many of the displaced Georgians were forced to flee their homes during the civil war in 1992. It feels strange to have finally reached the south of Abkhazia, after our epic diversion through the Caucasus Mountains.

A car from the Georgian controlled region of Abkhazia with "AZ" on the licence plate zooms past. During the Middle Ages Abkhazia was one of the most important kingdoms of Christian Georgia, but under Ottoman rule many Abkhaz converted to Islam between the 16th and 19th centuries. With a strong cultural identity and their own language, it seemed growing nationalism had risen quickly in Abkhazia. In actual fact, the process had been much more gradual. The Abkhaz speak a language that belongs to the north-western Caucasus group and they are closer culturally to the mountain people of southern Russia around the Sochi region, which from the 6th to the 11th centuries belonged to the kingdom of Lazica and kingdom of Abkhazia. From the moment Abkhazia fell under the control of the Georgian Soviet Republic in the

1930s, there had been official encouragement for the settling of large numbers of Georgians in the region. By 1989 only 18% of Abkhazia's population were Abkhaz and 46% were Georgian. With rising nationalism reaching its peak in 1991 following Georgia's independence from the Soviet Union, tensions rapidly developed into civil war.

At sunset, Si eagerly scans the Kolkheti wetlands for pelicans, storks and booted eagles as we skim alongside the vast national park. We soon arrive in the ancient Georgian port city of Poti and catch glimpses of the bustling commercial harbour, with towering spotlights that illuminate hundreds of sea containers in an eerie orange glow. The port is also home to the Georgian navy. It was severely bombed by Russian forces in 2008 and several ships were destroyed in the harbour. The Greeks founded Poti at the end of the 7th century BC and they established a trading colony here called Phasis. The city fell under Roman control following the invasion of the kingdom of Colchis by Pompey the Great in 73 BC, and it became a Roman client state for 400 years. During this period one of Eurasia's greatest roads was built, that is known today as the E70 highway. This spectacular 4,000km route crosses ten countries, from the Georgian port of Poti in the east to the Spanish town of A Coruña in Galicia in the west. Poti was later conquered by the Ottoman Empire in 1578, and was fortified into a Caucasian outpost with a large market dealing mainly in the slave trade of Circassian women who were famed for their beauty.

Travelling south towards Batumi and the Turkish Border, heavy rain forces us to park up for the night. We're disturbed around eleven o'clock by the blue and red flashing lights of a police vehicle. An officer in uniform appears at my window and shines a flashlight in my eyes.

He looks almost amused when he sees my surprised face wrapped up in a sleeping bag. He asks to see our passports and flicks through the pages. The police officer seems unsure what to make of us, and instructs us to follow him. Si hasn't got his contact lenses in his eyes, so we quickly swap seats in the small confines of the car. Driving with bare feet, I quickly reverse out onto the road and struggle to keep up with the speeding police car. We begin to fear the possibility of spending a night in the cells. After ten kilometres, the police car indicates and pulls off the highway opposite a brand new police checkpoint. The officer marches over and hands back our passports. He points in the direction of Batumi.

'Hotel, Batumi,' he orders.

We nod our heads obediently and throw him half a dozen "gmadlobts", before continuing swiftly south. Within minutes we cross into the autonomous region of Adjara, which we assume is outside of the officer's jurisdiction and one less problem he has to deal with tonight. We pass through the neon lit seaside resort of Kobulet, with its crowded bars and tacky nightclubs. Thumping dance music blasts from car speakers and boy racers in pimped up hatchbacks excitedly rev their engines and wheel spin between traffic lights. We devour a hamburger at a fast food kiosk. Si chats to the young guy working behind the counter and we discover Soloman is studying international business in Batumi. His name suggesting Jewish roots, he reveals there are many Jewish families living in Georgia. Keen to be of some assistance, he informs us there are a number of campsites close to the larger resort town of Batumi. Wishing Solomon luck we continue on our journey. A few kilometres north of Batumi, Si spots a small sign with a hand-painted drawing of a tent pointing towards the beach. We turn off the main highway and weave along a sand track that crosses the Batumi-Tbilisi coastal railway line. In the dead of night we park up beside the beach and I fall into a deep sleep to the atmospheric sound of the waves crashing against the shore.

An early morning passenger train bound for Batumi sounds its horn as it clatters past. Checking out my new surroundings, I find Si sat on the beach looking out to sea. The water is aquamarine with patches of blue-grey. Stripping down to my boxer shorts, I hobble across the pebbles and throw myself into the refreshing water. I feel an incredible sense of relief at having returned to the familiar setting of the Black Sea coast. We are now only 20km from the Anatolian peninsula, a region in the east of the Turkish Republic that was known to the Greeks as Pontus. This mountainous stretch of coastline, famed for its tea hills and mountain legends will carry us to the Bosphorus strait and the ancient capital of Istanbul.

The Batumi skyline looks like a miniature Dubai, with modern glass skyscrapers belonging to international hotels competing for space. We soon reach the suburbs of the city and pass a busy intersection near to the Chakvistskali railway station, with Turkish cafés, ATM machines and dozens of taxis waiting to escort tourists to the Mtirala National Park. The slogan "Batumi Miracle" welcomes us at the mouth of a tunnel, and Si blasts the car horn as the volume of traffic begins to increase. Fish bars and seafood restaurants are clustered on the quayside close to the port and the Batumi Passenger Ferry Terminal; the latter of which has connecting routes across the Black Sea to Kerch in Crimea and Illichivsk near Odessa. A fortified Roman port was first built here under the Roman Emperor Hadrian (117-138 AD), but was later deserted for the fortress of Petra in the times of Justinian I (527–565).

Crawling through Georgia's most popular party city, which was once a decrepit resort town 20km from the Turkish border, we catch a glimpse of the new Babillon Tower. When finished, this huge complex will be 170 meters tall and the highest residential building in Georgia. Following the coast that juts out to a point and then continues west, we crawl through the city traffic and begin to see hordes of holidaymakers wearing bikini tops and surf shorts wandering through Batumi's Bulvari Park. We skim alongside Evropas moedani "Europe Square", named by a pro-Western government in a newly independent Georgia. A monument to Medea, the daughter of the ancient King Aeetes, stands in the square. According to the mayor of Batumi at the time, "she had brought Georgia closer to Europe". Medea is the princess who married Jason in the ancient legend of Jason and the Argonauts, and I smile at this rather tenuous link to Georgia's ancient ties with Greece before Soviet rule. Batumi experienced a boom time under Russia in the 1890s, when industrial magnates such as Baron Alphonse de Rothschild and the Nobel brothers of Sweden transformed the city into a playground for the wealthy. With the completion of the Batumi-Tiflis-Baku railway line and the Baku-Batumi kerosene and crude oil pipelines in 1906 and 1930, Batumi became a major export terminal for oil from Azerbaijan. Expansion of this major transit route is currently underway, with the construction of the Baku-Tbilisi-Kars railway line, a project that has been labelled the new "Silk Road". When completed, this 826km BTK railway will connect Azerbaijan, Georgia and Turkey by rail to Western Europe for the first time.

* * *

We turn onto the wide Chavchavadze Avenue that passes renovated century-old apartment buildings. Novelty architecture reveals itself at every turn; a Sheraton Hotel designed in the style of the Great Lighthouse at Alexandria in Egypt, the Alphabet Tower celebrating Georgian script and writing, and an upside down restaurant resembling the White House. We drop by a quiet local café and the elderly woman behind the counter flicks on the TV. We grab a seat and watch Roy Orbison on stage singing 'Pretty Woman' to a live studio audience. Chris is curious to know if the woman is a fan of Roy, and his suspicions are confirmed when she slips on a pair of thick black framed glasses. A group of four girls sit at a table in the corner of the café; they look Turkish and are dressed casually in jeans. One of the girls has bleached blonde hair and is wearing a top that reveals a plunging cleavage. She glances over, and I quickly avert my gaze to a collection box for a Christian Church that is perched on the counter.

Under Ottoman control from the 16th century to the late 1800s, the majority of the local population of the autonomous republic of Adjara converted to Islam. But since the collapse of the Soviet Union and the re-establishment of Georgia's independence, the province has seen accelerated re-Christianisation, especially among the young. According to estimates by the Department of Statistics of Adjara, 63% are Georgian Orthodox Christians and 30% Muslim. Retaining its status as an autonomous republic until as recently as 2004, this region was once the personal regime of its pro-Russian president Aslan Abashidze. Adjara during this period was corrupt and authoritarian and tensions climaxed between Abashidze and President Saakashvili in 2004, when Abashidze sealed the Adjaran border from the rest of Georgia and raised fears of another Georgian civil war. Fortunately, Abashidze lost support from his Russian allies and days later he fled to Moscow in exile.

Keen to learn more about the history of this fascinating region of Eurasia, Chris suggests we drop by the ancient Roman fortress of Gonio-Apsarus; famed for being one of the best examples of Byzantine architecture in the world. Waving goodbye to the bright lights of Batumi, we drive 2km south of the city towards the Turkish border of Sarpi and park directly beneath the walls of this ancient fort. The oldest reference to Apsarus found is by Pliny the Elder, a Roman author and naturalist, as well as a naval and army commander of the early Roman Empire. Pliny mentioned the fortress in his encyclopaedic work Naturalis Historia in the 1st century AD. By the 2nd century AD, Apsarus was a well-fortified Roman city within the kingdom of Colchis. It later came under the influence of the Byzantine Empire, and was expanded in the 4th century AD and became the fortress we see today.

Exploring the ruins of an old theatre and a Roman-era bathhouse, we balance along high ledges between 18 towers and return through the well-kept gardens. Walking around the museum we study ceramics, small clay pipes, big chunky gold rings worn by Roman soldiers and a display of coins, including one silver coin found of Emperor Trajan (98-117 AD). The famous 19th century German archaeological excavator of Troy, Heinrich Schliemann, was interested in the study of the ancient fortress of Gonio-Apsarus based on myths of the Argonauts. Sadly, his proposed study had been declined by the Russian imperial court. Following the collapse of the Byzantine Empire, the Ottoman Empire eventually took control of the fort and, in 1762, the Ottoman troops despatched to Gonio won ill fame when they robbed the popular French traveller and merchant Jean Chardin.

With the border only a short drive away, we agree to enjoy a good feed before we cross into Turkey. Stumbling across a small restaurant with animal carcasses hanging in the window, we are served Turkish Black Sea tea in small tulip shaped glasses. The smart waiter has fair skin, black hair and blue eyes. Curious, I ask him where he is from and he reveals he was born in Rize, a city across the border in Eastern Turkey. Chris asks if he is Laz, an ethnic group of people native to this region of the Black Sea coast. He looks surprised and says "yes" and beams a smile. We discover he doesn't speak Laz, but occasionally returns to Rize to visit family. The Laz people had originated from the southern Caucasus and were one of the chief tribes of the ancient kingdom of Colchis. They were initially early adopters of Christianity, and most of them subsequently converted to Sunni Islam during Ottoman rule of the Caucasus in the 16th century. The Laz had at some point left the Caucasus and migrated to what is now present-day Turkey. Numbering around 200,000 people, they had spread to Istanbul and other cities in western Turkey and had even migrated back to Georgia hundreds of years after leaving the land where they had originated from. Our salad arrives, which consists of finely diced tomato, onion, green chilli and cucumber. It's accompanied by a fresh lemon dressing and a variety of vinaigrettes. A basket of fresh crusty bread is brought to the table, and is closely followed by a large plate of barbecued mutton. We devour the delicious tender meat that has been lightly salted and cooked in butter. I notice the place mats on the table are of Mount Kackar; a mountainous region of the Pontic Alps that rise from the south-eastern shores of the Black Sea. I smile at the experience of watching landscapes, boundaries and cultures entwine as we make a circuit around this fascinating sea.

Keen to cross into Anatolia before it gets too late, we drop by a busy petrol station and fill the fuel tank to the top with cheap gasoline. Holidaymakers crowd around a row of shops and purchase cartons of duty free cigarettes and bottles of alcohol. Caught up in the shopping fever, Chris withdraws money from an ATM machine and we change it into Turkish currency ready for the border. I ask the girl behind the money exchange counter if she is from Turkey, and she scowls at me and replies firmly that she is Georgian. We drive 6km south through the forested hills to the frontier town of Sarpi. Chris spots a huge traffic queue waiting to cross the border, so we pull over on top of the cliffs that plunge into the raging Black Sea below. Feeling restless, we look down towards the modern border checkpoint that barricades the road at the foot of the hill, and hear the azan call to prayer from a nearby mosque. Only feet away a sign reads in English, "Good Luck". The noise of the waves crashing against the rocks appears to intensify, sounding almost angry, as we're swallowed up by the night. Police cars thunder backwards and forwards along the road. We descend the hill and park the Volvo parallel to the beach. Perching on the sea wall along the promenade we watch the theatre of human life and trade between two nations. All of a sudden I notice my bag feels lighter. I whip the rucksack off my shoulders and discover the zip is open and my Nikon camera is missing. Marching back to the Volvo, we frantically search the inside of the car. It's nowhere to be seen. We gradually come to terms with the fact that 251 years after the famous French traveller Jean Chardin had been robbed at Gonio, we had fallen victim to the same fate. I feel foolish for allowing myself to drop my guard at a border crossing at night. We move closer to the border checkpoint and squeeze into a space beneath a street light. We take turns grabbing a few hours shuteye as we wait restlessly for the sun to rise.

PART 4
Turkey's Black Sea Coast

Fourteen

With a new stamp in our passports we enter ancient Anatolia. To our left the land rises steeply into the lush green Pontic Mountains, a range that stretches parallel with the southern Black Sea coast for a thousand kilometres. Studying the road atlas, Si reveals that directly south across this geological barrier lie Mount Ararat on the Armenian border and the predominantly Kurdish provinces in the southeast of the country bordering Iran, Iraq and Syria. Greek merchants first arrived on the Turkish Black Sea coast around 1000 BC, and formed colonial cities by the 8th and 7th centuries BC. The region became known as "Pontus", which was derived from the Greek name for the Black Sea "Euxeinos Pontos" (Hospitable Sea), a polite alternative to an earlier "Pontos Axeinos" (Inhospitable Sea). Strabo, the famous Greek geographer, historian and philosopher who lived in the 1st century BC wrote in his encyclopedia Geographica that he thought the Black Sea was called "inhospitable" before Greek colonization because it was difficult to navigate, and because its shores were inhabited by fierce tribes.

Curious to explore these mysterious green mountains that are covered by alder, chestnuts and hornbeams, we continue west on the E70 highway to the small coastal town of Ardesen. Si turns sharply inland, and we pass tea growing on the hillside and climb steadily through the Firtina gorge into the rugged Kackar Mountains. This picturesque region is home to the highest part of the Pontic Mountains, with the tallest peak, Kackar Dagi, reaching an elevation of 3,937 metres. We begin to see winch wires stretching across the gorge, which are used for hoisting goods up to the wooden tea houses. An elderly woman and a small boy crank a handle and send a small basket over the river to a man standing on the opposite hillside. Continuing to climb into the alpine mountains, we pull over beside a 17th century humpback bridge that was restored to commemorate the 75th anniversary of the establishment of the Turkish Republic. We look up into a lush green tea garden and see a man and a woman carefully trimming the tea bushes. Hessian sacks are tied beneath their shears to catch the falling leaves as they work methodically on the incredibly steep sided hill. Si waves to them and we admire their beautiful traditional wooden house that is elevated on stilts to the right of this tranquil garden paradise. Turkey is the fifth largest producer of tea in the world, with 225,000 tonnes of the leaf being grown in 2012. Tea was introduced to Turkey in the 1940s and 1950s and was offered as an alternative to coffee, which had become expensive and comparatively rare.

The road becomes incredibly steep as we enter the Kackar Mountains National Park; a region that is home to the rare Caucasian black grouse, salamanders and brown bears. Si grits his teeth as we squeeze past vehicles descending the mountain on a knife-edge. Driving through shallow streams we eventually arrive in the beautiful high-pasture village of Ayder. Hearing the Muslim call to prayer echo across the forest from a distant mountain mosque, I'm surprised to see a heaving mass of local day trippers spread out on picnic blankets across the hillside. Men attend to smoking charcoal barbecues, and women wearing colourful headscarves prepare salad and make tea in double-bodied teapots. We pass a girl walking along the roadside wearing a full length black burka with running shoes, which looks fantastically strange in this remote mountain location. A group of young guys wearing smartly fitted shirts sit in a circle and smoke a hooker pipe, the sweet smell of apple molasses drifts on the warm breeze. We mooch around the souvenir shops close to a row of charming alpine chalets and snack on Labana Sarmasi (stuffed cabbage rolls). I begin to notice many cars have German, Austrian, Belgium and French licence plates, and it occurs to me that they are most probably Turkish migrant workers who have driven home for the summer vacation. We look down over a circular arena and examine a sign that reads, "Kackar Daglari Milli Parki Galer Duzu Arena". A photo depicts two bulls with their heads locked together in a fight. Among the crowds of people, Si points out a woman wearing a traditional orange and red pattern Hemsin hijab that is decorated around the fringe with distressed silver metal coins. With a population numbering around 20,000 people, the local Hemsin community, who inhabit this remote southeast corner of the Black Sea, are descendants of Armenians who converted to Islam many centuries ago. They still speak Hamshenian, an old west Armenian dialect and have their own customs and dress. The Hemsin have taken on the role as tea farmers and river fisherman and, more recently, they are servicing the tourist industry that appears to have blossomed here in recent years. Reading from his notes, Si reveals the Hemsin can sometimes be seen in the summer months dancing the "horon" to music played by an instrument called a "tulum" that sounds similar to the bagpipes. I smile at the thought of the reluctant modern Hemsin teenagers being forced by grandma to perform a dance that is a cross between the conga and the hokey-cokey.

Winding our way back down the mountain road, we find a quiet spot to set up camp. Si stumbles across a forest cemetery and waves me over. One of the tombstones has an inscription both in the Turkish language and in the Roman alphabet. The person died in 1918, and I try to imagine how different life must have been here in this remote region of Turkey. Many Armenians from nearby Rize and Trabzon were tragically killed in a terrible genocide not long before this person had died. The Hemsin people, who migrated here from Armenia many centuries before, had been kept safe by their remote mountain location and their quiet conversion to Islam.

Making a small fire, we flame grill lamb chops with fresh wild mint and drink copious amounts of homemade Georgian wine beneath a clear night sky. In the eerie shadows of the forest, with the flickering fire illuminating our faces, Si tells the story of the Laz Big Foot. In Laz folklore, this giant mythological creature covered in fur is rumoured to live in these mountains. Called a Germakoci, it is said to walk on two legs like a human and would sometimes approach hunters in the high forest. Steeped in myth and legend, both Laz and Hemsin culture are rich in rules, superstitions and folklore that have assisted their survival and kept their children safe in these mountains. Si laughs at my concerned expression, but we both drop our smiles when we hear a strange hacking noise deep within the forest. Extinguishing the fire we call it a night and return to the relative safety of the Volvo.

Stirring from a deep sleep, I flick open my eyes and see a face peering at me through the window. It appears to be a woman in her late fifties. She is wearing a white headscarf and has masculine features. Her eyes scan the interior of the car owl-like. Curled up on the back seat, Si sits up and commands her to "go!" His voice startles the woman and she steps back from the Volvo and disappears into the forest.

The morning sun rises over the towering mountain peaks as we return through the picturesque Firtina gorge. Reaching the small town of Camlihemsin, we stumble across a local tea room. A group of elderly gentlemen sit on the pavement outside and Si greets them with a cheery "günaydin". The friendly owner, Silim, welcomes us inside. We study a photo on the wall of a man standing next to a bull.

'My father,' he smiles, offering us both a small tulip shaped glass of Black Sea tea.

We learn that Silim's father passed away quite recently and that the bull in the photo was called JR. A champion in the ring for two years running, we are fascinated to discover the circular arena we had seen in the high pasture village of Ayder, is actually a local stadium. During the mating season local Hemsin people can enter their bulls into a competition and watch them fight. JR apparently lived for ten years and when he died they had eaten him. Silim looks slightly ashamed, so I raise a toast to JR with my tea and we all clink glasses. Si asks Silim if he is Laz or Hemsin. He straightens his posture and proudly reveals that he is Hemsin, and explains that Hemsin and Laz people do not like each other. He knocks his fists together. They are clearly rivals. Admiring a large cast iron wood burner in the centre of the room, with a long pipe protruding out of the back, we are reminded that it gets cold here during the winter months. I imagine local men crowding around this fine wood burner drinking tea and eating Labana Sarmasi. I ask Silim how long the tea house has been here, and he scribbles down 1958. His father built the place with his bare hands. An old Turkish gentleman smoking a cigarette walks into the tea shop, but Silim snaps at him and turns him away. He explains smoking is prohibited in his tea room.

Enjoying a second cup of Black Sea tea, Silim holds his glass up to the sunlight and examines the strong red liquid with tea leaves floating at the bottom. Dropping a sugar cube into the glass, he gives it a quick stir with a miniature silver spoon and proudly informs us that his tea is organic with no artificial chemicals or fertilisers used in its production. Appearing to enjoy our interaction, he shows us photos on his mobile phone of river trout he caught further upstream, an electric smoke machine he bought recently for keeping bees and pictures of his dogs. Inviting us to meet his canine companions, Silim leads us around the side of the building. The river rushes through the valley a few metres away, and we look up into the green hills that disappear into the mist. Two huge Anatolian Shepherd dogs, the beige colour of lions, suddenly appear from out of the murky darkness and bark excitedly at the cellar bars. Silim commands them to heel. Unlocking the gates, he steps inside and the dogs leap up at him. Silim invites us to stroke them, but I hesitate at first before gently patting one of the huge dogs on the top of its head. Its tongue hangs from the corner of its mouth and it looks up at me with big watery eyes. Si reaches out a hand to stroke the second canine and it releases a deep bone shattering bark, before playfully leaping up at him and licking his face. Si looks petrified and Silim bursts out laughing. Returning to the front of the café, we sit in the sunshine with the group of old men and watch the passing traffic. After a final glass of tea, we pull ourselves away and thank Silim for his kind hospitality.

* * *

Chris taps his fingers in time to the Turkish pop music on the radio as we wind our way through the remainder of the gorge. We reach the confluence of the Firtina, where river meets sea, and rejoin the smooth coastal highway heading west to Rize and Trabzon. Huge yellow billboards advertising the Caykur tea company begin to appear on the outskirts of Pazar, and a mosque perched high on the hillside blooms like a white orchid in a lush green tea garden. Along the promenade an old man uses the free gym equipment and works hard to bring back the motion to his fragile legs. Chris fires a photograph out of the window of two smoking redbrick chimneys belonging to the Caykur tea plant. A second tea processing factory flashes by with its own harbour where the tea is cured, dried, blended and loaded aboard an awaiting cargo ship. Nearby, a colony of black cormorants on a cluster of rocks spread their wings majestically as they look to the horizon in the direction of Crimea.

Reaching the suburbs of Rize, we see more huge Caykur tea advertising billboards and zip by coastal apartment buildings painted peach and pastel blue. Dozens of Turkish national flags hang out of apartment block windows and it seems clear the citizens whether, Laz, Hemsin or ethnic Turks, feel a great sense of pride and patriotism towards their country and coastal mountain home. We take a stroll around the town that has the laid back ambience of a Mediterranean fishing port. The first written mention of Rize found to date, was by a

Greek called Arrian in a work named Periplus (Ship's Voyage) in 132-131 BC. The work records how its author, the governor of Cappadocia, made an inspection tour of the Eastern Black Sea territories that were part of his jurisdiction. In the centre of Rize we visit a café and join the all-male clientele perched on small plastic stools outside a shop selling spices and hazelnuts, dried dates, apricots and raisins. The waiter, who is wearing black trousers and a white shirt, brings us tea on a silver tray. I notice many of the Turkish men are sporting thick black moustaches and wearing shirts with pullovers and smart tailored trousers and leather shoes. Sat together in twos and threes, smoking cigarettes and chewing the fat, it is clearly evident that drinking tea here is as much an institution to these gentlemen as the pub is to the British or the coffee shop is to an Italian. We take a stroll around the main square "Ataturk Aniti", and pass a fish mongers, with large river trout in the window and kilos of Black Sea anchovies on a bed of ice. Along the busy commercial street, shops sell Levi jeans, headscarves, the popular Turkish game Okey, and music CDs by the artists, Cimilli Jbo, Resul Dindar and Crol Sahin. Dropping by a delicatessen, Chris purchases black olives and a kilo of korsas, a stringy dense rubbery cheese. Walking past the impressive Merkez Seyh Camii, the main city mosque, we run up a flight of stone steps to the town museum that is located inside an old reconstructed Ottoman house. A security guard sitting on a plastic chair leaps to his feet. Clutching a big bunch of keys, he unlocks the museum's front door and flicks on the lights. We wander through the rooms and view a large cast iron bell, ornate wooden furniture, weaponry, a decorative blue ceramic spoon, coins from the 4th to the 15th century, a collection of silver jewellery and a Fez style hat with tassels. Under Mehmet

II, the Rize Province was brought into the Ottoman Empire in 1461. But its first recorded occupation had been over two and a half thousand years earlier in the 8th century BC by the Greeks, who had created this chain of mountainous colony cities along the modern-day Turkish Black Sea coast.

After a swim, we drive to the bustling port city of Trabzon where we arrive in convoy with a procession of wedding cars decorated with flowers and lace. Joining the heaving crowds in Ataturk Alani, Trabzon's beating heart, Chris reveals camel caravans would gather here in the Byzantine and Ottoman periods before travelling across the mountains. The square today is the location of the city's main restaurants, hotels and tea houses.

Milesian traders first established a settlement here called Trapezous in 756 BC. Trapezous's advantageous location, with a direct path through the mountains linking the sea to the Silk Route, enabled the Trapezuntine rulers to amass great riches. Mithridates VI Eupator added Trapezous to the kingdom of Pontus in the 1st century BC, and it became the home port of the Pontic fleet. When the kingdom was added in 64-65 AD to the territory controlled by the Roman province of Galatia, the fleet became the Classis Pontica. Under Roman rule in the 1st century AD, Trebizond, as it was now called, grew in significance, with roads leading to the upper Euphrates valley and the Armenian frontier via the Zigana Pass. Under the rule of Vespasian new roads were built from Mesopotamia and Persia and, in the next century, the harbour was rebuilt under the orders of the Roman Emperor Hadrian. Acting as a gateway city to Iran in the southeast and to the Caucasus in the northeast, Trebizond grew into a vibrant multicultural city over the centuries, "a melting pot of religions, languages and cultures". In 258 AD, Trebizond's success under the Romans was brought to an abrupt end when the Goths pillaged the city. Although Trebizond was rebuilt, the city did not recover until the trade route regained importance in the 8th to 10th centuries. Son of the Byzantine emperor, Alexis Comnenos, established his new capital at Trabzon in 1204 after fleeing Christian soldiers of the Fourth Crusade, who seized and sacked Constantinople. The Trapezuntine rulers forced many of its noble families to seek refuge in Anatolia, and successfully balanced their alliances with the Mongols, the Venetians and the Genoese traders, who used Trabzon as an important seaport for trading goods between Europe and Asia.

The Comnenian Empire in turn came to an end with the arrival of the Ottomans in 1461. During this next period, the city became a focal point of trade to Iran and the Caucasus via its port. Maintaining its multicultural identity until late into the Ottoman period, Trabzon developed a wealthy merchant class and a local Christian minority that still had substantial influence in terms of culture. This was however to change. As Trabzon entered the modern era at the beginning of the 20th century, it experienced some tough and gruesome times. An escalation of events that had begun on 24th April 1915, when Ottoman authorities rounded up and arrested 250 Christian Armenian intellectuals and community leaders in Constantinople, had grown progressively into mass genocide across the Turkish Republic and Anatolia. An estimated 1 to 1.5 million Armenians are believed to have been exterminated during and after World War I, with around 50,000 believed to have been massacred in Trabzon alone. According to reports during the Trabzon trials series in 1919, thousands of women and children were placed on boats that where capsized in the Black Sea. Soon after, Trabzon had been the site of one of the key battles between the Ottoman and Russian armies during the Caucasus Campaign of World War I, which resulted in the capture of Trabzon by the Russian Caucasus Army in 1916. Russians banned Muslim mosques and forced Turks, which was the largest ethnic group living in the city, to leave. The Russian Army ultimately retreated from Trabzon, and also the rest of eastern and northeastern Anatolia with the Russian Revolution of 1917. Following the collapse of the Soviet Union in the late 1980s, Trabzon declined into a seedy port town, attracting travelling merchants from Russia and Ukraine.

Shuffling through the crowded bazaar in the carsi (market) quarter of the city, we admire the tall grey-stone buildings and look with intrigue at a Byzantine church that is now a mosque. Losing ourselves in the narrow side streets, I hear a Russian tour party and observe large groups of local women wearing fitted raincoats with headscarves, who shop eagerly for textiles in flat leather shoes. A large percentage of the population of Trabzon today are Circassian (Adyghe), a Sunni Muslim people we had met in the North Caucasus. They migrated to this region after being displaced during the course of the Russian conquest of the Caucasus in the 19th century. You would imagine this mass migration may have caused some division between the population, but many locals self-identifying as Turks living in Trabzon originate from a variety of different ethnic groups - mostly Chepni Turkmens, Laz people and a small community of Armenian Hemshin and Muslim Greeks.

In the rising heat we visit the Tashan, a centre of trade built around 1647 that is crowded with workshops, before making our way back along a busy pedestrian street to Ataturk Alani. We drink kiwi fruit juice, which grows in abundance in this region, and chat to the juice seller. He reveals he lived for ten years in New York City. The guy is bursting with personality and works at lightning speed to serve a long queue of customers. We sit in the main plaza and people watch for a while before returning once more to the mountainous interior of eastern Turkey.

Fifteen

Leaving behind the sticky streets of Trabzon, we head for the cooler altitude of the Altindere Valley National Park. Winding through the dense evergreen forests, we catch a glimpse of the breathtaking Monastery of the Virgin Mary at Sumela that is perched precariously at 1,200m on the side of a steep cliff. A stressed parking attendant waves Si into a narrow parking space adjacent to a Turkish biker gang. We admire their black and chrome motorcycles (their armoured horses) that are lined up at the foot of the trail that leads up to the monastery. Wearing red leather waistcoats without shirts and matching red bandanas, they stand out in stark contrast next to the Muslim women in long fitted raincoats that are buttoned up to the chin. An unshaven guy with a ponytail, with enormous hairy shoulders and a handle bar moustache, smokes a cigarette and jokes around with his fellow biker gang members. He looks like a medieval Seljuk Turk warrior. Making our way up the trail, we pass an old Turkish gentleman playing a kemenche (spike fiddle), a traditional Laz instrument similar to a violin. He suddenly stops in mid-performance to answer his mobile phone. The amused crowd waits patiently while he has a little chat and, slipping his phone back inside his pocket, he continues to play. Passing through a security barrier, we enter the monastery and duck into the guard quarters. Si waves me over to a small window with dramatic views high over the forest canopy.

The Sumela monastery was founded in 386 AD by the Greek Orthodox Church, during the reign of the Byzantine Emperor Theodosius I. It fell into ruin several times during its long history. It reached its present form in the 14th century after gaining prominence during the reign of Alexios III of the Comnenian Empire of Trebizond in 1204. The majority of the Greeks living in these hills during this period were Christian peasants, who farmed the land and reared cattle. They were allowed to remain here after the Ottomans captured Trabzon after a 42-day siege in 1461, but events that were to occur centuries later in 1923 saw the Pontic Greeks finally removed from this land forever. With the Ottoman Empire in ruins, the country of Greece had decided to take advantage of the Turks weak position and invade western Anatolia with the ultimate game plan of controlling the Aegean. The Greeks were defeated and in a bizarre twist of fate the last remaining Pontic Greeks were forced to leave their work, land and lives on the Turkish Black Sea coast and return home to Greece; a country where they had not lived for nearly 3,000 years.

Descending a steep flight of stone steps carved into the rock, Si squats down and photographs the main chapel that is covered in colourful frescoes from head-to-toe like a full body tattoo. The earliest frescoes date from the 9th century, although, most are actually 19th century work. Sadly, much of the artwork has been defaced by bored shepherd boys and covered in graffiti by USAF grunts that were here in 1965. Swifts and swallows nesting in the monastery walls zigzag above our heads, as we step inside the main chapel located next to a cave that was once a bakery. The large mural painted on the dome ceiling depicts biblical scenes, and tells the story of Christ and the Virgin Mary. A bald chap standing beside me takes a photo of the frescoes, but is quickly instructed by a security guard to refrain from using his flash. Stepping outside into the bright sunshine, I watch a mixed group of Muslim and Christian women reaching up their hands in a bid to catch drips of water falling from the overhanging cliffs. According to the Orthodox monks who once lived here, the sacred water room represents water falling from heaven. I smile as a Turkish woman wearing a headscarf superstitiously touches the water on her cheeks and forehead.

At first light, we scramble down a steep gorge and wash in an icy cold stream. Birds sing in the trees and a low mist hugs the forest canopy. It rained during the night, and there is an overwhelming scent of wet earth and ferns that fills the air. Back on the coastal highway, we catch a glimpse of the ruins of a 13th century Byzantine castle that is located on a small peninsula. We pull up outside a bakery in the town of Gorele, and Si returns with slices of pita (known locally as "pide") and an enormous round flat loaf of bread the size of the Volvo's steering wheel. In the small fishing town of Tirebolu, we begin to see hazelnuts drying in the sun on large square hessian sheets. Hazelnuts in this region are the mainstay of the local economy, and we see the occasional batch of a nut the Turkish call "findik", covered in a mass of curly leaves. Purchasing a large sack from a local farmer we cover the interior of the car with shells all the way to the town of Giresun. During Roman times, the port of Giresun was the location where Lucullus had first introduced the cherry to Italy. We look over the harbour where, according to the myth, Jason and the Argonauts moored up their Argo on their great voyage to the kingdom of Colchis. We visit a local museum housed in a disused 18th century Greek Gogora church, before cruising along a forested stretch of the coast that leads to the quaint town of Ünye. The town is eerily quiet, with many of its residence working in the countryside to gather the hazelnut harvest. We relax on the sea wall and watch fishermen in the harbour cleaning their boats and repairing fishing nets.

Predating the earliest Milesian trading colonies, this coastal settlement was once part of the Hittite civilisation. In the 15th century BC, these ancient Anatolian people thrived in this region. They established an empire at Hattusa that lies approximately 350km southwest of Ünye, close to the modern-day Turkish capital of Ankara. The Hittite Empire reached its peak during the mid-14th century BC under Suppiluliuma I, when it encompassed an area that included most of Asia Minor as well as parts of the northern Levant. According to archaeological evidence, it is thought that the Hittites arrived in Anatolia sometime before 2000 BC. It is not certain where they came from, but fascinatingly one theory traces their origins to the Pontic steppe (present-day Ukraine around the Sea of Azov) in the 4th and 3rd millennia BC. According to the Kurgan Hypothesis, it is believed that the Hittites may have originally emerged from the Dnieper-Volga region of modern-day Russia in the Copper Age (early 4th millennia BC). In the same way as the Scythians, these ancient people had been nomadic pastoralists, who, according to the model, by the early 3rd millennia BC, had expanded throughout the Pontic-Caspian steppe and into Eastern Europe.

Si leaps to his feet and paces up and down the sea wall, completely overwhelmed by the realisation that there had already been powerful civilisations inhabiting the Black

Sea thousands of years before the Scythians and the Greeks. I look to the horizon in the direction of Crimea and the southern Ukraine, and contemplate a region that has seen many great civilisations thrive (and decline) with the arrival of new bands of nomadic tribes migrating from the Volga region and around the Caspian Sea. After 1180 BC, the Empire of Hittite had disintegrated amid general turmoil in the Levant associated with the sudden arrival of a mysterious confederacy of seafaring raiders referred to as the Sea Peoples. Thought to have possibly originated from either western Anatolia or southern Europe (specifically a region of the Aegean Sea), the Sea Peoples were believed to have sailed around the eastern Mediterranean and invaded Anatolia, Syria, Canaan, Cyprus and Egypt towards the end of the 12th century BC. According to Egyptian records, those identified include Greek Danaoi, the Israelite tribe of Dan, Anatolian people of the Aegean, people of Sardis "Sardinians", the Italic people called Siculi (from Sicily) and a tribe of people from Crete who may have come with the Greek Teucrians.

Great civilisations have evolved and thrived in this region of the Black Sea since the birth of agriculture, but humans are a predatory species. With the rapid advancement of technology afforded by farming, perpetual war it seems is inevitable. Mastering the seas presented the Sea Peoples with opportunity, as the use of the horse and bow had been advantageous to the Scythians and in turn the evolution of heavy armour had been to the Sarmatians. Tribal war existed before farming, with some theories suggesting that it may have even prevented the emergence of agriculture occurring sooner. As long ago as 9000 BC, Jericho in the Levant had a wall around its settlement. Humans, it appears, instinctively seek out a chink in the armour of their rivals. This fear and threat from one another has driven the accelerated advancement of our entire modern society, and resulted in the development of aviation, space travel and the very real threat of extinction from nuclear war. Si looks glazed at the realisation that we exist in a period of human history, which urgently demands we open our eyes in order to prevent the total annihilation of our species.

* * *

Climbing aboard the Volvo, Chris accelerates west in the direction of Sinop. Within less than an hour we arrive in a region of Anatolia around the mouth of the Yesil and Terme rivers, known by the Pontic Greeks as the Themiscyra plains. This fertile region once produced a great abundance of grain, especially millet and in the parts near the mountains in the south, apples, grapes, pears and nuts.

Rolling through the suburbs of the nearby town of Terme, Chris parks the Volvo at the end of a bustling high street and we take a stroll around the main square. With a quaint pointed clock tower at its centre that is constructed from neatly squared blocks of stone, we pass a frothing water fountain and a group of men basking in the sun outside a tea house. A businessman in a suit rests his foot on an old brass plated foot stand with an embossed star at its centre, and an old chap with white hair shines his shoes in the shade of a multi-coloured ice cream umbrella. Stumbling across a butcher's shop I attempt to buy meat. Without the phrasebook I struggle to communicate with the guy behind the counter who is wearing a blood stained apron. Wielding a meat cleaver, he completely ignores me and mutters to the colourfully dressed woman working beside him. The guy points at the carcass of a cow in the window, and I smile. He throws his hands up in despair, and mutters "Uzbeki?" to the woman. She shrugs her shoulders. I get the distinct impression he dislikes foreigners coming to his town unable to speak a word of Turkish. I had witnessed the same hostile behaviour by my own countrymen in recent years, threatened by the sudden appearance of migrant workers travelling to the UK from Eastern Europe. Throughout its history, Turkey has been a nation of many races, being located directly at the crossroads of Europe, Asia and the Middle East. But assimilation is a slow ongoing process, and it would be the duty of individual people across the world to practise tolerance if we do not wish to participate in future wars. I feel ashamed for having not learnt more words in the Turkish language and, not wishing to enter into an argument with a man clutching a meat cleaver, I politely thank them both before returning to the street outside.

Heading out of town Chris reveals Terme was once known as the ancient settlement of Themiscyra, which was also the name of the fictional island-home of DC comic book superhero Wonder Woman. William Moulton Marston modelled Princess Diana of Themyscira on the Greek myth of a tribe of fierce female warriors who once lived in this region known as the Amazons; a legend that has inspired writers and artists for more than two thousand years. Back tracking along the highway, we see a statue of a female warrior at the roadside and turn sharply into a rest stop lined with tour coaches. Looking in awe at the life-size sculpture of the Amazon warrior who is drawing a bow and arrow, I notice she is dressed rather provocatively in an off the shoulder Roman-style toga, exposing her strong shoulders and bare arms. She expertly grips the fletching of a deadly arrow inside the drawn bow and aims it east in the direction of Georgia. The straps of her leather sandals encircle her calf muscles and are fixed tightly below the knee. Reading a sign at the foot of the newly built statue, that is written both in the Turkish and English language, we learn that it is believed these "fighting heroines of Anatolian Greek mythology lived in Themiskryia on the shore of Thermedon in the 1200s BC. Amazons used arrows and rode horses, and it is said that they even cut off their right breasts so as to draw the bow well. They exploited males as workers and servants and killed captives after having sex with them, killed male infants, raised female infants with care and trained them as strong fighters." Turning to the archaeological facts, the reality is that besides uncertified writings and legends of these women in Greek mythology, there is no physical evidence to prove that the Amazons truly lived here on the Pontus coast in the 1200s. Rather intriguingly though, not very far away, hidden in kurgan burial mounds on the north shores of the Black Sea, skeletons have been unearthed of high-ranking warrior women. These female warriors very real existence on the Pontic steppe in the 5th and 6th century BC, seven hundred years after the Amazons supposedly ruled the southern coast of the Black Sea, have inspired numerous theories.

In the book 'The Horse, the Wheel, and Language', David Anthony wrote, "About 20% of Scythian-Sarmatian "warrior graves" on the lower Don and lower Volga contained women dressed for battle similar to how men dress, a phenomenon that probably inspired the Greek tales about the Amazons." The nearby ancient town of Themiscyra (Terme) was first mentioned in the 5th century BC by Herodotus. He had travelled to the Greek colony of Olbia on the north shores of the Black Sea as part of a Periclean campaign. Widely referred to today as "The Father of History", he was the first historian known to collect his materials systematically and critically, and then to arrange them into a historiographic narrative. In the same pragmatic manner that he had written about the Scythian and Sarmatian nomadic pastoralists, he also explored old Amazonas tales known to the Greeks, and assimilated them to new narratives from sources of colonial Greeks on the Black Sea coast and Olbia. Herodotus stated that he believed this tribe of women was called Oiorpata in the Scythian language, Androktones in Greek, meaning "killers of men". He asserted that they lived in a region bordering Scythia in Sarmatia (modern territory of Ukraine). Neal Ascherson wrote in his book 'Black Sea', referring to the female nomads of the Pontic Steppe. "They ruled; they rode with armies into battle; they died of arrow-wounds or spear-stabs; they were buried in female robes and jewellery with their lances, quiver and sword ready to hand.' Ascherson also highlighted that, "In their graves, a dead youth sometimes lies across their feet. A man sacrificed at the funeral of a woman?"

Joined by two Muslim women wearing navy blue headscarves, who photograph the statue of this Amazon warrior with their mobile phones, I find myself wondering what they make of such a striking symbol of female independence and liberty. Neal Ascherson wrote referencing Herodotus. "After the Trojan wars (1184 BC)...the Amazons living on the south shore of the Black Sea had been overcome by the Greeks and herded into prison-ships. But they mutinied...settling 'three days' journey from Tanais eastward and a three days' journey from the Maeotian lake [Sea of Azov] northwards' and becoming the nation of the Sauromatae."

Herodotus documented this fascinating region in the 5th century BC, fairly soon after these female warrior kurgans had come into existence. His stories had been collated by talking to the local people and travelling to various regions around the Don delta. Although there is no hard evidence of the Amazons existence in Turkey, in light of the very real female warrior skeletons that have been found on the Pontic steppe, his work most certainly cannot be ignored. Ascherson wrote, "In the plains between the Ural and Volga rivers, nearly a fifth of the female Sauromatian graves dated between the sixth & fifth centuries BC have been found to contain weapons. Scythian graves all over the southern Ukraine have revealed women soldiers, sometimes buried in groups, equipped with bows, arrows and iron plated battle-belts to protect groins."

Picturing the landscape in my mind around the Don delta, Chris poses the question - why hadn't evidence of groups of similar independent warrior women been found in other parts of the world? Russian archaeologist Vera Kovalevskaya has an interesting theory, "During the time that the Scythians advanced into Asia and achieved near-hegemony in the Near East, there was a period of twenty-eight years when the men would have been away on campaigns for long periods. During this time the women would not only have had to defend themselves, but to reproduce and this could well be the origin of the idea that Amazons mated once a year with their neighbours."

Making a circuit around the statue, I smile at the thought that remnants of this ancient myth continue to exist to this present day in the form of the mighty Amazon River that winds its way across South America. An example of the power of this legend that captivated the minds of pioneering Portuguese sailors many centuries after the Greek Empire had collapsed.

Sixteen

Thrust into the large sprawling port city of Samsun it feels like we have suddenly been zapped back to the modern world. Car showrooms, computer and mobile phone outlets, a furniture warehouse and a Ramsey London clothes shop flash by my window. Si counts the many towering yellow cranes and brand new concrete apartment buildings that cast old ancient architecture into shadow. We wave goodbye to the mighty E70 highway as it disappears into the Black Sea and reconnects in the Bulgarian port of Varna. To our right, there is a stunning view of the large bay that is crowded with container ships, tankers and roll-on-roll-off ferries that sail between Samsun and Novorossiysk in Russia. Traversing a similar route to the ferry, the Gazprom Blue Stream pipeline is buried 2.2km beneath the sea bed and supplies Russian gas to Turkey. A large wrestling stadium zips by causing Si to flick through his notes. Oil wrestling has long been a national sport in Turkey. In fact, the annual Kirkpinar tournament held in Edirne since 1362 is the oldest continuously running sanctioned sporting competition in the world. The wrestlers, known-as "pehlivan" (meaning, hero or champion), smother themselves with olive oil and wear hand-stitched lederhosen called a kisbet that are made of water buffalo hide. Matches originally had no set duration and could go on for more than one or two days.

The region around Samsun has been inhabited for many thousands of years, throughout the Calcolithic, First Bronze Age, Hittite, Greek Hellenistic and Roman periods. Greeks from Miletus arrived here in 760 BC, and the city was later captured by the Persians in 550 BC and became part of Cappadocia. In the 4th century BC, the city came under the expanded rule of the kingdom of Pontus, with evidence of great wealth in the form of the Amisos treasure. In 1995, during roadwork construction in a suburb of Samsun, an ancient tomb was unearthed that was brimming with gold. Historians believe the Amisos treasure belonged to Mitridat, the 6th Pontus king. After World War I, Samsun and the Ottoman Empire lay in tatters, and reformist statesman Mustafa Kemal Atatürk established the Turkish Liberation Movement here on 19th May 1919. This marked the beginning of the Turkish War of Independence that was waged by Turkish nationalists against the Allies (France, Britain & Russia). Following yet more death during the Turkish-Armenian, Franco-Turkish and Greco-Turkish wars, the Treaty of Lausanne was signed in July 1923. The Allies left Anatolia and Eastern Thrace, and the Grand National Assembly of Turkey established a Republic that was declared on 29th October 1923. Mustafa Kemal Atatürk, a former Turkish army officer, became the first president of the Turkish Republic and served in office until 1938. His surname, Atatürk, meaning "Father of the Turks", was granted to him and forbidden to any other person by the Turkish parliament.

Returning to the wild open countryside, Si exhales a sigh of relief as the polluted urban sprawl is replaced with lush green paddy fields all the way to Bafra. This region around Samsun has long been known for its production of tobacco "Samsun-Bafra", which was popular and highly prized by the British for having small aromatic leaves. Cutting across huge fields of sunflowers that stretch to the horizon, it feels like we have been zapped back to the fertile Pontic steppe in the southern Ukraine. I overtake a gang of deeply tanned land workers hanging off the back of a tractor. Tobacco dries on racks outside small wooden houses and the minarets of small rural mosques sprout out of the landscape. We return to the Black Sea, where the water is the turquoise colour of the Caribbean. Passing Susan's Fish Factory, we wind along a tranquil coastal road to the pleasant seaside town of Gerze. Si takes over the driving, and we turn inland and explore the Sinop Midlands. I relax in the passenger seat and munch on hazelnuts. We follow a rushing river all the way to the small village community of Erfelek, a historically sparsely populated district that has an economy that until recently was almost totally self-sufficient. Using a mixed monetary and barter-oriented economy, the local people survive here on trade of forest products, small-scale farming, animal husbandry and income from family members living in large Turkish and European cities. The woodwork from this region of the Black Sea has been praised since Classical Greek times.

In search of the Tatlica waterfalls, we quickly become lost and find ourselves on a narrow country road climbing into the steep forested hills. We pass through a tiny hamlet locked in time, and Si weaves around two women carrying wicker baskets brimming with firewood. Wearing traditional baggy patterned Turkish shalvar trousers and headscarves tied like a bandana, the larger matriarchal mother has pale skin, big arms and a strong jaw. The road becomes unpaved, so we stop outside a traditional wooden stilt house and ask a friendly old chap leading a bull on a rope for directions to the falls. He points back down the hill and gestures with his hands that we need to cross a river. On the return journey we pass a second guy with a donkey heavily loaded with long tree branches. A hardy woman working in a nearby field gathers hay into a steep pepper pot shaped heap. At the foot of the hill we turn left at a house that is under construction, and I see a second woman carrying a long heavy plank of wood over her shoulder. It occurs to me that if a tribe of fierce female warriors did once inhabit this region of the world, these strong hardworking women would have almost certainly made the grade.

Crossing over a small bridge, we enter the private property belonging to the DSI Dam. We skirt around the perimeter of a large manmade lake and zip past a young kid standing at the side of the track who shakes a tin in the air. I glance in the rear view mirror and see the kid sprinting after our dust tail. Si slams on the brakes and we wait for him to catch up. Out of breath, he waves the tin in the air and we give him a couple of Turkish Lira as reward for his impressive stamina. Continuing along the narrow bumpy track, we reach the far side of the lake and approach the Erfelek Tatlica Waterfalls. Crossing a footbridge over the river, we join the dozens of families sat at picnic benches in the shade of the trees. A nearby charcoal barbecue smokes outside a wooden building with meat hung in the window. After checking out the waterfalls, I spark up a conversation with a smartly dressed Turkish guy named Ahmed. He reveals he works for a German telecoms company in Munich and is currently on holiday visiting his parents. He plans to drive home in two days time. Sharing the driving with his brother, they hope to complete the 2,500km journey through Bulgaria, Serbia, Slovenia and Austria in approximately 48 hours. Ahmed seems to be having an amazing time with his family and points out his beautiful wife and two children. He is keen to show us his new Mercedes, so we walk with them back to the car park. Witnessing the mass movement of the "New Europeans", despite Turkey not being an EU member state, it becomes clear that Europe is not dissimilar to the United States with few borders, good highways and endless opportunities for business and trade.

We leave the gates of the park, and set up camp on the edge of the lake ten metres from a waterfall that cascades down through the forest. We see a white tailed eagle glide effortlessly on the air currents, and I keep a sharp eye open for cypian vultures and European bee-eaters that inhabit this region. Hearing the familiar cry of a mosque drifting over the hills, we watch the red sun sink behind the hills.

* * *

Wading through knee length grass at first light, I absorb the breathtaking view of the emerald green lake. The whining sound of a two-stroke engine grabs my attraction. I glance over my shoulder and see a guy on a moped slowly making his way up the hill. Turning into the layby, he cuts the engine and leans the bike on its stand. He smiles as he approaches, and casts an inquisitive glance at the camping chairs on the back parcel shelf and at Chris snoring in the passenger seat.

'Fishing?' he asks.

I shake my head vehemently. 'No, tourists,' I reply.

The guy has a round face, hamster cheeks and a carefully groomed moustache, with wispy ends that give him the appearance of an artist. He asks if I speak French.

'Un petit peu,' I reply.

At hearing my response he launches into a musical monologue in the French language. He prompts me with a question.

I frown. 'Uh…qui.'

The guy laughs, and I manage to decipher that he lived in Provence for ten years and worked as a chef in a restaurant. He had since returned to Turkey and now lives in Erfelek and works for the DSI Dam. Seeming confident that we are not poaching fish out of the lake without a permit, he shakes my hand and welcomes me to Turkey. I watch as he straddles his moped and I bid him "bon voyage" as he accelerates down the track.

Hurtling through the countryside, we return to the coast and arrive in the bustling historic port of Sinop around mid-morning. Chris parks up beside the Kumkapi "Sand Gate"; an ancient section of wall and 25-metre tower made from large sandstone blocks. Patting one of the stones, Chris reveals that this wall is part of a later addition to a once grand 2km fortified circuit around the city that was built around 72 BC by the great king Mithridates VI, ruler of the Pontic Kingdom. According to archaeological evidence the Hittities first built a fortification in Sinop in 2000 BC, which had gradually been replaced over the many centuries by the Pontics, Romans, Byzantines, Seljuk Turks and Ottomans; each warring Empire toppling the next in an eternal cycle of power hungry humans.

Exploring the town on foot, we walk along the main street that is bustling with excited tourists from Istanbul and Ankara. I notice the men are wearing t-shirts and shorts and the women are wearing summer dresses and vest tops, which looks striking in contrast to the traditional clothes people predominantly wear in the east. Seeing bikinis for sale in clothes shop windows and crates of the Turkish brand of beer Efes Pilsen stacked outside a grocery store, we get a clear indication that we have crossed over into moderate Turkey. Purchasing Istanbul Simit from a street vendor, a delicious round ring of bread covered in sesame seeds, we stand in the street and admire the beautiful Alaadin Camii mosque. This large temple of worship that is set in a walled courtyard was built for Muinettin Suleyman Pervane, a powerful Seljuk grand vizier in the 13th century. As we had discovered in Georgia, the Seljuk Turks had originated from the Qynyq branch of the Oguz Turks ("Oguz", meaning "tribe"). They had migrated many centuries before from the Ural and Altai region of modern-day Russia and Siberia, and lived in the 9th century in Central Asia north of the Aral Sea and the Caspian Sea. The latter of which has recently dried up for first time in 600 years due to careless irrigation.

During the 10th century, some 300 years after the birth of the Islamic religion, the Oguz Turks had come into close contact with Muslim cities and around 985 AD the Oguz Turks had converted to Islam. Split by dissension among the tribes, one branch of the Oguz Turks had travelled to India while the other, led by descendants of Seljuk, struck out to the west. In the 11th century, the Seljuks migrated from their ancestral homelands into mainland Persia and defeated the Ghaznavid Empire in 1050-51. They established the Great Seljuk Empire, and became highly Persianized in culture and language and played an important role in the development of the Turko-Persian tradition. By 1081 the Seljuk Empire had spread west across Anatolia, and the Seljuk Turks captured the city of Sinop and founded a sizeable treasury. Sinop was eventually recovered by Alexios I Komnenos in 1204, ushering a period of prosperity under the Komnenian dynasty. But their reign was short lived, and in 1214 the Seljuk Turks of Rûm successfully recaptured the city. Muslim men, wearing their smart tailored tunics and prayer caps, enter the beautiful Alaadin Camii mosque. I smile at the thought of the transition the Seljuk Turks had undergone, over many centuries of migration and assimilation from their humble origins in the Ural and Altai Mountains.

Navigating the streets using a tourist map, I follow Chris through one of the seven original gates into the old walled part of the city. We emerge into a tranquil square that is dominated by half a dozen shops selling model ships. We peer through the window of a store that has been trading since 1953, and admire the beautifully crafted sailboats, steamers and war ships cleverly mounted inside glass bottles. Chris draws my attention to the fridge magnets and concludes they are for people who like model boats, but haven't the patience to build one. Crossing a cobbled road, we wander through the peaceful old town and pass a traditional tea house called Iskele Kiraathanesi. The tables are crowded with older gentlemen playing chess and cards, and a guy wearing black rimmed spectacles sits quietly reading a newspaper in the picture window. Inhaling the delicious scent of freshly baked bread drifting from the doorway of an upmarket delicatessen we pass a Turkish guy and his girlfriend embracing one another in the street. It's a display of public affection we had yet to witness in Turkey until now.

Reaching the waterfront, we sit outside a bustling restaurant on the quayside and watch luxury sailboats and yachts bob up and down in the marina. In 1999, maritime explorer Bob Ballard led an expedition off the coast of Sinop. His mission was to search the floor of the Black Sea in the hope of finding the remains of ancient settlements, and discover evidence that would support an exciting new theory known as the Black Sea Deluge Hypothesis. Published in 1997 by geologists William Ryan and Walter Pitman, the Black Sea deluge hypothesis proposed that a cataclysmic flood had struck this region around 7,000 years ago, swelling the sea and ultimately becoming the basis of the Noah story. The result of Ballard's awe-inspiring expedition to the bottom of the seabed revealed that an ancient untouched shoreline was indeed submerged underwater. If this discovery alone wasn't intriguing enough, the specimens of shells from freshwater and saltwater mollusk species, collected by the team from the sea floor, had shown through radiocarbon dating that a freshwater lake had indeed been overwhelmed by the Black Sea.

A National Geographic article on Ballard's expedition reveals that, "Almost every culture on Earth includes an ancient flood story. Details vary, but the basic plot is the same: Deluge kills all but a lucky few." The story most known to people today is the biblical account of Noah and the Ark, but earlier than Genesis is the Babylonian epic of Gilgamesh, about a king who set off on a quest to find the answer to immortality. During his odyssey, he met Utnapishtim, survivor of a great flood sent by the gods. Utnapishtim had been forewarned by the god of water, Enki, and had escaped death by building a boat. His actions had saved his family, friends, along with animals, artisans and precious metals. Fascinated to discover evidence of legends and folklore that pre-date the New Testament, the article also reveals that in Ancient Greek and Roman folklore the story of Deucalion and Pyhrra also existed, about a family and a group of animals who survived a flood in a box shaped ship. The thought that a monstrous flood could have occurred here on the Black Sea 7,000 years ago, has both myself and Chris grinning at the possibility that there may have been some truth in the stories and legends born in this region.

After the last Ice Age, the planet experienced a rapidly changing landscape. It is known that events such as the "Big Freeze" had taken place between approximately 10800-9500 BC; a period of cold climatic conditions and drought, which is thought to have been caused by the collapse of the North American ice sheets. According to the Black Sea deluge hypothesis, changes in world-wide hydrology around 5600 BC caused overall sea levels to rise, and may have been responsible for the Mediterranean finally spilling over a rocky sill at the Bosphorus. According to Ryan and Pitman, a volume of water 200 times the flow of the Niagara Falls, would have surged into the Black Sea for at least three hundred days. This catastrophic event would have significantly expanded the Black Sea shoreline (which was a glacial lake at the time) to the north and west. I glance across the calm surface of the water with new vision, and try to imagine the ancient farmland, settlements and thriving rural communities that are now located deep under water.

Continuing our stroll along the waterfront, we pass a row of tourist excursion boats and check out the Sehitler Çesmesi "Martyrs' Fountain". This simple stone block fountain was built in memory of the Turkish soldiers who died when the Russian Black Sea Fleet, under the command of Admiral Nakhimov, destroyed an Ottoman frigate squadron in 1853. This surprise attack on Sinop sparked the beginning of the Crimean War. Discovering the fountain was built using money recovered from the soldiers' pockets, I look in the direction of Crimea where our journey had first begun. In the distant past, the Greeks had referred to these waters as "Pontos Axinos" (Inhospitable Sea). Having learnt about the countless wars and massacres in this region during our journey, this description begins to resonate. Whether the Black Sea formed suddenly in a deluge 7,000 years ago, or, as some scientists believe, occurred slowly over time, the fact remains that the existence of this huge inland sea had caused hosts of civilisations over thousands of years to gather around its shores. Watching a small sailboat drift out of the harbour, Chris is reminded of Greek mythological tales warning sailors of mermaids luring their ships onto the rocks. These stories suddenly have new meaning. Seduced by this sea's promise of rich fishing grounds, fertile steppes and rivers of gold, the Black "Inhospitable" Sea exists at the crossroads of migrating civilisations, where those who establish empires here, discover only too late the dangers of others inhabiting this region at the central point of humanity. Sterile below the surface, with virtually no life existing below the depths of 150-200 metres, we begin to realise this sea isn't blue or black – its blood red.

Seventeen

To the haunting vocals of Nazan Öncel, Si powers the Volvo along a wild and deserted stretch of coastline. Soaring like an eagle over the salmon pink cliffs, I absorb our beautiful surroundings in what is quite frankly road trip heaven. Sweeping down a hill on a gradual bend, I look in surprise when a figure leaps into the middle of the road and starts flagging us down. Si slams on the brakes. A bearded guy wearing a red bandana, who is covered in tattoos, approaches the Volvo. We suspect it's a scam, so Si quickly whacks the gearbox into first and wheel spins away. I glance in the wing mirror and see the guy disappear in a cloud of dust. With adrenaline pumping through our veins, Si skids around a sharp bend only for us to realise we have driven slap-bang onto a Turkish movie set. A girl clutching a clipboard leaps out of the way and the angry face of the director peers over a movie camera attached to a crane. I flash a smile at three actors dressed like hippies who are standing beside a campervan covered in graffiti. The girl with the clipboard screams at us so loudly that her anger is almost amusing. We sit quietly like two naughty schoolboys, repressing our excited grins. She slowly calms down and takes a deep breath. Everyone on set looks unimpressed including the makeup artist and all of the extras huddled together in the shade of a makeshift canvas pagoda. I look sheepishly ahead as we are waved through.

With the fuel gauge kissing red, Si coasts the Volvo in neutral all the way to the small boat building community of Kurucasile. To the sound of nails being hammered into wood and the high-pitched squeal of electric wood saws and sanding machines, we wander around the boat building workshops close to the harbour. A deeply tanned chap wearing a baseball cap spray paints the bow of an old fishing boat, and I admire the skeletal frame of a large wooden ship near to the harbour beach. People swim in its shadow as we inhale the strong aroma of sawdust. A friendly guy working in a local grocery store called Mohammed kindly invites us to drink tea. We sit on the terrace outside and watch the day draw to a close.

We leave town an hour before sunset, and Si drives up a steep mountain road behind a truck heavily loaded with felled trees. Choking on diesel fumes, we penetrate the forested hills and park up for the night in a large clearing used by loggers for storing timber. By torchlight we prepare halal chicken fried in garlic with couscous, raisins and cream. Relaxing in my foldaway chair with a glass of frothy Efes beer, we listen to the sound of a deer calling from deep within the forest. In the eerie darkness, I suddenly notice a tiny red light the size of a cigarette end glowing in the trees. The light fades away, but appears again and looks disturbingly like an invisible person in the forest is smoking a cigarette. Unable to explain this phenomenon, we begin to suspect it could be either a species of firefly or a light inside the Volvo that has created a temporary optical illusion on our retinas. I raise an eyebrow at Si's suggestion that we could be slowly edging towards insanity. Drinking the last of the beer in the warm evening our conversation turns to the occult, orbs, theology and outer space.

Sometime during the night a car door slamming shut wakes me with a start. I wipe away the condensation on the window and peer into the eerie darkness. I look with concern at the presence of a saloon car nearby with its headlights on full beam. They suddenly cut out. A silhouetted figure circles the car and opens the trunk. I hear the disconcerting sound of heavy metal chains being dragged out and thrown onto the ground. Slipping the key into the ignition, I correct my seat and prepare to make a quick exit. I nudge Si awake and he pokes his head over his sleeping bag. He looks confused and wide-eyed. A second vehicle skids into the clearing and three men pile out of a van. They group together and talk loudly in either Turkish or Arabic; it sounds like they are having an argument. A bead of sweat drips from my forehead. I take a deep breath in a bid to slow down my heart rate. The men stop arguing. There is a deadly silence. What the hell are they doing? I hear the metal chains being dragged across the dry earth. It sounds like they are standing right behind the Volvo. I grab the key, but Si pushes my hand away and puts a finger to his lips. The men collapse into a second bout of angry chatter. I'm seconds away from starting the car when an engine suddenly roars into action. The throaty noise of a double exhaust vibrates inside my chest. All four men jump into their vehicles, and I release a deep sigh of relief as they disappear into the night.

We eagerly hit the road at dawn. Si overtakes a mule cart heavily loaded with wood and negotiates an unpaved red earth section of the highway. We pass through a small town with a colourful fruit and vegetable market, and climb once more into the green forested hills that morph into red rock. From the top of the cliffs there is a stunning view of the small town of Amasra below. Si turns inland when we reach the end of the coastal road and we move away from the Black Sea. We drive south towards Safranbolu and cross over the tail end of the Pontic mountain range. With the temperature outside increasing dramatically, we take the opportunity to refill our water containers from a natural spring. I spark up a conversation with a family from Ankara. They kindly share apples with us that they have picked from a nearby abandoned garden. The son speaks extremely good English, and we learn he is studying to be an engineer for high-speed trains. Si asks if there are plans to build a high-speed train line in Turkey. Under the watchful eye of his father, the son straightens his posture and informs us that 1,500km of railway network is due for completion at the end of the year, but he hopes to have the opportunity to work abroad. Helping us to refill our water containers, the mother generously shares more of their apples. We wave farewell and continue on our journey across the dry barren landscape.

We soon arrive in the beautiful Ottoman-era town of Safranbolu. Located in a ravine at 450 metres, we look over the terracotta roof tiles of the preserved Ottoman townhouses that are now shops, restaurants and boutique hotels. Added to the list of UNESCO World Heritage sites in 1994, we stroll through the narrow steep streets and admire the Kirankoy's Ulu Cami "Great Mosque", which had once been the principal church dedicated to St Stephen of the Ottoman Greeks. Safranbolu was a centre for growing the spice saffron during the 17th century, with the main Ottoman trade route between Gerede and the Black Sea coast bringing commerce, prominence and money to the town. Affluent residents in the 18th and 19th centuries constructed these grand houses from wood and sun-dried mud bricks. Before the 1920s Greeks had made up approximately 20% of the population of Safronbolu and, much to their reluctance, they had been forced to leave during the bizarre population exchange after WWI. Exploring the large market in the centre of the town, we browse stalls selling traditional textiles, jewellery and souvenirs. A guy with sunblock plastered across the bridge of his nose breaks free from his tour group and photographs a woman wearing a black burka standing outside a sweet shop. With a veil covering her face, she steps forward to offer him a sample of Turkish delight that is piled high on a silver tray. He recoils with fright and races back to his group. We peer in the window of a tailor's shop. I flash a smile at the white-haired gentleman wearing half-moon spectacles who is working at a Singer sowing machine. He looks uncannily like Mister Geppetto. Unable to find a local tea house to enjoy a refreshing çay, we pass expensive coffee shops and restaurants and see a guy dressed for the tourists in a burgundy Fez hat and matching waistcoat. I smile at the thought that the wealth that Safranbolu had enjoyed in the past is returning, only this time its riches would be made from tourism.

Weaving through the industrial city of Karabuk, we join the highway that will transport us west to Istanbul. We see signs of poverty at the roadside in the form of three men sat huddled together beneath tarpaulin around a steaming cooking pot, while a young mother rocks a baby to sleep in a blanket. Si exits the highway and turns into a bustling rest area with a Metro bus terminal. Charcoal smoke rises from the pink and blue neon lit kofte and fast food restaurants. A constant flow of cars and trucks speed in and out of the bustling services, and young Kurdish guys wearing yellow rubber boots wash vehicles with power hoses. Devouring a kebab served with sour cream, we excitedly debate the road ahead and the next stage of our journey to ancient Thrace, the Bosphorus strait and the legendary city of Istanbul.

* * *

A little after midnight, I'm woken by the sound of water hitting the passenger window. Struggling to focus, I see a Kurdish guy washing a nearby car. He points at the Volvo, and beams a smile. Nodding my head, he flicks up one of the windscreen wipers to claim his next job. I swing my legs out of the car and plant my feet firmly on the wet tarmac. Between my trainers two water trails race each other. The left wins before they merge with a puddle. Stretching my aching body I glance across the car park that is crammed full of cars, motorcycles, mini vans and long distance coaches. With the summer migration reaching its peak, it's comforting to see we are not the only people sleeping on the road.

Chris sticks his head out of the window. 'Coffee?' he croaks.

I nod and head over to the Metro bus terminal. On my return journey, I pass a red Ford Focus with British licence plates. I ask the driver where he is from. He grins at hearing my English accent and reveals he lives in South East London. Enjoying the relaxed conversation and slang that unites people from the same country, I ask him about his trip. He looks quite serious all of a sudden, and explains he has just driven to Baghdad to visit family. I'm completely amazed by his journey, and I wave to the guy's wife sat in the front passenger seat and his three teenage kids squeezed into the back. I ask him what it is like in Iraq now. He seems unsure how to answer my question, and then he tells me their journey had been trouble free and that they had seen many British cars on the road. Chris signals to me from across the car park and the guy smiles when he hears I'm travelling with my brother. He wishes us a fun road trip to the Danube Delta.

Excited by the prospect of a night drive, Chris eagerly slips behind the wheel of our shiny chariot. Joining a toll section of the highway that runs between Ankara and Istanbul, we relax in the slow lane and eat up the kilometres at a smooth and steady pace. Around 1am we begin to see signs for the ancient city of Adapazari, the location of the 480 metre Sangarius Bridge. An impressive feat of engineering, the Sangarius was built during the reign of East Roman Emperor Justinian I (527-565 AD), to improve communications between the capital Constantinople and the eastern provinces of his empire. We approach the large port city of Izmit in the small hours, and Chris points out the Sea of Marmara and a brightly-lit container ship with "Australia" painted across its hull. Twinkling lights along the shoreline reveal the town of Yalova, with a backdrop of silhouetted mountains against a purple sky. Thrust out of a tunnel, we pass hundreds of containers stacked on a quayside that are illuminated by towering spotlights. Drawn deeper into the urban chaos, lanes suddenly merge and a truck from Iran roars past with Arabic writing on the licence plate. We enter an industrial zone around 4am. Chris's eyes are fixed firmly on the road ahead, as we zoom past an open topped trailer with its loose tarpaulin flapping angrily in the wind. Passing the Miltas cement works, the sky overhead is heavy with dust. Newly constructed concrete apartment buildings rise fifteen-stories from the dry earth. A lunatic wearing a mustard-coloured boiler suit throws a metal pipe across the highway to his colleague standing on the central reservation. Brake lights immediately glow red. Brand new diggers for sale line up outside showrooms, with their hydraulic arms raised like giant metal monsters. A blue sign flashes overhead pointing in the direction of Istanbul. This is our gateway home, a colossal city of over 14 million people at the birthplace of the Black Sea.

We swap over the driving just as the sun begins to rise. I inhale one last deep breath before accelerating at speed onto the congested highway. Within a few kilometres the lanes begin to multiply and the many trucks and heavy goods vehicles exit onto a ring road that loops around the city. Approaching the Bosphorus Bridge, the highway becomes eerily quiet as we make our ascent towards towering suspension cables. Fearing that we are experiencing the calm before the storm, we reach the brow of a hill and look in awe at the stunning view of the Bosphorus that rises over the slender hood of the Volvo. To our right we look down over the wealthy district of Beylerbeyi that is located on the Asian side of the Bosphorus. This district of Istanbul is home to the grand Ottoman Beylerbeyi Palace and wooden beach mansions called "yali" that are among the most expensive properties in the world. Chris shoots photographs out of the window of the large passenger ferries, dwarfed in size, that cross this watery divide between the Anatolian Peninsula and ancient Thrace. Reaching the end of the 1.5km bridge, we catch a glimpse of a small yellow sign that confirms our arrival at the last stage of our journey. It simply reads, "Welcome to Europe".

PART 5
Istanbul to the Danube Delta

Eighteen

Concrete and stone, steel and glass sprawls to the horizon. Ottoman wonders stand strong next to billboards advertising designer clothes, watches and perfume. Apartment blocks spring up in every direction and fight for space next to sky rise office buildings. Si skids onto the Galata Bridge and enters into battle with a yellow taxi, while chilled out fishermen with their backs to the chaos cast out their lines into the mouth of the Golden Horn. We pull up alongside a minibus with the side door flung wide open. A guy with a long beard plays a reed flute. He wobbles his head from side to side and his fingers dance energetically over the holes. The atmospheric whining sound drifts over the traffic, as we nudge slowly towards the breathtaking and imposing city skyline. I can see the dome roof of the Yeni Cami "New Mosque" and the grand Sultanahmet Camii "Blue Mosque", with its many towering minarets.

During the Byzantine period, this district of Istanbul on the Golden Horn grew around a natural trading harbour. The Byzantine Empire began around 285 AD, when the emperor Diocletian split the Roman Empire into east and west administrative districts. Between 324 and 330 AD, Constantine I transferred the main capital from Rome to

Byzantium, later known as Constantinople "City of Constantine". Christianity became the Empire's official state religion and later the ruler Heraclius (610–641) adopted the Greek language, instead of Latin, for official use. Surviving the 5th century collapse of the Western Roman Empire, Constantinople continued to exist for an additional thousand years until it fell to the Ottoman Turks in 1453. The Golden Horn grew into a thriving port in Ottoman times; occupied by importers, warehousemen, sailors and traders of every description.

Following a tramline, Si swerves onto Kennedy Avenue and takes a sharp right at the Sirseci Railway Station. Famous as the terminating point for the Orient Express, this luxury train travelled between Paris and Vienna and later to Istanbul. Popular in the 1930s with diplomats, royalty and the bourgeoisie, the Orient Express is less of an attraction today with the arrival of high-speed trains and low cost airlines. In the next few months Istanbul will see the completion of the first stage of the Marmaray Project, the world's deepest undersea railway tunnel. Buried sixty metres below sea level, this high-speed train route will transport passengers and cargo 1.4km across the Bosphorus strait between Europe and Asia. In 2005, the project was delayed for four years, largely due to archaeological finds on the proposed site of the European tunnel terminal. Excavations revealed evidence of the 4th century Harbour of Eleutherios, later known as the Harbour of Theodosius. Traces of the city wall of Constantine the Great have also been uncovered and the remains of several ships, including what appears to be the only ancient or early medieval galley ever discovered. In addition, the oldest settlement in Istanbul has been found and artefacts such as amphora, pottery fragments and shells, pieces of bone, horse skulls and nine human skulls found in a bag dating back to 6000 BC. Glass artefacts and fragments date from the Hellenistic, Roman, Byzantine and Ottoman periods.

Entering the chaotic back streets around Ankara Caddesi, we find ourselves deep in the realms of Istanbul's hotel district. Weaving through the narrow cobbled streets, Si pulls up outside the Hotel Yeni that is located on the corner of Nobethabe Caddesi. We leave the Volvo in a secure parking area and throw our bags into a clean room with a black and white tiled floor. I dive into the communal bathroom and take the first proper shower I've had in weeks. Feeling revitalised, I meet Si in the lobby and we head out into the harsh midday sun. The overwhelming aroma of incense drifts through the ancient streets, where good-humoured shopkeepers tout for business and the azan call to prayer cries out over the rooftops. There have been complaints in recent years by local residents about the noise levels from the mosques; mostly concerning speakers that are turned up to deafening levels, as the muezzins battle against one another to be heard.

We drop by the opulent Topkapi Palace, the primary residence of the Ottoman sultans for over 400 years. Built around four main courtyards, at its peak the palace complex had approximately 4,000 people living inside its walls, and once covered a much larger area with a long shoreline. We seek out the Imperial seraglio (the living quarters of the Sultan's harem), which occupied one of the sections of the private apartments of the sultan. I admire the beautiful yellow and turquoise blue and green decorative tiles that cover the walls of one of the many rooms. Si tells the story of a seven-year-old boy who had been sent to the palace from Trabzon in 1502 to study science, history, literature, theology and military tactics.

He later became Suleiman I "the Magnificent"; the very same Sultan who married Roxelana, a young slave girl who was believed to have been born in the town of Rohatyn (in what was once Poland and is now modern-day Ukraine). With images of the beautiful Crimean Tatar rulers Khansky Palats "Khans Palace" in Bakhchysaray leaping into my mind, the full extent of the power and wealth of the Ottoman rulers in this vast and culturally rich region of the Black Sea becomes a very clear reality.

The Crimean Tatars profited enormously from the demand for slaves by the Ottomans, who needed to be foreigners, as Islam forbade enslaving local Muslims, Christians or Jews. The slaves were transported to the market in Kaffa (Feodosia), before being shipped southwest to Constantinople across the Black Sea. According to the legend, Roxelana, a former Christian girl converted to Islam from Suleiman's harem and subsequently became known and influential as Hürrem Sultan. She later became his legal wife, and their son, Selim II, succeeded Suleiman following his death in 1566 after 46 years of rule. Fascinated to learn what life would have been like in the harem for Roxelana, we discover that the girls would be taught Turkish and Islamic culture and languages as well as the arts of dress, make-up, reading and writing, music, dancing and embroidery. They would then enter a process of merit, first to the sultan's concubines and children, then to the sultan's mother and, finally, if they were the best, to the sultan himself.

We walk through Sultanahmet Park to the imposing Sultan Ahmed Mosque "Blue Mosque", built under the orders of Sultan Ahmet I (1603-17) as a monument to rival the nearby Aya Sofya. Si leads the way into the huge courtyard, and we look in awe at the walls and the ceiling that are covered in thousands of Iznik blue tiles, which are illuminated by the 260 windows that draw light into the vast central prayer hall. In turn we visit the Aya Sofya, Istanbul's most famous monument. We enter the building and walk into the inner narthex. Above the third and largest door the "Imperial Door", I see the mosaic of Christ as Pantocrator "Ruler of All". Stepping into the building's main space, that is famous for its dome, we look in awe at the huge nave and gold mosaics. Built during the reign of Emperor Justinian (527-65 AD), as part of his effort to restore the greatness of the Roman Empire, this exquisite structure was completed in 537 and was regarded as the greatest church in the Christian world until the Ottoman Conquest in 1453. Mehmet the Conqueror (1432-81) converted the building into a mosque, which it remained until 1935, when Atatürk "the first President of Turkey" proclaimed it a museum. Drawn to a mosaic portrait in the southern gallery of Byzantine Empress Zoe (1028-50), we discover this liberal minded ruler had three husbands during her life and had changed the mosaic portrait with each one. Zoe reigned as Byzantine Empress alongside her sister Theodora from 19th April to 11th June 1042. She was then enthroned as the Empress Consort to a series of co-rulers, beginning with Romanos III in 1028, until her death in 1050 while married to Constantine IX. According to Philip Sherrard in his book 'Byzantium', Zoe was fifty at the time of her first marriage and it was said that she was stunningly beautiful.

With a backdrop of dozens of enormous crimson Turkish national flags flapping in the warm breeze, we drink water from the German Fountain. Constructed to commemorate the second anniversary of German Emperor Wilhelm II's visit to Istanbul in 1898, it was built in Germany and then transported piece by piece to Istanbul where it was assembled on its current site in Sultanahmet

Square in 1900. The neo-Byzantine style fountain's octagonal dome has eight marble columns, and the interior is covered with golden mosaics. During the Ottoman period, paying for the construction of a fountain and creating a water supply was a noble gesture. The act of building a fountain was considered an expression of a sultan or sultan's mother or daughter's political and social standing. Refilling our water bottles, we weave through the busy streets to the atmospheric Grand Bazaar. Growing from a small emporium built during the time of Mehmet the Conqueror in the mid 15th century, the Grand Bazaar rapidly became one of the largest markets along the ancient trade routes. We explore the heavily scented labyrinthine of halls and interior courtyards crammed with over 3,000 shops selling Turkish ceramics, clothes, jewellery, carpets and textiles. An eccentric shopkeeper draws us in with his charm and we end up buying a few over-priced souvenirs for family and friends. Si haggles with humour, but fails to grab a cheap deal. Stumbling across a small restaurant located on a side street, we devour a delicious meal of garlic marinated beef served with an aubergine-yoghurt purée called ali nazik. The salad comes with fresh walnuts "Greek nuts", reminding us of the start of our journey on the crumbling sandstone cliffs of Odessa.

* * *

In the early evening, we leap aboard a tram and rattle towards Istiklal Caddesi "Independence Avenue" in the historic Beyoğlu district. Chris spots the Monument of the Republic at the heart of Taksim Square. Inaugurated in 1928, the eleven-metre bronze and marble monument portrays Mustafa Kemal Atatürk and his assistants, who together founded the Turkish Republic. Among the group of men is Mikhail Frunze (a Bolshevik leader during the Russian Revolution), and Kliment Voroshilov (a Marshal of the Soviet Union). The Soviet presence in the monument, ordered by Atatürk, symbolises the military aid and support given by Vladimir Lenin during the Turkish War of Independence in 1920. In the aftermath of World War I, one of the deadliest conflicts in history, the route was paved for major global political changes. Four of the major imperial powers in Europe; the German, Russian, Austro-Hungarian and Ottoman empires fell apart, and revolutions took place in many of the nations involved.

WWI had been sparked by the assassination of Archduke Franz Ferdinand of Austria, heir to the throne of Austria-Hungary, by Yugoslav nationalists on 28th June 1914. Four years later, ten million people had been killed, with the seemingly impossible scenario at the time of Britain and France going to war with Germany to defend Russia against Austria-Hungary over a dispute with Serbia. Anatole Kaletsky, an award-winning journalist and financial economist, warned in an article for Reuters that the short-sighted belief in 1914 that economic self-interest makes wars obsolete had led to the world's most devastating conflict. "The truth, as the world discovered in 1914 and is re-discovering today in the Middle East, Ukraine and the China seas,' wrote Kaletsky, 'is that economic interests are swept aside once the genie of nationalist or religious militarism is released."

When Mustafa Kemal Atatürk founded the Republic of Turkey in 1923 from what remained of the multi-ethnic Ottoman Empire, two groups, Kurds and Islamists, aggressively disagreed with the creation of a secular nation state. Kurds felt disenfranchised, and could see no opportunity for their ethnic and cultural rights to exist in the new Turkey, and Islamists who were against the westernisation of society and politics wanted the continuation of the sultanate and sharia law. Despite Kurds representing approximately 20% of the population, their resistance to Turkification was ignored and unrest was dealt with brutally by the Turkish military.

In the 1920s Mustafa Kemal Atatürk, "pursued a top-down project of radical modernization," wrote Ömer Taspinar, contributor to the book 'The Islamists Are Coming: Who They Really Are'. "Kemalist Turkey adopted Western legal codes together with the Latin alphabet and the Western calendar, Western holidays, and Western dress." Interestingly, despite these huge reforms, they had very little effect. During our journey travelling across eastern Anatolia, we had observed traditional dress and culture in the east of the country continuing to persist in striking contrast to the west of the country. "The rural and pious masses of Anatolia remained largely unaffected by the cultural reengineering in Ankara," wrote Omer, "in contrast to the military, the bureaucracy, and the urban bourgeoisie, who embraced or adapted to Kemalism's superficial Westernization."

The Justice and Development Party (AKP), a centre-right, social Conservative Party, came into power in 2002. Originally developing from the tradition of Islamism, it had taken nearly a century of evolution and the dissolution of four previous parties to create a party that the military would accept and that would win the support of the voters. Under the leadership of Recep Tayyip Erdogan, the AKP had grown strong over the years, with the help of a booming economy and by addressing welfare issues. Erdogan used the term "conservative democracy" rather than an Islamic reference to explain his political agenda. Ömer Taspinar believes, "Its evolution reflects how democratic traditions and institutions can both interact with and moderate political Islam, at least in one geostrategic country."

The success of the AKP, winning three terms of five years in a row since 2002, appears to be a natural readjustment to the balance of a country that was forcefully divided into Turkish versus Kurdish and secular versus Islamic identities, after the collapse of communism in 1991. Erdogan cleverly won favour with the secular business community, liberal intellectuals and middle class, by putting democratic reforms at the top of his agenda, and seeking to comply with EU membership guidelines. He also gave priority to social services that appealed to the poor underclass, securing votes on all sides. Ömer wrote, "Even as the AKP adopted a more liberal order, Kemalist segments of Turkish society grew increasingly suspicious that it had a hidden agenda. They feared that the AKP was exploiting the EU membership process to diminish the military's political role and, eventually, the Kemalist legacy."

We take a stroll through nearby Taksim Gezi Park, an area filled with sycamore trees that is one of the few green spaces left in central Istanbul. Only two months ago, the Turkish government unveiled plans to redevelop this tranquil park into a shopping complex with a cultural centre, an opera house and a new mosque. The announcement sparked a wave of protests in the city, and beyond. According to BBC News, "What started as a demonstration against urban redevelopment had transformed into a wider expression of anger against government policies." Sounding alarm bells, the use of excessive force by riot police had escalated tensions, and the event was (at the time) worryingly being compared with Cairo's Tahrir Square - the focus of the demonstrations, which toppled President Hosni Mubarak in 2011. Protesters' banners had claimed that redeveloping the park was like a commercial takeover of Hyde Park in London, or Central Park in New York.

Along with the construction of a shopping centre, there had also been the proposed reconstruction of an Ottoman-era military barracks that was demolished in 1940. The barracks had a symbolic significance. BBC News, "According to some accounts, it was at the barracks that a (failed) mutiny by Islamic-minded soldiers was initiated in 1909 intent on bringing in Sharia law, and attempts to rebuild them are seen by opponents to have the ring of Islamism."

The protest over Gezi Park is not the first time Taksim Square has been the location of political demonstrations. Many groups from all sides of the political spectrum, as well as many NGOs, have protested in the square throughout the 20th century. As early as 1955, during the anti-Greek Istanbul Riots, nearby Independence Avenue was sacked by looters and anarchists. In 1969, some 150 leftist demonstrators had been injured during clashes with rightwing groups in what is known as "Bloody Sunday". In the events known as the Taksim Square massacre, 36 left-wing demonstrators were killed by unidentified and allegedly right-wing gunmen on the square during the Labour Day demonstrations on 1st May 1977. For a period, group protests were banned in the square, but gradually the people have been allowed to return to voice their opinions. Tensions in Istanbul with regards to Gezi Park are by no means over. Turkish activists, who are alleged leaders of Taksim Solidarity (an umbrella group of civil society, union and political groups who helped launch the recent mass anti-government protests), may be caught and charged with founding a crime syndicate, violating public order and organising illegal protests through social media. If they do go on trial, it could cause outrage and spark further protests.

It seems clear a huge cultural and political divide still exists in Turkey, which had inevitably led to the election of the AKP in 2002 and the recent protests over Taksim Gezi Park. The Turkish Republic is still relatively new, and many Turks grandfathers (or great grandfathers) had died fighting during the Liberation War in 1923. The BBC reported, "critics say the decision to go ahead with the redevelopment was made too fast and without proper public and media debate."

Turkey's complex political situation will never be straight forward, but they have according to Ömer Taspinar so far managed to achieve and maintain in the 21st century, "arguably the most dynamic experiment with political Islam among the fifty-seven nations of the Muslim world." The process to maintain peace in this fascinating, multi-ethnic country will be a long arduous task, with many conflicting issues that may never be resolved. Ömer, "The AKP had long wanted to lift the ban on Islamic dress—or wearing of headscarves—in universities and end discrimination against graduates of Islamic high schools." With more than fifty percent of Turkish women covering their heads, this would forever be the subject of debate. "Under the AKP, Turkey is still not a liberal democracy, despite the pattern of multiparty elections." Wrote Ömer. "Compared to the lost decade of the 1990s; however, it has become a more multifaceted democracy, with elections, public opinion, opposition parties, parliament, the media and civil society all exerting more power. For the first time in the republic's history, Turkey's performance is also totally in civilian hands."

We join the city's night time revellers on nearby Independence Avenue, where beautiful neo-classical, neo-gothic and art nouveau architecture line the street. People sit outside pavement cafes and bars and drink Turkish red wine and beer and smoke Anatolian apple flavoured nargileh molasses in shisha pipes. During the Ottoman period, this avenue was called Cadde-i Kebir "Grand Avenue". It was popular with Ottoman intellectuals and was a centre for European foreigners and the local Italian and French Levantines. In the 19th century Constantinople was labelled the "Paris of the East"; a city with a tantalising blend of half-European and half-Asian culture. At a glance Istanbul is still an incredibly cosmopolitan and multicultural city, and I begin to find hope in the form of the future leaders and political thinkers who will shape our world. Our journey across Turkey, has allowed us to catch a glimpse into the lives of the many different people and cultures living together in this colossal melting pot at the frontier of Europe, the Middle East and Asia. On the surface, the majority of the Anatolian people we have met in the east appear to live happy and peaceful existences, and here too in Istanbul we witness youthful hope and expression. The protests over Gezi Park, however, should not be ignored, and should serve as a warning and reminder of Turkey's turbulent and volatile history. Here in this sprawling, over-populated metropolis, tensions can quickly rise. Rapid globalisation has created an ever-widening gap between the have and have-nots, and between those citizens looking to the West and those to the East. The world has signed up to the era of the megacity and, in a bid to prevent future unrest and the threat of violence and civil war, its people from multiple ethnic backgrounds will need to exercise extreme tolerance and consideration and work tirelessly to absorb and accommodate the continual influx of migrants seeking a role in the new world.

Lured by the buzzing atmosphere of a Turkish meyhane, Chris suggests we celebrate reaching the last stage of our journey by drinking copious amounts of raki. We enter the bar to the sounds of the fasil. Perched on stools, we lose ourselves in the night as the musicians playing the violin, lyre and clarinet, conjure up a spell that has the entire tavern dancing and singing until dawn.

Nineteen

Through half-closed eyes I reach for a bottle of water and struggle to unscrew the lid. My vision is cloudy and I begin to fear my brain has been removed during the night and replaced with kebab meat. Si rolls off his bed and staggers around the room, his hair is sticking up wildly and his t-shirt is inside out and back to front. Freshening up, we head down to reception in time for a strong Turkish coffee.

Flicking a coin, I choose tails and reluctantly slump behind the wheel. Within minutes, I'm battling against an army of bright orange Hyundai taxis on Kennedy Avenue. I see an IKEA to my right and a sign for the new Olympic Park that is already under construction for 2020. Joining the highway west to the Bulgarian border, a monster traffic jam grinds the speeding traffic to a sudden halt. Two police officers approach an unshaven guy who is selling bottled water at the side of the carriageway. He makes a sudden run for it. The cops leap into the back of a red pickup truck, and the civilian vehicle speeds up the hard shoulder. The water seller escapes with his freedom by scrambling down a steep bank. Two ambulances scream past and the traffic slowly begins to move once more. A few kilometres on, we pass the wreckage of three cars that have collided where the highway merges. I spot two guys wearing baseball caps standing on a bridge. They are both clutching assault rifles. A black SUV with tinted windows suddenly speeds past in convoy with four police motorcycles, two at the front and two at the back, and I wonder if it is the President of Turkey or some neighbouring politician.

Breaking free of the congestion we traverse the north shore of the Sea of Marmara, which is flooded in soft lemon light. A strong, hot wind blows through Si's window from the direction of the Dardanelles strait in the southwest that connects the Black Sea to the Aegean Sea. It was here that Alexander the Great, the king of the Greek kingdom of Macedon, launched his expansion plans and invaded the Achaemenid Empire "First Persian Empire" in 334 BC. Tutored by the philosopher Aristotle until the age of 16, Alexander succeeded his father to the throne after he was assassinated in 336 BC. Inheriting an experienced army and strong kingdom, he was awarded the generalship of Greece and used this authority to launch his father's military expansion plans. In 334 BC, aged 22, he crossed the Hellespont (Dardanelles) with approximately 48,000 soldiers (many Thracian), 6,100 cavalry and a fleet of 120 ships with crews numbering 38,000. On the south shores of the Sea of Marmara, near the site of Troy, he fought the Battle of the Granicus River; the first of three major battles fought between Alexander the Great and the Persian Empire. Successfully ruling Asia Minor, he began a campaign that lasted ten years. Overthrowing the Persian King Darius III, he conquered the entirety of the Persian Empire that stretched all the way from the Adriatic Sea to the Indus River in modern-day Pakistan and India.

After a few hours, we turn off the highway and drive north to Kirklareli. This small ancient town 15km from the

Bulgarian border claims to be the location of one of the first organised settlements on the European continent, with artefacts from the Palaeolithic and Neolithic periods. The Persians conquered Kirklareli in 513–512 BC and the Ottoman Turks took the city from the Byzantines in 1363. We pass the Kırklareli Dam and cruise along a quiet two-way road that cuts across the rural landscape to the small 'Aziziye - Malko Tarnovo' border crossing with Bulgaria. Si throws his passport onto the dashboard and I nod to a stony-faced border guard. He casually points his rifle in the direction of the immigration building. After our passports have been stamped we are directed to the back of the building, where we greet an old man sitting in the shade in a crumbling part of the border crossing. We hand him our car documents and he whacks a stamp on one of the pages. After changing the last of our Turkish Lira into euros, I get chatting to a Turkish guy from London. He seems keen to know where we have been in our Volvo, and smiles at hearing we have driven around the Black Sea. Hussein hands me a business card and invites us for a free drink in his bar in Shoreditch the next time we are in London. He seems keen for us to know that it is not a kebab shop, but rather a trendy restaurant and bar. Shaking him firmly by the hand he flicks on his shades and leaps behind the wheel of a convertible Audi A7. The engine roars and he accelerates away.

At Bulgarian customs we approach an official slumped behind the counter with dark circles under his eyes.

'Cigarettes?' he asks.

We shake our heads and with a grunt he sends us away.

Having successfully made it back to the European Union, we drive to the small settlement of Malko Tarnovo and pass a group of cyclists. They look like a professional racing team. Filling up with fuel, I notice three overland jeeps from Poland parked up at the adjacent pumps. The vehicles look brand new and are covered in sponsorship stickers. Si points out two incredibly thickset guys walking across the forecourt. They look to be of Roma ethnicity.

With little written history the origins of the Roma was for a long time a complete mystery. Arriving in Europe in the 14th century, we now know from clues in the various dialects of their language "Romani" that they migrated from northern India to the Middle East a thousand years ago. Europeans had initially mistaken them for being Egyptians, and gave them the shortened name "Gypsies". The fact that the Roma people originated from India had always puzzled me. But after learning about the Persian Empire and the Greek kingdom of Macedon under Alexander the Great, which reached as far as the Indus Valley in eastern Pakistan and northwest India, it no longer seems so incredulous. In the one-thousand years that the Roma have called Europe their home, they have not achieved anywhere near the same level of acceptance as, for example, the Scythians, who migrated onto the Pontic steppe around the time the Greeks first began to colonise the Black Sea. Arriving in a world very different to their own, there was little opportunity for the Roma to develop a symbiotic existence, whereby two very different ways of living, the settled and the nomadic could exist in harmony.

From the moment of their arrival in Europe, the Roma had been subjected to persecution with the modern state viewing their nomadic existence as anti-social and their spiritual beliefs and fortune-telling being contradictory to the philosophy of the church. According to Peter Godwin in an article published by National Geographic, "At various times they have been forbidden to wear their distinctive bright clothes, to speak their own language, to travel, to marry one another, or to ply their traditional crafts. In some countries they were reduced to slavery and it wasn't until the mid-1800s that Gypsy slaves were freed in Romania."

Life for the Roma in Eastern Europe, where the majority live today, had been somewhat more complicated. Under communism, they were forced to settle and to assimilate and today few of them are now nomadic. For multiple generations many Roma have lived across Eastern Europe in slums on the edge of towns and rundown concrete tower blocks in cities. It is difficult for Roma to find work, because no one wants to employ them. Very few Roma children in areas of Slovakia have been to school; instead they are placed into special schools for kids with learning difficulties and consequently the cycle of poverty is passed on from one generation to the next. Peter Godwin wrote, "After World War II many rural Slovakian Gypsies were relocated by the government to work in the factories of the industrial heartlands of the Czech territories. But when the Velvet Revolution toppled communism in 1989, Gypsy jobs tended to be the first lost as the economy lurched from central to market control. And while there is a small, assimilated Gypsy intelligentsia, today Czech Gypsies typically live in grim tenements in the cities."

The prospect of new opportunities in Western Europe, as the Cold War drew to a close, had predictably attracted many members of the Roma to move to EU member states to work illegally, beg, or claim political asylum. Panicked members of the European Union have introduced restrictions to visas in an attempt to control immigration. These new regulations once again upsetting the Romanian and Bulgarian gadje (non-Gypsies), who blame the

Gypsies for slowing down the integration process into Europe. Fuelling tensions further, a minority of Roma who have profited from their new opportunities in Europe, have built large new houses with decorative roofs known as, "Gypsy Mansions". This has provoked yet more fanatical behaviour by skinheads and neo-Nazis, who have victimised the Roma for the past few decades. But violence and hostility is nothing new for the Roma. In their bleak history, approximately half a million perished in the Holocaust, caught up in Nazi ethnic hysteria. Peter Godwin wrote, "Their horses have been shot and the wheels removed from their wagons, their names have been changed, their women have been sterilized, and their children have been forcibly given for adoption to non-Gypsy families (a practice in Switzerland until 1973)."

Against all odds, the Roma have survived in Europe for a thousand years and show no signs of disappearing. In France, life has got better for the Roma. "Every town in France with a population over 5,000 has to have a field reserved for Gypsies, by law," wrote Godwin. In the old days they didn't go to school, they travelled constantly and they were chased away from one town to the next and often hid in the forest. But the Roma is starting to live differently. They are buying property, they are intermarrying and consequently the culture is becoming diluted. For Western Europe the difficulty with knowing how to manage the Roma people is just beginning, but for the Roma people themselves, they also have a challenging future ahead of them as they struggle to hold on to their traditional culture and their place in a settled society.

Si points up into the cloudless sky at a huge Great White Pelican that glides overhead. We watch this magnificent bird soar above Lake Burgas in a region that was once inhabited by tribes the Greeks called Thracians. The first historical record found that mentions the Thracians is in the ancient Greek epic poem, "the Iliad", which describes them as allies of the Trojans in the Trojan War against the Greeks. Thracians were considered to be a fierce race of warrior tribes and were seen as "barbarians" by the Greeks and the Romans. Plato in his "Republic" considers them, along with the Scythians, extravagant and high-spirited and in his "Laws" considers them a war-like nation, grouping them with Celts, Persians, Scythians, Iberians and Carthaginians. The Thracians left behind the ruins of sanctuaries and sacrificial altars and dolmens (megalithic tombs) in this region. With no written history, as with the Pagans, where the Thracians originate from is unknown. It is widely thought by archaeologists and historians that a proto-Thracian people developed from a mixture of indigenous peoples and Indo-Europeans, who are believed to have emerged from the Pontic-Caspian steppe in Central Asia, around the time of Proto-Indo-European expansion in the Early Bronze Age around 1500 BC.

The city of Burgas was first settled by the Thracians, who built the mineral baths of Aqua Calidae and the fortress of Tyrsis. Under Darius I (550 BC) it became part of the Achaemenid "First Persian Empire", and the Greeks built a marketplace in the Sladkite kladenzi district for trade with the Thracians kings during the rise of the Odrysian kingdom. The Odrysian State was the first Thracian kingdom that acquired power in the region, by the unification of many Thracian tribes under the rule of King Teres in the 5th century BC. During this period the state extended from the Black Sea to the east, Danube to the north, the region populated with the tribe called Triballi to the northwest, and the basin of the river

Strymon to the southwest and towards the Aegean.

According to the Greek historian Herodotus, a royal dynasty emerged from among the Odrysian tribe in Thrace around the end of the 5th century BC, which came to dominate much of the area and peoples between the Danube and the Aegean for the next century. With evidence of its survival into the 1st century AD, the dynasty's power progressively declined following a second wave of Persian encroachment, followed by Macedonian (Alexander the Great) and later Roman expansion. The extent of Greek influence in this western corner of the Black Sea was clearly evident, as under the Odrysians, Greek became the language of administrators and of the nobility. Milesian traders had been successfully exporting Greek culture around the shores of the Black Sea for centuries, first with the Scythians and then with the Sarmatians. Greek customs greatly influenced east Balkan society, and the Thracian kings were among the first to be Hellenized; adopting Greco-Roman dress and military equipment and spreading it to the other tribes.

* * *

On the outskirts of Burgas, Chris draws the car to a halt outside a rundown apartment building opposite a fish-processing factory. We grab coffee from a vending machine, and recruit the assistance of two Roma women waiting at a bus stop with two children. They are wearing beautiful jewellery and colourful skirts. Deeply tanned, the women look strong and laugh hysterically as they help the clumsy foreigners operate the machine.

Driving into town we stretch our legs along the pleasant tree-lined waterfront around Burgas Bay, and see fishing trawlers that operate at the heart of the Bulgarian fishing industry. Heading north, we see chimneys belonging to the LUKOIL Neftochim Burgas, the largest oil refinery in south-eastern Europe. We hug the coast and skim alongside the shores of Lake Atanasovsko, home to marsh harriers, pelicans and red-footed falcons. Chris reveals that due to the lake's high salinity, sea salt has been produced here since 1906 with approximately 40,000 tons of the mineral being extracted each year. We pass a number of large seaside resorts and the Burgas airport, with a number of old planes deteriorating on the runway. Billboards advertise the 100 Gypsy Violins Concert, campsites, hotels, endless nightclubs and the cage fighting event "Cage of Glory IV". On the road to the seaside resort of Sunny Beach, we see holidaymakers covered from head-to-toe in black mud basking on the sand. The mud is a sedimentary product of the salt from Lake Atanasovsko, and is thought to alleviate symptoms associated with various skin diseases and gynaecological health issues. Apparently, even Adolf Hitler was a fan of the mud, and he ordered two wagon loads to be delivered to Berlin when he left Bulgaria during the Second World War.

After enjoying a quick dip in the blue, Chris powers the Volvo into the eastern end of the Balkan Mountains, which stretch for 560km across the entire width of the country from the border with Serbia to the Black Sea. This region of the Balkan Mountains was the site of numerous battles between the Bulgarian and the Byzantine Empires in the 9th and 12th centuries. One of those great battles was the battle of Varbitsa Pass in 811 AD, when Khan Krum defeated an enormous Byzantine army. Known as 'Krum the Fearsome' during his reign, the Bulgarian territory doubled in size and spread from the middle Danube to the Dnieper in Ukraine and from Odrin to the Tatra Mountains. From our elevated vantage point we look out towards Cape Emine, a headland that forms the tip of Stara Planina "Old Mountain" where it meets the sea. Stara Planina acted as a natural fortress protecting the Bulgarian Empire that existed between the 7th and 14th centuries. The Byzantines feared these mountains, and on several occasions soldiers had pulled back only on the news of approaching Stara Planina. During Ottoman rule, outlaws, highwaymen and freedom fighters from the Balkans and Central and Eastern Europe, known as "haiduks", also found refuge in these hills.

A Roma prostitute wearing bright pink lingerie touts for business at the roadside, and we pass a group of shady looking youths standing around a pimped up hatchback. I glance over my shoulder and smile when I see a civilised picnic spread out on the rear parcel shelf. We pause for fuel in the upmarket port town of Obzor and watch a cream Bentley skid onto the forecourt. A clean-cut guy wearing a sports jacket and shades leaps out, while his attractive female passenger checks her makeup and reapplies lipstick. Driving to the edge of town in the late evening, we spot a small zoo located in a tranquil forest. Two motor homes with Italian licence plates are parked up in a clearing so we choose to spend the night here. We cook delicious Bulgarian sausages and drink a glass of beer to the atmospheric hooting call of a peacock.

The roaring engine of a tourist coach looms over the Volvo. The doors gasp open and dozens of weary holidaymakers disappear zombie-like into the undergrowth. Chris grumpily strikes the engine and moves the car closer to a huge pile of felled trees. Stretching my aching back, I inhale the fresh morning air that is scented by the faint odour of animal dung. Outside the gates of the small zoo, a guy wearing khaki shorts and a cowboy hat chats casually to an older chap wearing a smart shirt and trousers. There is a truck parked a short distance away, and I smile at the company name "Hunland" written across the back. Climbing aboard the Volvo we point the car north and drive to the final frontier of our journey. Within an hour we find ourselves in a heaving traffic jam as we approach the 2km Asparuhov Bridge, which was built in 1976 to cross a newly constructed canal linking Lake Varna and the Black Sea. In the rising heat of the day the temperature inside the Volvo grows unbearable, so we join dozens of other road users seeking the shade of the trees. With a mixture of locals and tourists wandering around the highway, there is a relaxed carnival atmosphere in the air. A middle-aged guy wearing a smart polo shirt reaches inside the trunk of his car and raids the cool box.

He looks over, and smiles. 'You are British?'

'Yes,' I reply.

'There is big accident on bridge. We could be here for much time.'

He kindly offers us both a ham and cheese sandwich. We gladly accept and soon learn Dimitri is a business executive from the Bulgarian capital of Sofia. He explains he comes to Varna every year with his family and would love to travel to the UK and work in London. Our conversation turns to politics, and he explains that since the end of communism and the adoption of a democratic constitution in 1991, it has been an uphill struggle for Bulgaria. Working as a renewable energy consultant, he explains the strongest sectors of the economy are heavy industry, power engineering and agriculture, all of which rely on local natural resources. In his opinion, the EU needs to follow the example of China and Germany and throw all of its resources into creating clean renewable power.

Bulgaria had taken a massive hit economically when it joined the EU, largely because it had been required to close down its communist-era nuclear power station in January 2007. With a negative population growth since the early 1990s, Bulgaria is in a state of demographic crisis. Economic collapse had caused mass emigration, with over one million people, mostly young adults, leaving the country by 2005; a substantial number when you consider the total population is only a little over 7 million. A third of all households consist of only one person in Bulgaria, and 75% of families do not have children under the age of 16. Consequently, population growth and birth rates are among the lowest in the world, while death rates the highest. I ask Dimitri about the Socialist backed government under Prime Minister Plamen Oresharski, and the recent student-led protests in Bulgaria over high energy costs, low living standards and corruption, that had led Boiko Borisov's GERB conservative party government to resign on the 20th February 2013.

Dimitri furrows his brow. 'People are tired of corruption. They want better management of our economy. The students do not want a Socialist government, they want real democracy.'

Our conversation is interrupted by the noise of an ambulance screaming past. People begin to walk towards the bridge to grab a closer look. It appears to be very serious. Dimitri's two small children run over and lighten the mood, as they fight excitedly over the contents of the cool box. After two hours, I hear car engines spark up into action. Dimitri shakes our hands and we wish him a fun vacation. Chris leaps behind the wheel and we inch slowly across the fifty metre high bridge, with stunning views over Varna Lake. We pass the scene of the accident, and see a red VW Golf with alloy wheels that has virtually been crushed beyond recognition. Pushing through the city traffic, we arrive at the Varna Archaeological Museum and make our way through the crowds to catch a glimpse of one of the most astounding archaeological discoveries around the Black Sea.

In 1972, excavator operator, Raycho Marinov, accidentally stumbled across a necropolis right here in Varna. Archaeologists investigated the site and discovered graves containing gold coins, weapons and jewellery over 6,000 years old. The largest prehistoric cemetery in south-eastern Europe, 294 graves have been found in the necropolis on the north shores of Lake Varna. Three of these were found to contain sophisticated examples of copper and gold metallurgy, with 3,000 gold artefacts uncovered with a combined weight of approximately 6kg, along with 600 pieces of pottery (some gold-painted) and high-quality flint and obsidian blades, shells and beads. Examining the many beautifully handcrafted gold artefacts, dating from 4600-4200 BC, which occupy three separate exhibition halls, we are left completely mesmerised at seeing evidence of a highly evolved civilisation that thrived in this region in the 5th millennium BC. The Varna culture had existed only a thousand years after the proposed catastrophic flood (according to the Black Sea deluge hypothesis), and I try to imagine what the world might have been like here thousands of years before the arrival of the Scythians on the Pontic steppe and the birth of Abrahamic religions in the Levant.

Predating the Ancient Greeks by more than 3,000 years and the earliest Ancient Egyptians by 1,000 years, the Varna Necropolis treasure belonged to an ancient Eneolithic Varna culture. With 30% of the estimated necropolis area yet to be excavated, Chris smiles at the prospect of the secrets that may still lie hidden beneath the earth. Findings at the site have led archaeologists to believe that the Varna culture may have had trade relations with distant lands, in particular with tribes inhabiting the lower Volga region in the east and the Cyclades in the south (a Greek island group in the Aegean Sea between mainland Greece and Turkey). It is thought they may have exported metal goods and salt from the Provadiya rock salt mine, along the shores of the Black Sea. Studying a display of Mediterranean spondylus shells that were found in the graves; images flash through my mind of a powerful civilisation trading goods for these precious shells, which are thought to have been an early form of currency. Peering into a tomb with a skeleton inside belonging to a man, who it is believed was approximately 45-50 years old and either a chief or priest; it seems some kind of hierarchy existed in their society as he was buried with 1.5kg of gold objects. In the grave sites, 99 tombs were found to contain skeletons lying straight on their backs (most of whom were men), and in 67 tombs the skeletons were found to be lying on their right sides in bending position (who were found to be mostly female). In 57 of the graves there had been no skeleton at all, only grave gifts "cenotaphs". Intriguingly, it was these symbolic empty graves that contained the richest gold artefacts, with grave 43 containing 1,000 objects, including 31 gold necklaces, which represent the oldest worked gold pieces on Earth found to date.

Based on the incredible findings around these fascinating Black Sea shores, it seems clear this region flourished economically during the second half of the 5th millennium BC. According to extensive archaeological excavation of this region, by the end of the Eneolithic Age this primitive society on the Balkan Peninsula appears to disappear. With evidence of a period of movement of large human masses from east to west across the Pontic steppe shortly after this period (as revealed by the Kurgan hypothesis), it is thought the end of the Varna civilisation may have been caused by the arrival of warring steppe tribes. Marija Gimbutas, founder of the Kurgan hypothesis, claims that at the end of the 5th millennium BC the transition to male dominance began in Europe. The high status male was buried with large amounts of gold, held a war axe and wore a gold penis sheath.

We exit the museum and I debate with Chris the crystal clear realisation that an ongoing pattern seems to repeat itself over and over again in this region of the world. Since the formation of the Black Sea 7,000 years ago, a sizeable shoreline has existed where civilisations flourished. The Black Sea was the world's first "Grand Bazaar", a central meeting point of multiple evolved cultures born out of the rise of modern humanity, and made possible by the evolution of agriculture. The eastern nomadic tribes came to dominate the steppe, and in turn would thrive very rapidly through trade with the existing advanced civilisations living around these waters. But with few predators, inevitably a stronger tribe born out of the hostile east would eventually emerge out of the grasslands and replace it. It suddenly occurs to me that the romantic idea of living a nomadic existence exists only in times of peace. The settled and the nomadic ways of life had collided here, often existing in symbiosis. Nomadic pastoralists became merchants, farmers and soldiers of empires, wealthy agrarian landowners, aristocracy and even kings. Seduced by the riches and power a settled existence offers nomadism quickly dissolves, but it never entirely disappears.

Twenty

The Dormition of the Mother of God Cathedral slides into view. Si nudges through the city traffic and we see a road sign for the mighty E70 highway, which emerges out of the Black Sea and continues on its epic journey west to A Coruña in Galicia. We make our way steadily north to the Romanian border, and pass a continuous chain of hotels and villa communities that link Varna for 17km all the way to the seaside resort of Golden Sands. The forests in this region of Bulgaria were first mentioned by Pliny the Elder, a Roman author and naturalist from the 1st century AD. He wrote Naturalis Historia, which became a model for all other encyclopaedias. Bizarrely, Pliny described these old-growth forests between ancient Odessos and Dionysopolis, as the home of mythical dwarfs visited by the Argonauts. Perhaps more interestingly, later in his life Pliny was tragically killed by the volcanic eruption that destroyed Pompeii.

The forests disappear at the resort town of Kavarna and are replaced by flat barren plains. Like an army of Thracian soldiers, wind turbines guard this stretch of the Bulgarian coast all the way to the Vama-Veche border crossing. They turn majestically as they embrace the warm easterly breeze that blows from the steppes across the

Black Sea. At the control booth we flash our passports at the Romanian immigration officer, and he casually glances at our photographs before waving us through. Si buys road tax from a small brick building and returns reciting the word "multumesc", Romanian for thank you.

Romania has an ancient prehistoric human history, with archaeological evidence of Homo sapiens living in this region 40,000 years ago. The first known inhabitants of Romania were the Cucuteni-Trypillian culture, who lived mainly centred around the territory of Moldavia around 5500 to 2750 BC. This ancient indigenous civilization, were Danubian farmers who practised agriculture, raised livestock, hunted and made intricately designed pottery. According to the Kurgan hypothesis, they gradually became absorbed by the Proto-Indo-European expansion of tribes of nomadic pastoralists, who (predating the Scythians) migrated from the Pontic-Caspian steppe and into Eastern Europe in the 3rd millennium BC. Indo-Europeanization was complete by the beginning of the Bronze Age, and the people described as proto-Thracians later developed into Danubian Getae (from the Lower Danube), and the Dacians (from the Carpathian Mountains north of the Danube). The Getae, a name given to several Thracian tribes inhabiting this region, were later brought into close contact with the Ancient Greeks; being at the hinterland of the Greek colonies. Fascinatingly, evidence has been found right here in the nearby town of Mangalia of Scythian presence who, by this time, had begun to be pushed west into modern-day Romania by the Sarmatians. The Dacians in the north of Romania and the Getae in the south both spoke the Thracian language, but the Dacians were culturally more influenced by the neighbouring Scythians and the Celtic invaders from the west.

At the start of our journey we had imagined the only connection the Scythians had with the Greeks was via their trading colonies around the Pontic steppe. But drawing closer to making a loop around this large inland sea, we begin to realise mainland Greece also expanded north into Bulgaria and Romania and was geographically very near to the Scythians, who migrated west over the north shore of the Black Sea as early as 600 BC.

Following the conquests in 335 BC of Alexander the Great from the neighbouring Greek kingdom of Macedon, Dacia became a province of the Roman Empire and later came under the control of the Ottoman Empire. The principalities of Moldavia and Wallachia, located north of the River Danube and south of the Southern Carpathians, unified in 1859 to form the basis of the modern state of Romania. It gained independence from the Ottoman Empire in 1877, and by the end of World War I, Transylvania, Bukovina and Bessarabia united under the sovereign Kingdom of Romania. The name Romania derives from the Latin "romanus", meaning "citizen of Rome" and the word is not known to have been adopted by the Roma (Gypsies), who derive their name from the word "rom", a masculine noun in the Romani language, meaning "man of the Roma ethnic group".

Our first introduction to Romania is the grand sight of three enormous ships on a production line. We look with intrigue at the freshly painted black and yellow vessels that tower above the road. On the outskirts of Mangalia, Si spots a beautiful golden sandy beach and he swings the Volvo into a parking space overlooking the sea. Slipping on my swimming shorts, I tiptoe across the hot sand and dive into the turquoise blue water. From our current location we are now only a three-hour drive to Tulcea on the Danube delta, where we could treat ourselves to a cold beer, a hot meal and sleep in the comfort and safety of a hotel. Si hasn't mentioned the idea, so I decide to remain quiet…one more night on the road…one more night living on the Black Sea.

Si introduces me to a guy with long, wavy black hair called Stefan. He kindly offers us both a can of beer, and we stand around the trunk of his red Dacia hatchback and soak up the healing rays of the sun. Stefan reveals he was born in Moldavia and moved to the capital of Bucharest a few years ago to study information technology at university. He now works for a leading computer security company, and proudly informs us Romania is home to some of the most talented computer hackers in the world. I ask him about life in Romania before independence. Stefan explains that it had been tough growing up in Iasi, a city in the western part of Moldavia, which is today part of Romania. The east of Moldavia around Bessarabia was annexed in 1940, as part of Russia's grand plan to pursue a potential communist revolution in Romania. It became the autonomous Moldavian Soviet Socialist Republic later that year within the Ukrainian SSR. Lasting until 1991, Moldova declared itself an independent state following the dissolution of the Soviet Union. The country, officially known as the Republic of Moldova, is a member of the UN and aspires to join the EU. We talk about the breakaway region of Transnistria, and Stefan jokes about how the Transnistrians are living in the past and yearn for the old days under Soviet rule. A thin strip of Moldova's internationally recognised territory on the east bank of the river Dniester has been under the de facto control of the breakaway government of Transnistria since 1990. Unlike the rest of Moldova they had not wanted to separate from the Soviet Union, and events had escalated into a military conflict that started in March 1992 and was concluded by a ceasefire in July 1992. Although the ceasefire has held, the territory's political status remains unresolved and Transnistria is an unrecognised, but independent presidential republic with its own government.

For Stefan, his childhood in Moldavia was shaped by the terrible events that his grandparents had endured during World War II. With the threat of Soviet invasion hanging over their heads, Romania had agreed to cooperate with the Germans during their planned 1941 Axis invasion of the Soviet Union. Invading their close neighbours in the territories of Bessarabia, northern Bukovina and Transnistria, Romanian forces, with an army of 1.2 million men, fought the Russians and deported or exterminated approximately 300,000 Jews and Gypsies, including 147,000 from Bessarabia and Bukovina. Romania's decision to side with the Germans against the Soviet Union saw the country become the target of intense bombing by the Allies (France, Britain and Russia); partly because the country was now the main source of oil for the Third Reich. In August 1944, with King Michael's Coup, the country switched sides and joined the Allies. Changing sides cost the Romanians the loss of 170,000 men, and after the defeat of Germany by the Allies the country fell under Soviet occupation. The communist-led government called for new elections in 1946, and rapidly established them as the dominant political force. In 1947, King Michael I was forced to abdicate and leave the country and Romania was proclaimed a peoples' republic. Romania remained under the direct military occupation and economic control of the USSR until the late 1950s.

According to Stefan, during this period, Romania's vast natural resources were allegedly drained by mixed Soviet-Romanian companies set up for unilateral exploitative purposes. His grandparents had been teenagers during the war, and they had been worst affected after 1948 when the state began to nationalize private firms and to collectivize agriculture. The family lost their farm and lived in fear of the Securitate (the Romanian secret police). During this period a campaign of purges was introduced in which numerous "enemies of the state" were imprisoned for political or economic reasons, tortured and eventually killed. In 1965, a couple of years after Stefan's parents were born Nicolae Ceausescu came to power as the General Secretary of the Romanian Communist Party. In 1967, he became head of state and over the following two decades he gradually morphed into a dictator. He ordered the construction of the infamous Palace of Parliament that was built in Bucharest in 1984, an enormous 12-storey building with 1,100 rooms. During Ceausescu's lengthy rule, he gradually lost touch with the realities of life for the people in his country.

'People had money in their pockets,' Stefan reveals, 'but there was no food to buy in the shops. Under the communist system, education was good and my father managed to get a place to study engineering at university in Bucharest. It was difficult times. He wanted to excel in his education, but his parents were practically starving to death in the countryside.'

Ceausescu's brutality meant that he ruled with an iron fist, muffling the growing desperation of the people. In 1989, with the goal of paying off Romania's large foreign debt, Ceausescu's ordered the export of much of the country's agricultural and industrial production. This decision had the catastrophic affect of creating huge shortages of basic necessities such as medicines, food and fuel. Consequently living standards were dramatically lowered sparking widespread protest.

Stefan takes a swig of beer and speaks matter of fact about the events in his country. 'People were so frightened of Ceausescu, that even his closest advisors would hide the problems with food distribution in our country. They would stock shops with food wherever he went to visit. I think he did not realise the extent of the problem.'

Ceausescu's regime collapsed after he ordered his security forces to fire on anti-government demonstrators in the city of Timisoara on 17th December 1989. Stefan's father had bravely joined the many anti-government demonstrations, which spread to Bucharest and became known as the Romanian Revolution. Ceausescu and his wife, Elena, fled the capital in a helicopter, but were later captured by the armed forces. On 25th December the couple were hastily tried, convicted and shot by firing squad. Following the 1989 Revolution, Romania began a slow transition towards democracy and a capitalist market economy. Si asks Stefan what life is like in Romania now, and he pauses in thought.

'It is not perfect,' he replies. 'The government are thieves. We have huge mineral deposits in the mountains, and oil. They sell pieces off for their own financial gain whenever they think they can get away with it. Life is still pretty bad for the people here. If we want to earn good money we have to work abroad. Under communism we had more money and job security, but nothing to buy. Under democracy we have no jobs and no money and everything to buy.'

A guy waves to Stefan from across the beach and he signals back. We thank Stefan for the beer and for giving us an insight into the complex and fascinating world of Romania. Respectfully shaking our hands, Stefan wishes us luck on the remainder of our journey. He runs across the sand and turns around sharply and punches the air.

'Say hello to London from Stefan!" he laughs.

* * *

A smooth arrow-straight highway with a freshly painted yellow line transports us across a vast open landscape of rolling hills. I catch snapshots of a small substation, a brick ruin and an old abandoned farmhouse. A large herd of goats munch on stalks of harvested wheat in a dusty brown field; the soothing jangle of bells floats through the humid air. A field of petrified sunflowers, charred by the sun, stand with their backs to the road; their heads hung low. I develop the sudden urge to start cutting them down, it seeming cruel to leave them to suffer in the blistering heat. Reaching the small town of Babadag, we see dozens of Roma women and children at the roadside. A teenage girl, who looks to be of pure Indian origin, is wearing a bright purple sari and enormous gold earrings. A woman wearing the same colourful fabric clutches an infant to her breast and watches us pass with curiosity. The Roma still hold onto much of their heritage, marital rights, folklore, music, dance and language, which has many linguistic connections to Hindi and Punjabi. Fascinated to have stumbled across a Roma community living out here, who do not appear to have given up their cultural identity in any way, we pause near to a railway crossing and watch a horse drawn cart turn sharply into the road. A muscular guy wearing a white vest and black trilby hat tugs on the reins and skilfully drives the cart standing up. A young kid with mousy brown hair sits atop a mountain of hay. The proud gentleman driving the cart looks less Indian and more Turkish or Southern European than the Roma we had seen in the town. The evolution of a fairer phenotype through intermarriage is present within the Roma across Europe and nowhere more strikingly than among the Romanichals. Commonly known as "Gypsies" or "Travellers" in the United Kingdom and Southern Ireland, the Romanichals are a closely related subgroup of the Roma in continental Europe. Displaying cultural, linguistic and genetic markers distinct from those of other people of the British Isles, they are more closely related to continental Roma groups like the Sinti from Germany and Austria, and the Roma people from Eastern Europe. Two of Britain's notable Romanichals are Charlie Chaplin, who is believed to have descended from a thriving Roma community on the industrial edge of Birmingham, and the English Hollywood actor Bob Hoskins. The Romanichals distant origins are also in the Indian subcontinent, where they began their migration westwards long ago in the 11th century. The first groups of Roma people migrated to Great Britain in the late 15th century, escaping the Ottoman conquest of the Balkans. Fearful of this nomadic people living outside of the norms of British settledness, laws were quickly passed aimed at stopping the Roma immigration and, during the reign of Henry VIII, the Egyptians Act (1530) banned Gypsies from entering and required those living in the country to leave within 16 days. The punishment for not abiding to this law resulted in imprisonment, confiscation of property and deportation.

We witness the ice white moon expand and rise in the east, flooding the surrounding countryside in eerie blue light. Chris drives the last 35km to Tulcea, a city at the gateway to the mighty Danube delta. Flowing into the Black Sea, the Danube delta is the second largest in Europe (after the Volga) with the greatest stretch of reedbeds in the world. Over 300 species of bird have been recorded living here. It seems fitting to witness the spectacle of nature at the end of our journey. Traversing the Bucharest-Tulcea railway line, we soon arrive in this quaint little town and park near the waterfront outside the Hotel Delta. Chris cuts the engine. We both sit in silence and take a moment to acknowledge that we have finally completed our quest to drive our twenty year old Volvo around the Black Sea.

Boats of varying shapes and sizes line the colourfully lit promenade, with brightly painted signs offering excursions of the delta. Loving couples, retired pensioners and a group of teenagers absorb the cool evening air. We stand outside a lively waterfront bar and consider going inside. I feel hesitant. It seems a shame not to enjoy such a beautiful night. Strolling along the promenade, we sit beneath a street lamp overlooking the river. Chris fishes Annalise's bottle of Ukrainian red wine out of his bag, a gift that we have carried with us all the way from Odessa. Toasting Annalise, we sip the sharp tasting alcohol and absorb the warmth of the moonlight.

Reminiscing about our journey over the past few weeks, we recall the many colourful people we have met along the way; Kristina, Yana, Aleksander, Sasha, Jan, Robert, Nina, Vladimir, Yuriy, Anna, Pavel, Olga, Mzia, Giorgi, Zurab, Marine, Silim, Ahmed, Hussein, Dimitri and Stefan. These names we are unlikely to ever forget. The kindness of strangers reaffirming to us that maybe, "we are not all so different". We have passed through ancient kingdoms, explored great legends and found clarity during our mission to unravel this fascinating region of the world at the birthplace of civilisation.

A guy with a beard exits a small wooden boat and climbs awkwardly onto the promenade. The boat looks badly in need of repair. A name is painted across the hull, it reads, "Ochi Negru". The sailor approaches us and lights a slim cigar with a zippo lighter. A cloud of grey smoke spirals into the air. I struggle to see his face in the dark shadows.

'Black Sea tour?' he wheezes, his deep voice interrupting the silence.

I cast Chris a sideways glance and he breaks into an enormous smile.

261

Chronology

850-800 BC Scythians arrive on the Black Sea steppes

750-700 BC First Greek colonies established

480 BC Greek colonies form the Bosporan state

450 BC Herodotus travels to Olbia

438 BC Bosporan Kingdom ruled by Spartocid dynasty

334 BC Alexander (the Great) Defeats Persia

300s BC Sarmatians enter Black Sea steppes

44 BC Julius Caesar becomes Roman Dictator

27 BC Roman Republic falls, the Roman Empire begins

240 AD Goths invade Roman colonies on Black Sea

300s Georgia adopts Christianity

313 AD Roman Empire accepts Christianity

370 AD Huns destroy Olbia and Tanais

610 AD Emperor Hercalius attains power of the Roman Empire now known as Byzantine

632 AD Prophet Mohammed dies

700s Allying with Byzantine, Khazars establish Black Sea empire

882 AD Kiev becomes centre of Russia-Viking state

1096 First Crusade

1100s Jewish Sect known as Karaite arrive in Crimea

1204 Venetian trading colony of Sudak established in Crimea

1204 Comnenian Empire of Trebizond founded during Fourth Crusade

1206 Mongols under Genghis Khan launch Asian conquests

1223 Russia invaded by Mongols

1240 Mongols (Golden Horde) control Volga

1241 Tatar-Mongol invasions of Europe

1261 Byzantine Empire regain control of Constantinople

1275 Venetian explorer Marco Polo arrives in China

1280 Kaffa founded by the Genoese in Crimea
1347 Black Death spreads to Europe via Kaffa
1423-40 Tatar Khanate separates from Golden Horde
1453 Constantinople seized by Ottoman Turks
1461 Turks takeover Trebizond
1774 Turks driven out of part of the Black Sea by the Russians
1783 Tatar Khanate ends with Russian annexation of Crimea by Catherine the Great
1789 French Revolution
1853-6 Crimean War
1905 Revolution in Russia
1914 First World War
1917 Bolshevik Revolution
1939 Second World War
1944 Stalin's deportation of Crimean Tatars, Chechens & Ingush
1953 Death of Stalin
1954 Crimea ceded to Ukraine
1965 Nicolae Ceausescu comes to power in Romania
1986 Chernobyl
1989 Romanian Revolution
1991 Dissolution of the Soviet Union
1991-1992 Russo-Georgian War – South Ossetia
1989-1992 The East Prigorodny Conflict in North Ossetia-Alania
1992 Abkhazia-Georgia War
1994-6 First Chechen War
1999 Second Chechen war
2004 Beslan School Hostage Crisis
2013 Euromaidan demonstrations and civil unrest in Ukraine
2014 Sochi Winter Olympics
2014 Russian Federation annex Crimea

Bibliography

Adas, Michael. Agricultural and Pastoral Societies in Ancient and Classical History. Temple University Press, 2001.

Anthony, David W. The Horse, the Wheel, and Language. Princeton University Press, 2007.

Apollonius Rhodius. The Argonautica. Tr.T.C.Seaton. London, 1912.

Archibald, Z. H. The Odrysian Kingdom of Thrace: Orpheus Unmasked. Oxford University Press, 1998.

Bagby, Lewis. Lermontov's "A Hero of Our Time": A Critical Companion. Northwestern University Press, 2002.

Baldick, Chris. Oxford Dictionary of Literary Terms. Oxford University Press, 2008.

Bartmann, Barry; Bahcheli, Tozun. De Facto States: The Quest for Sovereignty. Routledge, 2004.

Bellwood, Peter. First Farmers: The Origins of Agricultural Societies. UK, 2004.

Boardman, John. The Cambridge Ancient History (vol. 3). Cambridge University Press, 1970.

Boardman, John. The Cambridge Ancient History (vol. 3). The Prehistory of the Balkans. Cambridge University Press, 1982.

Brackman, Roman. The Secret File of Joseph Stalin: a Hidden Life. Portland, Oregon: Psychology Press, 2000.

Brighton, Terry. Hell Riders: The Truth about the Charge of the Light Brigade. Penguin Books, 2005.

Burger, Michael. The Shaping of Western Civilization: From Antiquity to the Enlightenment. University of Toronto Press, 2008.

Cardona, George; Hoenigswald, Henry M.; Senn, Alfred. Indo-European and Indo-Europeans. University of Pennsylvania Press, 1970.

Chekhov, Anton. Letter to brother Mihail, 1 July 1876.

Chekhov, Anton. Letter to cousin Mihail, 10 May 1877.

Childe, V.Gordon. Man Makes Himself. Oxford University Press, 2003.

Christopher Walter. The Warrior Saints in Byzantine Art and Tradition. UK, 2003.

Clot, André. Suleiman the Magnificent: The Man, His Life, His Epoch. Saqi Books, 1992.

Conquest, Robert. The Nation Killers: The Soviet Deportation of Nationalities. MacMillan, London, 1970.

Cox, Cynthia. Talleyrand's Successor (Armand Emmanuel du Plessis Duc de Richelieu 1766-1822). London, 1959.

Crofton, Henry Thomas; Smart, Bath Charles. The Dialect of the English Gypsies. London, 1875.

Davies, Brian L. Warfare, State and Society on the Black Sea Steppe. Routledge, 2007.

Davies, Norman. Europe: A History. Oxford University Press, 1996.

de Waal, Thomas. The Caucasus: an Introduction. Oxford University Press, 2010.

Dubin , Marc; Lucas, Enver. Trekking in Turkey. Lonely Planet, 1989.

Dumitrescu, Vlad; Boardman, John; Hammond, N. G. L; Sollberger, E. The Cambridge Ancient History (vol. 3): The Prehistory of the Balkans. Cambridge University Press, 1982.

Erickson, John. The Road to Stalingrad: Stalin's War with Germany. Yale University Press, 1999.

Figes, Orlando. The Crimean War: A History. London, 2011.

Fisher, Alan W. The Crimean Tatars. Hoover Institution Press, Stanford, USA, 1978.

Fisher, Mary Pat. Living Religions: An Encyclopaedia of the World's Faiths. Tauris Publishers. 1997.

Fouracre, Paul. The Barbarian invasions: The New Cambridge Medieval History (vol. 1). Cambridge University Press, 2005.

Fraser, Antonia. Marie Antoinette: The Journey. New York, 2001.

Garstang, John. The Hittite Empire. University Press, Edinburgh, 1930.

Gimbuta, Marija. The Prehistory of Eastern Europe Part 1. American School of Prehistoric Research, 1956.

Gimbutas, Marija; Dexter, Miriam Robbins; Jones-Bley, Karlene. The Kurgan Culture and the Indo-Europeanization of Europe. Institute for the Study of Man, 1997.

Grousset, R. The Empire of the Steppes. Rutgers University Press, 1991.

Hancock, Ian; Karanth, Dileep. Selected Essays: Danger! Educated Gypsy. University Of Hertfordshire Press, 2010.

Harutyunyan, Angela; Horschelmann, Kathrin; Miles, Malcolm; Kathrin, Hörschelmann. Public Spheres After Socialism. Bristol, UK: Intellect, 2009.

Heckel, Waldemar; Tritle, Lawrence A. Alexander the Great: A New History. Wiley-Blackwell, 2009.

Herodotus. The History. Translated by David Grene. University of Chicago Press, 1987.

Hinnells, John. The Routledge Companion to the Study of Religion. UK, 2009.

Hoddinott, Ralph F. The Thracians. Thames & Hudson, 1981.

Hornblower, Simon; Spawforth, Antony. The Oxford Classical Dictionary. Oxford University Press, 2012.

Hupchick, Dennis. The Palgrave Concise Historical Atlas of the Balkans. Palgrave Macmillan, 2001.

James Stuart Olson. Cherkess: An Ethnohistorical Dictionary of the

Russian and Soviet Empires. Greenwood Publishing, 1994.

Kazhdan, Alexander P. The Oxford Dictionary of Byzantium. Oxford University Press, 1991.

Khodarkovsky, Michael. Russia's Steppe Frontier. Indiana University Press, 2004.

Kun, Miklós. Stalin: An Unknown Portrait. Central European University Press. New York City, 2003.

Leach, John. Pompey the Great. Routledge, 1986.

Lermontov. Random House Webster's Unabridged Dictionary. 2005.

Liu, Li. The Chinese Neolithic: Trajectories to Early States. Cambridge University Press, 2007.

Ludwig, Arnold M. King of the Mountain: The Nature of Political Leadership. University Press of Kentucky, 2002.

Macrobius, Ambrosius Theodosius. Saturnalia. Book I: XI, 33, Latin.

Malcolm, Janet. Reading Chekhov: A Critical Journey. Granta Books, 2004.

Mallory, J. P.; Adams, Douglas Q. The Oxford Introduction to Proto-Indo-European and the Proto-Indo-European World. Oxford University Press, 2006.

Maloney, Allison. St George: Let's Hear it For England! UK, 2010.

Mayor, Adrienne. The First Fossil Hunters: Paleontology in Greek and Roman Times. Princeton University Press, 2000.

Miller, William. Essays on the Latin Orient. Cambridge University Press, 2014.

Nagle, D. Brendan; Burstein, Stanley M. Readings in Greek History: Sources and Interpretations. Oxford University Press, 2006.

Neal Ascherson 'Black Sea'. Vintage Books. London, 2007.

Nicolle, David; Mcbride, Angus. Attila and the Nomad Hordes. Osprey Publishing, 1990.

Olson, James Stuart. An Ethnohistorical Dictionary of the Russian and Soviet Empires. Greenwood, 1994.

Ostrogorsky, George. History of the Byzantine State. Rutgers University Press, 1969.

Pindar (c. 475 BC)

Polomé, Edgar C. The Indo-Europeans in the 4th and 3rd Millennia. Karoma Publishers, 1982.

Reeves, Francis B. Russia Then and Now (1892-1917): My Mission to Russia During the Famine of 1891-1892.

Rives, James B. Religion in the Roman Empire. Wiley-Blackwell, 2006.

Robbins, Richard G. Famine in Russia, 1891-1892. Columbia University Press, 1975.

Roisman, Joseph; Worthington, Ian. A Companion to Ancient Macedonia. John Wiley & Sons, 2010.

Rose, Mark. Under Istanbul (vol. 60). Archaeological Institute of America, 2007.

Roth, Klaus; Lauth Bacas, Jutta. Migration In, From, and to Southeastern Europe. The British Library, 2004.

Ryan and Pitman. Black Sea deluge hypothesis. 1997.

Savory, R. M. Introduction to Islamic Civilisation. Cambridge University Press, 1976.

Sebag Montefiore, Simon. Young Stalin. New York City. Random House. 2008.

Sherrard, Philip. Byzantium. Time-Life, 1966.

Simmons, Ernest J. Chekhov: A Biography. University of Chicago Press, 1970.

Simms, J.Y. The Crop Failure of 1891: Soil Exhaustion, Technological Backwardness, and Russia's "Agrarian Crisis". Slavic Review (vol. 41). 1982.

Simonian, Hovann. The Hemshin: History, Society and Identity in the Highlands of Northeast Turkey. Routledge, 2007.

Speer, Albert. Inside the Third Reich. Simon & Schuster, 1997.

Stark. Archaeology of Asia: Wiley Blackwell Studies in Global Archaeology. UK, 2005.

Stillwell, Richard; MacDonald, William L; McAllister, Marian Holland. Trapezus. Princeton Encyclopedia of Classical Sites. 1976.

Strabo. Geography (vol. 3). Cambridge, Mass and London, 1983.

Taspinar, Omer. Contributor. The Islamists Are Coming: Who They Really Are. United States Institute of Peace Press, 2012.

Todorova, Khenrieta. The Eneolithic Period in Bulgaria in the Fifth Millennium B.C. British Archaeological Reports, 1978.

Verner, Andrew M. The Crisis of Russian Autocracy: Nicholas II and the 1905 Revolution. Princeton University Press, 1990.

Watton, Victor. A Student's Approach to World Religions: Islam. Hodder & Stoughton, 1993.

Webber, Christopher; McBride, Angus. The Thracians 700 BC-AD 46 (Men-at-Arms). Osprey Publishing, 2001.

Welch, Alford T. Contributor. Encyclopedia of Islam. UK.

Wilkes, J.J. The Cambridge Ancient History (vol. 10). Cambridge University Press, 1996.

Williams, Brian. The Crimean Tatars: The Diaspora Experience and the Forging of a Nation, 2001.

Wood, James. The Broken Estate: Essays on Literature and Belief (Anton Chekhov). Pimlico, 2000.

Woodard, Colin. Ocean's End Travels Through Endangered Seas. Basic Books, 2001

Yenne, Bill. Alexander the Great: Lessons From History's Undefeated

General. Palmgrave McMillan, 2010.

Yermolenko, Galina. Essay. Roxolana: "The Greatest Empresse of the East". Pennsylvania, 2005.

Reports, Papers and Statistics

Human Rights and Human Development Action for Progress: Armenia, 2000.

US State Department Country Report on Human Rights Practices: Abkhazia. 1993.

Forbes Rich List: Rinat Akhmetov, 2015.

Biological Sciences H90: Black Sea. University of California, Irvine.

Tanais Archaeological Reserve Museum Online.

The Don Readings in Physical Anthropology: Collection of Papers. Russian Academy of Sciences.

Russian Federal State Statistics Service: Population Census (vol. 1) 2011.

Russian Census 2010: Population by Ethnicity.

First Chechnya War 1994-1996. GlobalSecurity.org

Prominent Russians: Mikhail Lermontov. Russapedia, 2012.

Kabard Distribution. Ethnologue.com. 2013.

Elbrus: Summary. Global Volcanism Program. Smithsonian Institution. 2010.

The Ingush-Ossetian Conflict in the Prigorodnyi Region. Helsinki Human Rights Watch. Library of Congress.

Christianity and the Georgian Empire. The Library of Congress. 1994.

Christianity in Georgia (Tbilisi). Catholic Encyclopedia.

Georgia, Azerbaijan Debate Control of Ancient Monastery's Territory. Eurasia.Net, 2006.

Official Government Site of Kutaisi, Georgia.

A Modern Field Investigation of the Mythical "Gold Sands" of the Ancient Colchis Kingdom. Journal Quaternary International. 2014.

Constitutional Court of Georgia: Brief History. constcourt.ge.

Georgian Autonomous Republic of Adjara: Department of Statistics.

Tea in Turkey. Euromonitor. 2014.

Sumela Monastery. Republic of Turkey Ministry of Culture and Tourism. 2007.

Hittites. British Museum. London, 2014.

Buying a Table in Erfelek: Socialities of Contact and Community in the Black Sea Region. academia.edu.

Tugba, Binnaz. A Historical Panorama of an Istanbul Neighbourhood. Sasanlar. Bogazici University, 2006.

CIA World Fact Book. 2014

Boonstra, Jos. Moldova, Transnistria and European Democracy Policies. Democratisation Programme: FRIDE.ORG. 2007.

Saint Nino. Orthodox Church of America.

Berger, W. H. The Younger Dryas Cold Spell – A Quest for Causes. Scripps Institution of Oceanography. University of California, 1990.

Varna Museum of Archaeology Online.

Genetic Studies of the Roma (Gypsies). BMC (Biomedical Central). Australia, 2001.

A Newly Discovered Founder Population: The Roma/Gypsies. Stanford School of Medicine, 2005.

Bell, George. Notes and Queries: Gypsies in England. Oxford University Press, 1855.

Vaux, Bert. Hemshinli: The Forgotten Black Sea Armenians. Harvard University, 2001.

Lonely Planet: Ukraine, Russia, Georgia, Turkey, Bulgaria, Romania.

Media Sources

American and Russian Combat Dolphins. Will Stewart. UK, 2014

South Russia Blast Kills Minister. BBC News, 2006.

Putin Orders Vast Expansion of Russia's Black Sea Fleet. Ted Thornhill. UK, 2014.

What You Don't Know About Sochi. Eve Conant. National Geographic, 2014.

Chechen Rebels Said to Kill Hostages at Russian Hospital. Michael Specter. New York Times, 1995.

Narzan Water Bubbling to the Top. Simon Ostrovsky. The Moscow Times, 2004.

Kabardino-Balkaria Profile. BBC News, 2015.

Nalchik. Marina Marshenkulova. The Moscow Times, 2012.

An Explosion of Islamic Militancy Across an Entire Region. Nick Paton Walsh. Guardian, 2005.

History of Chechen Rebels' Hostage Taking. Gazeta.Ru, 2002.

Land Rover Defender Climbs Mount Elbrus. ExplorersWeb, 2004.

3 Days in Hell: Russia Mourns Beslan School Siege Victims 10 Years On. rt.com. 2014.

Militant Leader Reported Killed In Ingushetia. Radio Free Europe-Radio Liberty (RFE/RL), 2012.

Georgian Jailed for Bush Attack. BBC News, 2006.

Christianity: Saint George. BBC News, 2012.

Stalin: Among the Dead. MississippiReview.com. 2008.

Russian Jets Bomb Georgia. Reuters, 2008.

Putin Accuses US of Orchestrating Georgian War. Matthew Chance. CNN, 2008.

Energy Pipeline That Supplies West Threatened By War Georgia Conflict. Robin Pagnamenta. The Times. UK, 2008.

Georgia's Oil Pipeline is Key to US Support. Anne Gearan. Associated Press, 2008.

Professor Unearths 8,000 Year Old Wine. David Keys. The Independent. UK, 2003.

World's Earliest Wine. Mark Berkowitz. Archaeological Institute of America. 1996.

Russia Set to Resume Imports of Georgian Wine. Steve Gutterman. Reuters, 2013.

Glamour Revives Port of Batumi. Dinah Spritzersept. New York Times, 2010.

Kars-Tbilisi Agreement. Railway Gazette International, 2007.

Tea Industry's Future Depends on Corporate Collaboration. Richard Anderson. BBC News, 2014.

Ataturk Alani: Trabzon. Fodor's Online.

Turks Slay 14,000 In One Massacre. Toronto Globe, 1915.

Ballard and the Black Sea. National Geographic Online, 2000.

World Spectacular Infrastructure Projects. Eoghan Macguire. CNN News, 2013.

Lost Treasures of Constantinople Test Turkey's 21st-century Ambition". Guardian News, 2010.

Nautical Archaeology Takes a Leap Forward. The Times Online, UK.

Center of Ottoman Power. Marlise Simons. New York Times, 1993.

World War One: First war was impossible, then inevitable. Anatole Kaletsky. Reuters, 2014.

Turkey Clashes: Why are Gezi Park and Taksim Square so important? BBC News, 2013.

Suicide Blast Hits Istanbul. Al Jazeera, 2010.

Wars of Alexander the Great: Battle of the Granicus. John R. Mixter. Historynet.com, 2013.

Gypsies. Peter Godwin. National Geographic Online, 2001.

Will EU Entry Shrink Bulgaria's Population Even More? Deutsche Welle, 2006.

Bulgaria: Country Profile. BBC News. 2014.

Romania's Bloody Revolution: Nicolae Ceausescu. BBC News. 1999.

Was Charlie Chaplin a Gypsy? Matthew Sweet. The Guardian, 2011.

42341788R00163

Made in the USA
Charleston, SC
23 May 2015